# Entrepreneurship, Money and Coordination

# NEW HORIZONS IN INSTITUTIONAL AND EVOLUTIONARY ECONOMICS

**Series Editor**: Geoffrey M. Hodgson
Research Professor, University of Hertfordshire Business School, UK

Economics today is at a crossroads. New ideas and approaches are challenging the largely static and equilibrium-oriented models that used to dominate mainstream economics. The study of economic institutions – long neglected in the economics textbooks – has returned to the forefront of theoretical and empirical investigation.

This challenging and interdisciplinary series publishes leading works at the forefront of institutional and evolutionary theory and focuses on cutting-edge analyses of modern socio-economic systems. The aim is to understand both the institutional structures of modern economies and the processes of economic evolution and development. Contributions will be from all forms of evolutionary and institutional economics, as well as from Post-Keynesian, Austrian and other schools. The overriding aim is to under the processes of institutional transformation and economic change.

Titles in the series include:

The Evolution of Scientific Knowledge
*Edited by Hans Siggaard Jensen, Lykke Margot Richter and Morten Thanning Vendelø*

Evolutionary Economic Thought
European Contributions and Concepts
*Edited by Jürgen G. Backhaus*

Economic Institutions and Complexity
Structures, Interactions and Emergent Properties
*Karl-Ernst Schenk*

The Economics of Knowledge Sharing
A New Institutional Approach
*Edited by Ernst Helmstädter*

The Economics of Energy and the Production Process
An Evolutionary Approach
*Guido Buenstorf*

Institutional Economics and the Formation of Preferences
The Advent of Pop Music
*Wilfred Dolfsma*

Globalization, Economic Development and Inequality
An Alternative Perspective
*Edited by Erik S. Reinert*

Entrepreneurship, Money and Coordination
Hayek's Theory of Cultural Evolution
*Edited by Jürgen G. Backhaus*

# Entrepreneurship, Money and Coordination

Hayek's Theory of Cultural Evolution

*Edited by*

Jürgen G. Backhaus

*Krupp Chair in Public Finance and Fiscal Sociology, Erfurt University, Germany*

NEW HORIZONS IN INSTITUTIONAL AND
EVOLUTIONARY ECONOMICS

**Edward Elgar**
Cheltenham, UK • Northampton, MA, USA

Published by
Edward Elgar Publishing Limited
Glensanda House
Montpellier Parade
Cheltenham
Glos GL50 1UA
UK

Edward Elgar Publishing, Inc.
136 West Street
Suite 202
Northampton
Massachusetts 01060
USA

A catalogue record for this book
is available from the British Library

**Library of Congress Cataloguing in Publication Data**
Entrepreneurship, money, and coordination : Hayek's theory of cultural evolution / edited by Jürgen G. Backhaus.
    p. cm. — (New horizons in institutional and evolutionary economics)
    Includes bibliographical references.
    1. Hayek, Friedrich A. von (Friedrich August), 1899– 2. Entrepreneurship. 3. Money. 4. Evolutionary economics. 5. Institutional economics. I. Title: Hayek's theory of cultural evolution. II. Backhaus, Jürgen G., 1950– III. Series.

HB101.H39E58 2006
330.1—dc22

2005046193

ISBN 1 84542 130 2

Typeset by Manton Typesetters, Louth, Lincolnshire, UK
Printed and bound in Great Britain by MPG Books Ltd, Bodmin, Cornwall

# Contents

# Contributors

Jürgen G. Backhaus, Professor, Krupp Chair in Public Finance and Fiscal Sociology, University of Erfurt, Germany.

Martin T. Bohl, Professor of Finance, Faculty of Economics, European University Viadrina Frankfurt (Oder), Germany.

Alexander Ebner, Assistant Professor, Krupp Chair in Public Finance and Fiscal Sociology, University of Erfurt, Germany.

Dr. Horst Feldmann, Privatdozent of Economics, University of Tübingen, Germany.

Walter W. Heering, Dr. rer. pol., Senior Lecturer in Financial Economics, Brighton Business School, University of Brighton, England.

Jens Hölscher, Dr. rer. pol., Reader in Economics, Brighton Business School, University of Brighton, England.

Brian J. Loasby, Honorary and Emeritus Professor, Department of Economics, University of Stirling, Scotland.

Christian Schubert, Dr. rer. pol., Research Fellow, Evolutionary Economics Group, Max Planck Institute for Research into Economic Systems, Jena, Germany.

# Introduction

## Jürgen G. Backhaus

Hayek's theory of cultural evolution has been the topic of some controversy in recent years – with this volume, we want to explore the relevance of Hayek's theory for its own sake and for evolutionary economics more generally.

Horst Feldmann's critique of the critiques actually provided the impetus for this book.[1] He largely refutes the criticisms by basing his argument on Hayek's writings, taking his place in answering the critics.

*The Sensory Order* is Hayek's much less well-known attempt to explain how the human mind works in making distinctions between objects which may not necessarily correspond to distinguishing features of them.[2] It is discussed here by Brian Loasby.

The emergence of institutions through legislation is discussed against the background of Hayek's theory of economic policy. It appears that Hayek provides quite specific precepts for economic policies relating to legal institutions which can be far-reaching in scope but must adhere, as the editor of this volume points out, to specific criteria of consistency and functionality. Christian Schubert likewise addresses the problem of designed institutions, i.e. the outcome of legislation, and what Hayek's theory can contribute to a wider understanding of them. Both Backhaus and Schubert incorporate Hayek's theory of entrepreneurship. The entrepreneur is a driving force in cultural evolution. Alexander Ebner therefore discusses Hayek's theory of entrepreneurship. Money, a central concern in Hayek's political economy, is the topic of two chapters. Martin Bohl and Jens Hölscher put Hayek's proposal for a de-nationalization of money in the somewhat contrasting context of the establishment of the Eurozone. They provide some support for the proposition that money supply by private banking is related to monetary stability. Finally, Walter Heering advances his monetary theory of reciprocity in order to gain a better understanding of the concept of money on Hayek's terms.

# NOTES

1. A conference on this topic was hosted by the Max Planck Institute for Research into Economic Systems, Jena (Germany) on 17 November 2003. We gratefully acknowledge the hospitality of the Institute, the third time in a row. Previous conferences there led to the following publications: *Modern Applications ...* and *European Evolutionary Thought ...*
2. Hayek, Friedrich A. von (1952), *The Sensory Order*, London and Chicago: University of Chicago Press.

# 1. Hayek's theory of cultural evolution: a critique of the critiques

## Horst Feldmann

The gradual evolution of certain rules of behavior and other institutions has resulted in an enormous increase in the human population and an unprecedented improvement in the standard of living over the past three centuries. Friedrich A. von Hayek thoroughly analysed this process of cultural evolution, developing a theory that some scholars regard as one of the most significant social theories of the twentieth century.[1] The growing number of publications discussing Hayek's theory shows that interest in it is rising. At the same time, the theory itself is very controversial and has been harshly criticized by many scholars. Is this criticism justified? This chapter takes a critical look at the major points raised by Hayek's critics.[2]

## SYNOPSIS OF THE THEORY

The starting point of Hayek's theory is the fact that for millions of years, humans and their hominid ancestors lived in small groups in which every member knew all the others personally.[3] Life in such a group was characterized by concrete common goals and a similar perception of the environment, an environment recognized by all members chiefly as a potential source of food and danger. Cooperation within the group was narrowly circumscribed. It was during this period that certain instincts evolved and became genetically fixed. They guided individual behavior. These instincts were adapted to life in small groups and served to ensure the cohesion and continued existence of the group (in particular instincts of solidarity and altruism that applied to the members of one's own group but not to others).

According to Hayek, the emergence of today's civilization became possible because some of these small groups gradually developed other modes of behavior. A tradition of learned rules evolved that enabled people to acquire knowledge that gave them more and more power over their environment and allowed individuals to cooperate with a growing number of other individuals. These rules, which were passed on to succeeding generations through teaching and imitation and which were gradually improved over the course of time, made it possible to coordinate the activities of a larger number of people. Thus the groups that adopted these rules were able to increase in number. They were more successful in procreation and also attracted additional members from outside the group.

Most of these learned rules that grew to increasingly override and replace innate instincts are specific moral rules such as honesty, truthfulness and contractual fidelity. Other social institutions such as the family, language, law, private property, the market and money also emerged in this manner and played a decisive role in this process of cultural evolution. Many of the more recent rules repealed former prohibitions. Instead of prohibiting certain acts and prescribing others, the rules that gradually developed in the course of cultural evolution came to afford the individual more effective protection against arbitrary violence from third parties and enabled him to create a protected area into which others were not allowed to intrude and within which the individual had the right to apply his knowledge for his own purposes. Hayek cites as examples the toleration of barter trade with members of other groups; the recognition of delimited private property, especially in land; the enforcement of contractual obligations; the permission of competition with fellow craftsmen in the same trade; the variability of initially customary prices; and the lending of money, particularly against payment of interest. According to Hayek, all these innovations were originally infringements of innate instincts or older customary rules.

Hayek stresses that the rules that led to the emergence of civilization were usually not introduced deliberately and with a purpose, but were in most cases discovered by chance and passed on to succeeding generations even though their functions were not fully understood. According to Hayek, reason was not the driving force behind cultural evolution, but rather co-evolved in the course of this process.

## IS THE SCOPE OF APPLICABILITY OF THE THEORY VERY NARROW?

Vanberg (1984, pp. 96–7) claims that the scope of applicability of Hayek's theory is very narrow because it allegedly only deals with rules that evolved spontaneously and not with those that were deliberately created (see also Steele 1987, p. 176, who argues in a similar way). With respect to processes of deliberate rule making and rule enforcement, he thinks that 'an evolutionary conception is hardly useful', and regards the public choice theory as more helpful (Vanberg 1984, pp. 110–11).

Nobody disputes that the analysis of spontaneously evolved rules is the focus of Hayek's studies. There are two reasons for this: first, the processes involved in the unplanned evolution of rules are particularly hard to explain, whereas deliberate acts through which institutions are created or changed are relatively easy to understand through the analysis of the motivations and scope of action of the persons involved (Hayek [1952a] 1979, pp. 61–76; 1967, p. 71). Second, and this is particularly stressed by Hayek ([1978] 1979, p. 163; 1988, p. 12), all the major institutions that have made modern civilization and today's prosperity possible (especially language, morals, law, markets and money) originally developed spontaneously and not according to a deliberate plan. The analysis of these institutions is thus much more significant than the analysis of deliberately created rules.

At the same time, however, Hayek also stresses:

> that systems of rules of conduct will develop as wholes, or that the selection process of evolution will operate on the order as a whole; and that, whether a new rule will, in combination with all the other rules of the group, and in the particular environment in which it exists, increase or decrease the efficiency of the group as a whole, will depend on the order to which such individual conduct leads. (1967, p. 71)

For this reason, and considering that the originally deliberately created rules are also subject to processes of variation and selection in the course of cultural evolution, such rules must also be covered by a theory of cultural evolution, which is precisely what Hayek's theory does. Hayek closely studied the characteristics, the emergence and the changes as well as the effects of deliberately created rules, such as the rules of organizations (for example, enterprises), legislation and statute law, and the institution of democracy.[4] In these studies, his evolutionary view turns out to be very productive, contrary to the opinion of Vanberg. Moreover, in his analysis of democracy Hayek also takes into account the findings of the public choice theory (in particular, Olson 1965).[5]

Neither would it be possible to focus exclusively on the processes of spontaneous evolution of rules, as originally unplanned rules are also repeatedly subject to deliberate changes in the course of cultural evolution. Contrary to what some authors, such as Steele (1987, pp. 188–91), have claimed, Hayek understood this fact and analysed it in detail in the context of his theory:

> Although undoubtedly an order originally formed itself spontaneously because the individuals followed rules which had not been deliberately made but had arisen spontaneously, people gradually learned to improve those rules. ... The spontaneous character of the resulting order must therefore be distinguished from the spontaneous origin of the rules on which it rests. (Hayek 1973, pp. 45–6)

For example, he studied in detail the evolution of law and how norms which originally had arisen spontaneously were deliberately changed over time, as the evolution of law progressed, and he stresses that '[the system of legal rules] is the outcome of a process of evolution in the course of which spontaneous growth of customs and deliberate improvements of the particulars of an existing system have constantly interacted' (Hayek 1973, p. 100).

## DOES HAYEK'S METHODOLOGICAL INDIVIDUALISM CONTRADICT HIS EVOLUTIONARY APPROACH?

Hodgson claims that Hayek's methodological individualism does not help to explain evolutionary processes:

> In short, according to the methodological individualist, individuals do not evolve. Clearly, assumptions of this type are typical of neoclassical economics, as well as the economics of Hayek. ... With investigations into short-run processes, or partial equilibria, tastes and preference functions could be taken as given. But in an unfolding and evolutionary perspective, involving long-run changes and developments in a social context, this compartmentalization is arguably out of place. ... Thus there is an inconsistency in Hayek's work between, on the one hand, the ideas emanating from his individualist roots, and, on the other, his growing commitment to an evolutionary perspective. In an evolutionary context, methodological individualism has to be either redefined or abandoned. (Hodgson 1993, pp. 153–7)

This criticism is incorrect. It ignores the special features of Hayek's approach, which is fundamentally different from that of neoclassical economics.[6] Hayek modified methodological individualism so as to create a sound foundation for the analysis of cultural evolution. Neoclassical economists usually assume that individuals always have all relevant information at their disposal, have unlimited mental capacities for processing information and under all circumstances are able to select the option maximizing their personal utility. Furthermore, they assume that preferences remain constant over time.

By contrast, Hayek ([1937] 1948; [1945] 1948) points out that all the knowledge used in any given society is dispersed among all members of this society and cannot be known in its entirety by any single individual. He speaks of the 'constitutional limitations on knowledge' (1973, p. 15) and also stresses that human reason as such is limited. His theory explains how reason itself evolved only in the course of cultural evolution: 'It was when these learnt rules, involving classifications of different kinds of objects, began to include a sort of model of the environment that enabled man to predict and anticipate in action external events, that what we call reason appeared' (Hayek [1978] 1979, p. 157). In psychological studies that form an important basis of his theory of cultural evolution,[7] Hayek (1952b; [1963b] 1967; [1969] 1978) showed that humans are only able to partially perceive their external environment. The organs of the senses unconsciously classify sensory impressions. Certain types of sensory impressions trigger certain responses, also often subconsciously. Human beings learn, usually subconsciously in early childhood, certain rules of perception and behavior, enabling them to adapt to the external world – which they only perceive in part – and to coordinate their actions with those of the other members of society. This makes it possible for them to pursue their own plans. The rules of perception and behavior have developed in the course of history according to specific evolutionary principles and have enabled members of society to better pursue their individual goals. This evolution and its impacts on the size and standard of living of different groups were analysed in detail by Hayek when he developed his theory. In accordance with methodological individualism, he starts out with the individual members of society, but takes into account not only their individual interests and objective scope of action, but also their limited cognitive capacities, their subjective knowledge and their subjective values, which are shaped by the respective society and are variable over time (Hayek [1952a] 1979, pp. 41–60).

Hayek's methodological individualism is therefore not only fundamentally different from neoclassical methodological individualism, but also defines the necessary starting point for explaining social institutions and their evolution. Hodgson (1993, pp. 252–67) has proposed a holistic alternative. He defines cultural institutions as completely separate beings and does not consider the individuals who use these institutions in his attempt to analyse the latter. This approach, however, is useless. Institutions can only be explained via the notions and the behavior of individuals because the latter are responsible for the creation, expression, effects and change of the former. By discarding methodological individualism and using institutions as the basic units of analysis, Hodgson fails to provide a precise explanation of these institutions, their evolution, change and significance.[8]

## IS HAYEK'S CONCEPT OF FOLLOWING RULES NATURALISTIC?

Kley (1992, p. 23) criticizes Hayek's concept of following rules as naturalistic. According to Kley, Hayek assumes that the behavior of people is determined by social rules in the same way as natural events are determined by those 'causal regularities that are described by the laws of nature'. In Kley's opinion, Hayek fails to recognize that social rules are not the cause of rule-following behavior; the rules would, if anything at all, 'merely describe some causal chains of events'. Hayek's concept of compliance with rules 'does not leave any latitude for actually taking action', says Kley, arguing that this implies 'a mechanistic perception of society and social processes. There is no room for individual autonomy, for people capable of making judgments and pursuing their own goals, or for engaging in a critical assessment of existing rules and rule systems.'

The criticism expressed by Gray (1986, p. 53) is similar in that he postulates: 'The problem with the natural-selection approach is that in accounting for individual character traits, dispositions, and so on by reference to their survival values, it deprives individual choices and purposes of their place at the terminal level of social explanation.' At the same time though, Gray undermines his own critique in his presentation of Hayek's theory by saying that Hayek does not deny people's capacity to deliberately pursue individual objectives, but rather that he – in contrast to the neoclassical theorist Gary Becker – additionally takes into account that this capability is shaped by traditional social rules (Gray 1986, pp. 49–53). Gray's statement (1986, pp. 47–8) that Hayek acknowledges the fact that human beings are capable of changing rules also invalidates his own criticism.

Hayek by no means assumes that social rules are the sole cause and the only determinants of human behavior, as is illustrated by the following statement:

> It is important always to remember that a rule of conduct will never by itself be a sufficient cause of action but that the impulse for actions of a certain kind will always come either from a particular external stimulus or from an internal drive (and usually from a combination of both), and that the rules of conduct will always act only as a restraint on actions induced by other causes. (Hayek 1967, pp. 68–9)

Neither can social rules of behavior be viewed exclusively as a restriction on the scope of action of individuals, according to Hayek. On the contrary, these rules are also 'a device for coping with our constitutional ignorance' (Hayek 1976a, p. 8).

Moreover, Hayek (1976a, p. 14) emphasizes that social rules only define some attributes of actions. This is often also seen in the animal world, he says: 'It must be particularly emphasized that these propensities or dispositions possessed by higher animals will often be of a highly general or abstract character, that is, they will be directed towards a very wide class of actions which may differ a great deal among themselves in their detail' (Hayek 1973, p. 76). In the Great Society of humans it is all the more important that rules of conduct be general and abstract and allow individuals as much freedom as possible to pursue their own goals, because the 'utilization of factual knowledge widely dispersed among millions of individuals is clearly possible only if these individuals can decide on their actions on the basis of whatever knowledge they possess' (Hayek 1976a, p. 8). If an individual is allowed to use his knowledge to pursue his own goals, this knowledge will be used, under certain conditions, 'in the service of the needs of his fellows' (Hayek 1976a, p. 9).[9] How anyone, given these statements, can claim that Hayek's concept of following rules is naturalistic is not really understandable.

## IS THE THEORY INCOMPLETE?

### Does it Fail to Explain the Emergence of New Rules?

Another charge is that Hayek's theory is incomplete in several respects. For example, Schmidt and Moser (1992, p. 195) as well as Hodgson (1993, pp. 176–7, 179) accuse Hayek of failing to explain how new rules emerge. This criticism is also unfounded. Hayek not only formulated general hypotheses about the emergence of new rules of conduct, giving a number of empirical examples to support his hypotheses, but also analysed the prerequisites for the emergence of new rules of conduct. As regards these prerequisites, Hayek points out that biological evolution has endowed humans with a much higher capacity to learn from their peers than other species. The extension of the duration of childhood and adolescence was a decisive step in the biological evolutionary process that has enabled humans to learn many different rules of behavior. By contrast, reason was not a prerequisite for the evolution of cultural norms, according to Hayek, because reason itself developed only in the course of cultural evolution (Hayek 1988, pp. 21–3).

Hayek repeatedly stresses that new rules of conduct that later would turn out to be useful probably were often originally discovered by chance. At first sight, this hypothesis may appear very vague but it is not at all unusual in the context of an evolutionary theory, given that the genetic changes (mutations) that drive biological evolution are always random. Moreover, Hayek ([1978] 1979, pp. 161–2) also proposes a more concrete hypothesis concerning the emergence of new rules of conduct. According to this hypothesis, a few individuals broke some of the traditional rules of conduct and started specific new practices that were advantageous for them and subsequently proved to be advantageous for the group in which they predominated. As empirical examples, Hayek names barter trade with members of other groups, the mutual recognition of private property (originally of weapons and tools, in particular), the change in initially customary prices, and the lending of money for interest. Although Hayek in his last book, (1988, ch. 2 and 3), provides a more detailed description of the historical emergence of the institution of private property and the market, historical and anthropological studies that specifically examine Hayek's hypothesis have yet to be undertaken. Moreover, the theory behind Hayek's explanation of the emergence of new rules could also be elaborated in more depth. In this context, Sugden (1986; 1989) and Heiner (1983; 1986; 1989) have already made valuable contributions in recent years.

## Does the Theory Fail to Explain How Rules are Sustained and Disseminated?

Closely related to the allegation that Hayek fails to explain how new rules emerge is the claim that his theory is functionalist. For instance, Hodgson states[10]:

> Hayek's argument has a functionalist quality; it assumes that the contribution of a rule to the maintenance of a system is sufficient to explain the existence of that rule. Absent in Hayek's argument is the specification of a process by which a rule that is advantageous to the system is sustained in operation within that system. (1993, p. 168)

This critique is also unjustified. Although Hayek stresses the social functions of rules of conduct, at the same time he explains in detail how the rules that contribute to prosperity and allow people to have more children are maintained and how they spread. These rules are passed on to succeeding generations through teaching and imitation, with the education of children in the family playing a pivotal role. In some instances, the members of other groups adopt successful rules or these individuals join the more successful groups (Hayek 1988, ch. 1). Moreover, the desire to be accepted by other people also motivates people to observe the traditional rules of society (Hayek [1978] 1979, pp. 164–5).

Hayek emphasizes that humans, at least in the early phase of cultural evolution, were not aware of the beneficial functions of traditional rules of conduct and even hated the restrictions on behavior imposed by such rules because they went against their innate instincts. It is therefore very important for his theory to explain how the traditional rules of conduct nevertheless managed to remain in place throughout the centuries. In his theory, Hayek (1983, pp. 185–9; 1988, ch. 9) provides an answer to this question, too. His explanation is that magical and religious beliefs were crucial in this respect. Taboos and the belief in spirits that punished persons who violated traditional rules and customs served to motivate people to act in accordance with the rules very early on. This allowed certain traditions to be sustained and passed on long enough to develop their beneficial effects. Of the thousands of religions that were founded in the course of history, only those have prevailed that support the institution of family and private property in their system of mores. In the course of cultural evolution, which thus also involved a selection process among different religions, useful rules and institutions were selected and preserved in this way, although people initially did not recognize the benefits of these rules and institutions.

## Does the Theory Ignore the Significance of State Power and Historical Accident?

Finally, Hayek's theory is criticized as incomplete on the grounds that it ignores major factors that are of great significance for the long-term development of human societies. In this context, Gray (1986, p. 138) cites first, the power of the state and second, historical accident. Because of historical accident, he argues, the history of mankind cannot be explained in a theory.

As regards chance events, what should be mentioned first is that Hayek explicitly takes account of this factor in the discovery of new rules. Second, it should be kept in mind that scientific research is always an endeavor to explain a multitude of actual events and phenomena by general laws or principles (Popper [1934] 1959). The scope of application of a theory should be as large as possible, and each theory has to explain reality in a uniform manner. Ad hoc explanations that attribute historical events to varying and often random factors and do not contain any general laws or principles are therefore not scientific. By contrast, Hayek's theory provides a uniform explanation for the long-term development of human societies and their institutions on the basis of general principles of evolution.

The role of the state is very systematically analysed in Hayek's theory. His main hypotheses in this context are, first, that a state that protects private property and the freedom of its citizens facilitates cultural evolution and the expansion of the spontaneous order. Second, he says that a strong state will sooner or later curb cultural evolution, and third, that competition between different political powers will reduce the obstructive influence of the state and may thus help new institutions to emerge, which will then become predominant as unintended by-products of the political power struggle (see, for instance, Hayek 1988, p. 32).

Hayek discusses the role of state power also in his empirical studies, and he points out historical accidents if they were significant for a specific context. For example, in his writings on the Glorious Revolution of 1688 he states that the individual liberty of modern times came about 'as a by-product of a struggle for power rather than as the result of deliberate aim' (Hayek 1960, p. 162). It was the 'the great struggle between king and Parliament ... from which emerged as a by-product the liberty of the individual' (Hayek 1960, p. 167). In a similar vein, he stresses in his analysis of the historical development of private property and the market that the far-reaching long-distance trading networks that were created thousands of years ago by merchants around the Mediterranean emerged irrespective of the views of the local ruling powers and often even against their resistance (Hayek 1988, ch. 2 and 3).

## IS THE THEORY TELEOLOGICAL?

Voigt (1992, pp. 465–6, 468) claims that Hayek's theory is teleological. He states that cultural evolution, according to Hayek, after leading through a sequence of specific social development stages, eventually leads to the Great Society as the final stage and ultimate objective of cultural evolution. Hodgson (1993, pp. 152–80) makes a similar allegation. He states that Hayek's theory is essentially of an ontogenetic nature. In the same way as biological ontogeny describes the development of an individual, from the fertilized ovum to the final stage of full maturity, Hayek – in Hodgson's view – claims that cultural evolution inevitably leads from the groups in which humans lived in prehistoric times to the Great Society as the final stage.[11] In the course of this process, the breadth of variation of the system is seen to diminish successively: 'Hayek's theory of socioeconomic evolution ... is asymptotic to ontogeny as the kind of variety that is introduced into the system becomes confined, or even progressively dries up' (Hodgson 1993, p. 180).

The claim that Hayek's theory is teleological is downright grotesque. Hayek distanced himself time and again from the notion that evolution consists of an unavoidable sequence of specific steps or stages that invariably lead to a certain final state. The evolutionary principles of his theory – especially the unpredictable, often random, emergence of new rules as well as the selection of rules for the continual adaptation to unknown and unpredictable, often chance, circumstances – categorically exclude a teleological understanding of evolution. For this reason, Hayek states very clearly:

> None [neither biological nor cultural evolution] knows any 'laws of evolution' in the sense of a necessary sequence of stages in an evolutionary process that a given species has to go through. Although this view, which is derived from the pseudo-historical theories of Hegel, Marx and Comte and is still being taught by Marxists, is often confused with the theory of evolution, it has nothing to do with it and is utterly incompatible with that theory. ... The fundamental nature of evolution, which means that we are dependent on adapting to unforeseen circumstances and changes, excludes the possibility that this type of development theory will lead to laws of evolution. (1983, pp. 174–5, 186)[12]

Hayek himself mentions and discusses various factors that may hinder the development towards a Great Society (or the continued existence of such a society) and have sometimes halted or even reversed such a development in the past. For example, he points out that strong governments tend to abuse their power and to suppress their citizens, mentioning ancient Egypt, the Roman Empire as of the second century AD and imperial China as examples (Hayek 1979, pp. 2–3; 1988, pp. 31–3). According to Hayek, today's democracies also pose a threat to the functioning of market economies and the rule of law. Since the power of politicians is not sufficiently limited and since they depend on the support of organized interest groups, political interventions in favor of these interest groups occur repeatedly in violation of the principles of the market economy and the rule of law, increasingly endangering the order of a free society (Hayek 1979, ch. 12). The notion of 'social justice' today also threatens the functioning of this order, because it is very often used as a reason for interventions that do not conform to this order (Hayek 1976a, ch. 9).

Hayek also attributes fundamental significance to the fact that human reason frequently objects to traditional rules of conduct whose purpose is not immediately evident (Hayek 1988, pp. 48–62). One example given by Hayek (1960, pp. 236–9) is legal positivism, which gained widespread influence as of the second half of the nineteenth century and rejected traditional rules and principles of law that were not rationally explainable and implied a limitation upon the power of legislation. Legal positivism thus helped to pave the way for National Socialism and Communism, the greatest threats to the Great Society in modern times.

In Hayek's view (1988, pp. 11–23) it is no less threatening that the instincts suppressed by traditional rules of conduct revolt against these rules from time to time. This is expressed, for example, in the theories of Sigmund Freud and the Communists (Hayek [1978] 1979, pp. 169–75). In Hayek's view, there is thus the risk that humans may fall back on the notions of tribal society, threatening the existence of the extended social order to which they owe not only their material welfare, but even their lives.

The above arguments also go to show that Hodgson's claim of an ontogenetic nature of Hayek's theory is untenable. Hayek (1973, p. 24) himself wrote: 'Although it must be admitted that the original meaning of the term "evolution" refers to such an "unwinding" of potentialities already contained in the germ, the process by which the biological and social theory of evolution accounts for the appearance of different complex structures does not imply such a succession of particular steps' (see also Hayek 1988, p. 26). Neither is Hodgson right in claiming that, according to Hayek's theory, the breadth of variation in the system is continuously narrowing during the evolutionary process. The contrary is correct. According to this theory, cultural evolution leads to a continuous increase in diversification and differentiation:

> [D]ifferences among individuals increase the power of the collaborating group beyond the sum of individual efforts. Synergetic collaboration brings into play

distinctive talents that would have been left unused had their possessors been forced to strive alone for sustenance. Specialization releases and encourages the development of a few individuals whose distinctive contributions may suffice to provide them a living or even to exceed the contributions others make to the total. … Thus the development of variety is an important part of cultural evolution, and a great part of an individual's value to others is due to his differences from them. The importance and value of order will grow with the variety of the elements, while greater order in turn enhances the value of variety, and thus the order of human cooperation becomes indefinitely extensible. (Hayek 1988, p. 80)

## CAN THE THEORY BE FALSIFIED?

A number of critics[13] charge that Hayek's theory cannot be falsified because he does not name the characteristics of the beneficial institutions independently of their success in the process of evolution. They say that Hayek simply claims that beneficial institutions survive in the evolutionary process and that institutions are beneficial if they survive in competition with others in the evolutionary process. They reproach him for an argument that is tautological, circular and devoid of empirical content. In order to be falsifiable, Hayek's theory would have to name the characteristics of beneficial institutions irrespective of their success in the evolutionary process.

This is another inaccurate reproach. Hayek's theory is indeed falsifiable because he clearly names the institutions that were decisive for the growing prosperity and the increase in the human population and lists each of their characteristics, irrespective of their success in the evolutionary process to date. He also explains why they have endured and proven to be beneficial for the groups that created or adopted them. According to Hayek (1988, pp. 12, 67), the most important institutions that promote prosperity are private property, individual liberty, the market and certain moral rules (especially honesty and contractual fidelity). In the case of the institution of private property, for example, the main issue is that it must be clearly defined and protected by the state (Hayek 1988, pp. 30–7). This ensures that every individual has a certain area in which he can rule alone, Hayek says. As long as the legal rules defining individual liberty are known, abstract and general, apply equally to all and ensure the largest possible scope of action, every individual has the option and the incentive to use his own private property and knowledge for his own purposes (Hayek 1960, ch. 10 and 14; 1973, ch. 5; 1976a, ch. 8). Since this type of use under the rule of law is only feasible if the individual satisfies the needs of others, the overall welfare of society increases (Hayek 1960, ch. 2). Hayek also stresses that the market contributes to a general rise in prosperity (Hayek 1976a, ch. 10; 1988, pp. 75–85). If the property of market participants is protected, if contracts are enforceable and market prices flexible, then a large extent of division of labor evolves and resources are efficiently allocated. Furthermore, Hayek also thoroughly analysed the opposite of the market economy, the centrally planned economy, and showed in detail why it is inefficient. He already predicted its downfall at a time when this economic system was spreading to more and more countries during the expansion era of socialism (Hayek [1935a] 1948; [1935b] 1948; [1940] 1948).

Some critics claim that Hayek's theory is not falsifiable because Hayek fails to state the period of time over which the institutions he considers beneficial are able to develop their benign effects.[14] If in a specific case the benign effects of the institutions considered beneficial do not occur, advocates of Hayek's theory could always claim that more time is needed. In this manner the theory could be made immune to criticism.

It is true that Hayek's theory is a theory of the long-term development of institutions and societies. However, as the theory covers the entire human history to date, and since Hayek studied specific institutions and their development in detail, an ex-post testing of his theory is possible. For example, Hayek himself applied his theory to the emergence and early development of the institution of private property and the market, deducing concrete hypotheses that are falsifiable (Hayek 1988, ch. 2 and 3). He also studied the Glorious Revolution of 1688, a key event in the establishment of individual liberties in the modern era, from the perspective of his evolutionary theory (Hayek 1960, ch. 11). His hypotheses in this context are also falsifiable. Moreover, the theory may be applied to the development of other institutions in earlier periods. The hypotheses deduced would also be falsifiable. Claims that Hayek's theory cannot be falsified because of its indeterminate time horizon are therefore also unfounded.

## IS THE PRECISENESS OF THE HYPOTHESES LOW?

According to recognized methodological opinion, preference is given to theories that are able to deliver the more precise statements and forecasts, that is, those with a higher degree of preciseness in their hypotheses (Popper [1934] 1959). According to Paul (1988, p. 260), the degree of preciseness of the hypotheses deduced from Hayek's theory is low, as they do not allow one to make any precise forecasts. Therefore, she even doubts if Hayek's theory meets the criteria required to qualify it as scientific: 'Hayek's evolutionism seems to be reduced to a claim that social institutions must be understood as the result of the historical development of a particular society. This would hardly constitute a scientific discipline but rather simply an historical exercise.'

As with biological evolution, cultural evolution consists of the adaptation to future, unpredictable circumstances that are unknown at present. For this reason, it is in indeed true that it cannot be precisely predicted which new rules and institutions will emerge or how existing ones will change in the future. Even if the future overall conditions were known, it would still be impossible to make precise forecasts because the scope of possible options for the emergence of new or the variation of established institutions would still be very large. In the case of complex phenomena such as cultural evolution – but also biological evolution – it is impossible to predict individual events or the exact consequences of a concrete situation due to the numerous variables involved and their uncertainty. In several in-depth methodological studies, Hayek himself has shown that in the case of complex phenomena it is nonetheless possible to arrive at explanations of the principles that lead to them (Hayek [1952a] 1979; [1955] 1967; [1964] 1967). Scientific laws in the narrow sense of the word (that is, rules by which two phenomena are connected with each other according to the principle of causality) cannot adequately describe complex phenomena because in the case of such phenomena the number of variables and parameters is very large and their values are often unknown. Since the principles according to which cultural evolution progresses cannot be determined through direct observation, it is nonetheless a scientific and useful approach to attempt to reveal and explain these evolutionary principles. This type of explanation that Hayek supplies with his theory not only gives us a general understanding of the long-term development of the rules and institutions of a society, but also of the long-term development of a society's prosperity and size, and of the conditions on which these depend.

Although the theory of cultural evolution does not allow any precise predictions of individual events, it is possible to make so-called pattern predictions, that is, predictions stating that under certain general conditions a certain type of pattern will occur. It is possible to make predictions of future developments as well as a posteriori predictions. These types of predictions are falsifiable. At the same time, however, they only have a relatively low degree of empirical content because they only allow us to make predictions or give explanations of a few general features of a situation. Still, they are useful because they supply insights into chief influencing factors and mechanisms of society's development. Furthermore, they also illustrate that Hayek's theory is scientific not least because it is falsifiable.

Therefore, it is obvious that Paul's criticism is completely exaggerated. It is based on a very narrow methodological understanding that would even classify the modern biological theory of evolution as unscientific.

# ON THE CONCEPT OF GROUP SELECTION

## Does the Concept Contradict Methodological Individualism?

The concept of group selection is of pivotal significance for Hayek's theory, because 'cultural evolution operates largely through group selection' (Hayek 1988, p. 25). According to Hayek, the rules of conduct that he considers to be crucial for the emergence of Western civilization spread because the rules made it possible for the groups that adopted them to be more successful at procreation and at attracting outsiders. The process also led to the displacement of other groups, which often, but not always, involved the use of violence. In any case, the former groups grew in numbers faster than the others, and they achieved relatively greater prosperity (Hayek 1973, pp. 9, 17–18, 99; 1988, pp. 16, 70, 121).

Hardly any other part of Hayek's theory has been criticized as harshly as his concept of group selection. The main charge is that it contradicts the principles of methodological individualism.[15] The selection of rules of conduct is allegedly explained at the group level and not by the preferences and actions of the members of a group. According to Vanberg (1984, p. 104), Hayek fails to deliver a specification of the group selection mechanism that could be interpreted as individualistic; neither does it seem at all feasible to arrive at such a specification. In this context Vanberg (1994b, p. 83) also claims that Hayek added the concept of group selection to his initially strictly individualist theory only at a later date: '[T]here is a tacit shift in Hayek's argument from the notion that behavioural regularities emerge and prevail because they benefit the individuals practising them, to the quite different notion that rules come to be observed because they are advantageous to the group.'

This criticism is wrong. As early as 1960, Hayek (1960, p. 36) explicitly mentioned the notion of group selection: 'Within any given society, particular groups may rise or decline according to the ends they pursue and the standards of conduct that they observe. And the ends of the successful group will tend to become the ends of all members of the society.' In this context he also stresses that individual preferences have to be subordinate to whatever is needed to perpetuate the existence of the group: 'It is not only in his knowledge, but also in his aims and values, that man is the creature of civilization; in the last resort, it is the relevance of these individual wishes to the perpetuation of the group or the species that will determine whether they will persist or change' (Hayek 1960, p. 36). Consistent with this view, Hayek (1960, p. 32) defends the system of individual liberty not by stating that it serves the interests of the individuals, but rather of society: 'What is important is not what freedom I personally would like to exercise but what freedom some person may need in order to do things beneficial to society.' The shift asserted by Vanberg from individual to collective utility as a selection criterion for rules of conduct does not exist in Hayek's theory. Hayek always stressed that such rules must benefit the group as a whole.

In 1967, thus also in an early phase of the development of his theory of evolution, Hayek (1967) explained the mechanism of group selection (see also Hayek 1973). He differentiated between the rules that guide the behavior of individual members of a group, and the overall order of actions that results from these rules for the group as a whole. According to Hayek, the whole order of actions is crucial for a group's productivity and survival. The evolutionary selection of the various rules of individual conduct is also driven by the efficiency of the order of actions created on the basis of these rules.

Thus Hayek differentiates two levels: the level of individual, rule-guided behavior, and the collective level of the group, encompassing the social order of actions determined by this behavior. This order may be more or less efficient and welfare-increasing, depending on how well the rules of conduct are adapted to the environment and to what extent the members of the group can be made to act efficiently, using the knowledge dispersed throughout society. If the order of actions is relatively efficient in comparison to that of other groups, the needs of its members can be satisfied relatively well, and therefore they will have better chances of procreating. For the same reason, members of other groups are attracted to it. It is thus able to grow relatively faster than the others.

Since a relatively efficient order of actions benefits the members of the group concerned, these members have a fundamental self-interest to observe the rules that lead to this order, and to improve them over time. The members of the group do not necessarily have to be aware of the meaning of the rules, as the more efficient rules are selected by a process of trial and error, according to Hayek (1988, p. 20): 'That rules become increasingly better adjusted to generate order happened not because men better understood their function, but because those groups prospered who happened to change them in a way that rendered them increasingly adaptive. This evolution was not linear, but resulted from continued trial and error, constant "experimentation" in arenas wherein different orders contended.'

All this illustrates that Hayek systematically explains the mechanism of group selection through the behavior of individuals, contrary to the contentions of his critics. His explanations are fully in line with methodological individualism.[16]

## Does the Problem of Behavior Detrimental to the Group Remain Unsolved?

Hayek's critics concede that although rules of conduct do exist, which, if followed, would serve to increase the welfare of the members of the group as compared to other groups, there is an incentive for individual members of a group to break many of these rules, because by breaking such rules they can increase their personal welfare even further at the expense of the other members of the group.[17] Hayek's critics mainly refer to situations of the type illustrated by the Prisoner's Dilemma. They claim that Hayek does not explain which mechanisms hinder this type of opportunistic behavior and how the preventive mechanisms emerged. Without such mechanisms, the maintenance and spread of superior rules would not be possible.

This claim is also unfounded. Not only does Hayek recognize the problem of behavior detrimental to the group, but he also analyses virtually all of the significant mechanisms that can be used to deter such behavior:

- The first mechanism to emerge in the history of evolution came about, according to Hayek, through the ignorance of people.[18] Even before humans acquired the capacity to interpret observed events through the use of reason, the traditional rules of conduct told them (and their hominid ancestors) what an individual should do or not do under certain circumstances. This made it possible for them to adapt to their environment. Since humans did not yet understand the complexities of their environment, but their survival depended on the right behavior, they must have developed a strong instinctive preference to act according to established rules and a great fear of the unknown consequences of deviant behavior. As humans in the course of evolution gradually came to develop an awareness of a few of the regularities of their environment, this must have, according to Hayek, reinforced their preference for those kinds of conduct which produced expected effects. It must also have triggered an aversion to doing something unfamiliar and fear when it has been done. The individuals must have felt that they were exposing themselves to dangers by transgressing the rules, even if no one was there to punish them.
- A second mechanism, according to Hayek, also developed in the early history of humans and became innate. At the beginning of cultural evolution, humans and their hominid ancestors lived in small groups for millions of years and individuals were only able to survive as members of such groups. This encouraged the development of a strong preference to follow the group's rules. The fear of punishment, especially the fear of expulsion from the group, served to assure rule-abiding behavior to a large extent.[19]

- Another mechanism that Hayek points out is the need that exists to this very day in every human to be accepted by other group members.[20] It probably also emerged in the course of the long history of humans living as members of small groups on which an individual's survival depended. Even today, according to Hayek, the varying degrees of respect towards other people are influenced largely by the extent to which such people are seen to live by the rules of society. This continues to create a strong incentive for individuals to follow those rules.
- Additionally, Hayek (1988, ch. 9) maintains that mystical and religious beliefs also contributed to motivating people to adhere to social norms, even if breaches of such norms would be advantageous for an individual in the short term. Early on, the violation of such norms was declared a taboo in mystical beliefs and was later on branded as a sin by religions. Humans were induced to fear the revenge of the spirits and gods, and to dread hell. This also contributed to the prevention of behavior detrimental to the group, and continues to do so in many cases to this day.
- The upbringing of children in the family also plays a key role according to Hayek (1988, pp. 18, 23). Mostly the family passes on traditional values and norms to succeeding generations. The long phases of childhood and adolescence make the upbringing of children over long years an important mechanism that contributes to a large extent to the prevention of opportunistic behavior.
- Finally, Hayek (1973, pp. 47–8) also mentions the state. State institutions such as the police and judiciary are in his opinion indispensable especially for the Great Society in order to ensure obedience with the general rules of conduct.

Thus Hayek obviously does not only identify and explain the significance of practically all important mechanisms that may be used to largely prevent behavior detrimental to the group. He also explains their emergence and development as part of the process of cultural evolution. Hayek's exposition in this context is therefore a constituent part of and consistent with his theory of evolution in general, and his concept of group selection in particular.

Over the years, a number of other scholars have also conducted in-depth theoretical and empirical research on the mechanisms that contribute to the prevention of behavior detrimental to groups. This research, which has been carried out largely without any connection to the works of Hayek, deepens and impressively corroborates his hypotheses. Of the large number of the more recent studies, we would like to mention those of only two authors as examples:

- Axelrod (1984) studied how various behavioral strategies compete in an iterative Prisoner's Dilemma situation within the scope of computer tournaments. The strategy of tit-for-tat proved to be superior. This strategy enforces rule-abiding behavior by responding to the uncooperative behavior of one player with uncooperative behavior by the opponent, who otherwise acts cooperatively. This strategy came to prevail in computer tournaments and resulted in rule-abiding behavior by all players in the end. Axelrod's computer tournaments illustrate that cooperative behavior may come about through an evolutionary process under certain conditions and can remain in place even without deliberately being planned or foreseen by the actors involved, and without the need to enforce cooperative behavior through an external authority.[21] The strategy of tit-for-tat serves as the mechanism for suppressing behavior detrimental to the group.
- Ostrom conducted a series of very instructive field studies about how most diverse groups ensured rule-abiding behavior themselves (without using the assistance of coercive state power) to govern the use of common resources (such as game population and irrigation systems).[22] The members of the group invested in the surveillance and sanctioning of the other group members to prevent behavior detrimental to the group. The surveillance and sanctioning mechanisms emerged through evolution. In laboratory experiments Ostrom analysed in depth the preconditions and the mechanisms involved in the emergence and success of such informal regulatory systems by applying experimental game theory. In an overview of her research and of numerous other recent similar studies, Ostrom arrives at the following conclusion: 'Both laboratory experiments and field studies confirm that a substantial number of collective action situations are resolved successfully, at least in part. ... Indeed, recent developments in evolutionary theory – including the study of cultural evolution – have begun to provide genetic and adaptive underpinnings for the propensity to cooperate based on the development and growth of social norms' (Ostrom 2000, p. 154).

## DOES EMPIRICAL EVIDENCE CONTRADICT THE THEORY?

A theory must be repeatedly subjected to the most stringent examinations (Popper [1934] 1959). What needs to be examined is whether it can be used to explain or predict empirical facts. Empirical corroboration is a crucial methodological criterion. Some critics charge that Hayek's theory or at least some of his hypotheses contradict empirical facts. However, none of them have taken the trouble to empirically examine Hayek's theory in depth. Often, criticism is even voiced without citing any concrete evidence.

## Economic Development

### Historical studies

Hayek himself uses his theory to explain, above all, what is nowadays usually referred to as the rise of the Western world. In Hayek's view, the Industrial Revolution that started in the eighteenth century in the United Kingdom and the increase in population and prosperity of the Western world ever since are the result of a wide-ranging application of the principle of individual liberty, especially the freedom of contract, trade and commerce; the prevalence and effective protection of private property; and the rule of law. In this context, Hayek stresses that individual liberty was not deliberately introduced to bring about these prosperity-creating effects. These effects were not foreseen. Hayek himself shows in detail how individual liberty became prevalent for the first time in England as the by-product of a political power struggle (Hayek 1960, ch. 2, 3, 11).

Bouillon (1991, p. 43) questions Hayek's explanations and asks if, 'Erich Weede had not been right in contending that catallaxy was a specialty of Europe that was more favored by geographical circumstances than by respect for several property'. The term 'catallaxy' is meant to characterize an extended order of production and exchange that does not serve a unitary hierarchy of ends. Hayek (1988), Mises (1963) and other Austrian economists prefer this term to the terms 'market economy' or 'capitalism' that are more common but less precise and, to some extent, even misleading. In fact, the author quoted by Bouillon is fully in agreement with Hayek's explanation. Although Weede says that the geographical conditions in Western Europe favored the rise of the Western world, he assesses the same factors as crucial that Hayek did:

> The fragmentation of political and economic power, and the resulting competition, have been the driving forces behind the necessity and the possibility to progress, because many had the option, and also the need, to experiment. This is a very fundamental issue, which has been pointed out time and again especially by Hayek (1971). [... In Britain,] property rights of manufacturers and merchants were especially designed to promote economic growth. Nowhere on the European continent were they better safeguarded from intervention by the state. ... Moreover, England was freer than the European continent: serfdom, barriers to class mobility and absolutism had been overcome earlier than in France, and especially earlier than in Central Europe. England also became a single market earlier and thus did not have any internal barriers to trade in the form of road tolls, river tolls or city gate tolls. This must have had a positive influence on the division of labor and on productivity'. (Weede 2000, pp. 244, 248–9)[23]

Over the years, a number of profound studies in economic history have corroborated Hayek's explanation of the rise of the Western world – usually, however, without specifically testing his theory. For example, in his monumental study Landes (1998, ch. 15) states that in order to develop, a society needs institutions that secure rights of private property and personal liberty, enforce rights of contract, and provide stable, responsive, honest, moderate, efficient and ungreedy government. In analysing why Britain was the first to enter the Industrial Revolution, he stresses that it came closest earliest to this ideal social order. 'Political and civil freedoms won for the nobles (Magna Carta, 1215) were extended by war, usage, and law to the common folk. ... [B]y comparison with populations across the Channel, Englishmen were free and fortunate' (Landes 1998, p. 220). Similarly, North and Weingast (1989) point out that it was the successful evolution of the institution of secure property rights – including judicial independence and the elimination of confiscatory government – following the Glorious Revolution of 1688 that permitted economic growth to take place in early modern England. In an earlier book, North and Thomas (1973) analysed in detail how the evolution of institutions securing private property rights led to the rise of the Western world. Rosenberg and Birdzell (1986, p. 34) also stress the importance of secure property rights, the rule of law and 'a large measure of freedom to experiment' for the rise of the Western world. In addition, they point out the role of Europe's political division as a source of economic growth. 'Competition among the political leaders of the newly emerging nation-states, each anxious to retain the revenues and credits available from a merchant class and each aware of the political danger of allowing neighboring states to increase their capacity to finance military power, was an important factor in overcoming the inherited distaste of the rural military aristocracy for the new merchant class' (Rosenberg and Birdzell 1986, pp. 136–7). Analysing the diffusion of the European institutions to countries colonized by European powers during the past 500 years, Acemoglu et al. (2002, p. 1279) conclude that 'in previously sparsely settled areas, Europeans settled in large numbers and created institutions of private property, providing secure property rights to a broad cross section of the society and encouraging commerce and industry. ... [T]hese societies took much better advantage of the opportunity to industrialize.' Thus all of these studies corroborate Hayek's theory. As Landes (1998, p. 516) puts it: 'If we learn anything from the history of economic development, it is that culture makes all the difference.'

## Regression analysis

The 'Economic Freedom of the World (EFW)' index, which has been developed since the late 1980s by a group of North American economists under the auspices of the Canadian Fraser Institute and which is regularly updated and revised by a worldwide network of economists, is exceptionally well suited to econometrically test Hayek's theory.[24] This index measures precisely those factors that Hayek considered crucial. Specifically, it covers rule of law, security of property rights, limited government, access to sound money, the absence of regulatory constraints that limit the freedom to exchange in domestic credit, labor and product markets, and the absence of tariffs, regulatory trade barriers and capital market controls that limit the freedom to exchange and transfer goods, services and capital across national boundaries. The rating scale that is being used to calculate the index ranges from 0 to 10, with 0 representing the lowest and 10 the highest degree of economic freedom.

Tables 1.1 and 1.2 illustrate the relationship between economic freedom, as measured by the EFW index, and log income per capita and economic growth, respectively. To measure the effects on economic growth, we use the growth rate of real GDP. Most other researchers have used the growth rate of real GDP per capita instead. However, Hayek argues that countries may improve their competitive position in cultural evolution not only by becoming more productive but also by increasing in population size and that this growth in population initially may even lower real GDP per capita. Thus the growth rate of real GDP, which captures both increases in productivity and increases in population size, is much more appropriate.

The country group consists of 105 countries (see Appendix A1.1 for a complete list of them). Using the most recent methodology and data, the Fraser Index was calculated for every fifth year from 1970 on, plus for the years 2001 and 2002. As no data were available for years prior to 1980 with respect to some control variables, the following regressions are based on data for the years 1980, 1985, 1990, 1995, 2000, 2001 and 2002.

In our baseline regressions, the coefficients are estimated using the random effects, generalized least squares (GLS) procedure that incorporates time-invariant country effects. This enables us to exploit both the cross-country and the time-series variation included in the sample, while simultaneously controlling for unobserved country effects. Allowing for cross-country differences in economic performance that reflect the influence of omitted variables is highly desirable, but the random-effects method for doing so produces biased estimates if variables included as controls are correlated with country-specific error terms. Therefore, a Hausman test for misspecification of the random-effects model is shown for each random-effects GLS regression. As the results from this test indicate, only the estimates in regression (3) of Table 1.1 are biased. Thus, in all but one regression, the random-effects GLS method is the appropriate choice. In any case, we also report the coefficients on economic freedom from pooled regressions, to check whether the different methods yield similar results (each method has advantages and drawbacks).

*Table 1.1* *Regressions to explain log income per capita*[a]

|  | (1) | (2) | (3) |
|---|---|---|---|
| Economic freedom[b] | 0.72 | 0.70** | 0.70** |
|  | (1.00) | (2.45) | (2.17) |
| Investment share |  | −0.01* | −0.01 |
|  |  | (−1.73) | (−1.44) |
| Secondary enrollment rate |  |  | −0.00 |
|  |  |  | (−0.23) |
| Latitude | 1.04 | 1.08 | 1.01 |
|  | (0.43) | (1.09) | (1.17) |
| Ethnolinguistic fractionalization | −0.48 | −0.56 | −0.57 |
|  | (−0.42) | (−1.21) | (−1.31) |
| War | −0.02 | −0.02 | 0.11 |
|  | (−0.17) | (−0.25) | (1.05) |
| Transition country | 0.06 | 0.07 | 0.07 |
|  | (0.04) | (0.11) | (0.10) |
| Regional dummies | Yes | Yes | Yes |
| Year dummies | Yes | Yes | Yes |
| Number of observations | 722 | 713 | 683 |
| $R^2$ | 0.71 | 0.71 | 0.72 |
| Standard error of regression | 0.37 | 0.37 | 0.36 |
| F-statistic | 164.46*** | 153.48*** | 177.01*** |
| Hausman test | 0.01 | 7.12 | 59.53*** |
| Memorandum item: |  |  |  |
| Coefficient on economic freedom[b] | 0.70*** | 0.66*** | 0.27** |
| estimated using pooled IV[c] | (6.32) | (6.02) | (2.32) |

*Notes:*

[a] Two-stage generalized least squares estimates with country-specific random effects (Swamy-Arora method). The dependent variable is the natural logarithm of gross national income divided by mid-year population, converted into current international dollars using purchasing power parity rates. Economic freedom is instrumented; the instrumental variables are English language, Western European languages, English legal origin, French legal origin, and German legal origin. Data for 105 countries from the years 1980, 1985, 1990, 1995, 2000, 2001 and 2002. Heteroskedasticity-consistent t-statistics in parentheses (White method). *** (**/*) denotes statistically significant at the 1% (5%/10%) level. All regressions also contain a constant term.

[b] Economic Freedom of the World (EFW) summary index.

[c] The pooled IV regressions are also estimated using two-stage least squares. The control variables and the instrumental variables used for economic freedom are the same as the ones used for the random-effects GLS regressions. Heteroskedasticity- and autocorrelation-consistent t-statistics in parentheses (Newey-West method).

*Table 1.2 Regressions to explain economic growth[a]*

| | (1) | (2) | (3) |
|---|---|---|---|
| Economic freedom[b] | 0.86*** | 0.51** | 0.53** |
| | (3.52) | (2.41) | (2.36) |
| Investment share | | 0.21*** | 0.21*** |
| | | (7.07) | (6.85) |
| Secondary enrollment rate | | | −0.02 |
| | | | (−1.18) |
| Log income per capita | −0.49 | −0.81** | −0.58 |
| | (−1.29) | (−2.51) | (−1.18) |
| Latitude | −3.64 | −2.23 | −1.74 |
| | (−1.52) | (−1.13) | (−0.88) |
| Ethnolinguistic fractionalization | −1.79 | −0.61 | −1.09 |
| | (−1.62) | (−0.67) | (−1.19) |
| War | −1.39* | −0.98 | −0.61 |
| | (−1.73) | (−1.38) | (−0.78) |
| Transition country | 1.27 | −0.26 | −0.24 |
| | (1.08) | (−0.27) | (−0.24) |
| Regional dummies | Yes | Yes | Yes |
| Year dummies | Yes | Yes | Yes |
| Number of observations | 720 | 711 | 681 |
| $R^2$ | 0.09 | 0.17 | 0.18 |
| Standard error of regression | 3.89 | 3.87 | 3.79 |
| F-statistic | 4.17*** | 8.40*** | 7.59*** |
| Hausman test | 8.92 | 14.12 | 19.47* |
| Memorandum item: | | | |
| Coefficient on economic freedom[b] | 0.72*** | 0.48** | 0.47** |
| estimated using pooled OLS[c] | (3.07) | (2.25) | (2.14) |

*Notes*:
[a] Generalized least squares estimates with country-specific random effects (Swamy-Arora method). The dependent variable is the annual percentage growth rate of real GDP. Data for 105 countries from the years 1980, 1985, 1990, 1995, 2000, 2001 and 2002. Heteroskedasticity-consistent t-statistics in parentheses (White method). *** (**/*) denotes statistically significant at the 1% (5%/10%) level. All regressions also contain a constant term.
[b] Economic Freedom of the World (EFW) summary index.
[c] Pooled OLS regressions. The control variables are the same as the ones used for the random-effects GLS regressions. Heteroskedasticity- and autocorrelation-consistent t-statistics in parentheses (Newey-West method).

Rich countries may be able to afford, or perhaps prefer, more economic freedom. Thus causality may run from income per capita to economic freedom, not vice versa. To solve this reverse causality problem, the regressions presented in Table 1.1 are based on two-stage least squares. A major feature of the sixteenth through nineteenth centuries was the spread of Western European influence around the world. The extent of this influence varied widely across countries and may safely be thought of as exogenous to income per capita today. We use two types of variables that are good proxies for this influence: European languages (two variables) and legal origins (three variables). In using these five variables as instruments in our regressions to explain log income per capita, we follow the most recent literature.

In each of the regressions, we use the following basic set of controls (for definitions and sources of all variables, see appendix A1.2):

- latitude, because countries that are closer to the equator tend to have more tropical climates that may hinder production;
- ethnolinguistic fractionalization, because in ethnically and linguistically heterogeneous societies, the group that comes to power may implement growth-reducing policies (for example, policies that expropriate the losing groups and prohibit the growth of industries that threaten the ruling group);
- a dummy variable for wars, because these may considerably affect prosperity and growth in the countries involved;
- a dummy variable for those countries that are in transition from planned to market economy, because this process has a major impact on prosperity and growth as well;
- dummies for various regions of the world, to account for special regional aspects;
- year dummies, to largely eliminate year-specific effects such as exogenous shocks.

In the regressions to explain economic growth, log income per capita is also part of the basic set of controls. This variable is meant to account for the effects of the huge cross-country differences in the level of economic development.

As Tables 1.1 and 1.2 illustrate, the 'economic freedom' variable is statistically significant in all but one regression. The higher the level of economic freedom, the higher is both income per capita and real GDP growth. This result holds even if we add the investment share, a standard variable in neoclassical economics, and the secondary enrollment rate, a standard variable to measure human-capital accumulation, to the model (see regressions (2) and (3) in Tables 1.1 and 1.2). The regression results indicate that economic freedom is an important determinant of both the level of economic development and economic growth, even when investment in physical and human capital, geography, ethnolinguistic fractionalization and other potentially important factors are taken into account.[25] They fully corroborate Hayek's hypothesis of the prosperity-increasing effects of individual liberty.

For two reasons, the results for the 'economic freedom' variable are even likely to understate the effects of economic freedom on income per capita and economic growth. First, people only tend to invest in physical and human capital if they are free to use their capital and to collect the fruits of their investments. Thus the 'investment share' and 'secondary enrollment rate' variables probably capture some of the indirect effects of economic freedom. Hall and Jones (1999) provide evidence of such indirect effects for a cross-section of 127 countries. Second, for a cross-section of 72 countries, Easterly and Levine (2003) found that geographic endowments affect GDP per capita only indirectly via institutions like security of property rights, the rule of law and a light regulatory burden. Thus the 'latitude' variable probably also captures some indirect effects of economic freedom.

**Population Growth**

Hayek is also criticized for claiming in his theory that free societies have larger population growth, which is said to be refuted by empirical evidence. His critics point out that population growth in developing countries is much higher than in the highly developed industrial countries in which the institutions of freedom are the most advanced (Witt 1994, p. 184; Vanberg 1994a, pp. 461–3).

In order to examine whether this criticism is justified, we must first of all clarify precisely what Hayek did say about the relationship between demographic development and institutions. Hayek's central hypothesis in this context is that the size of the human population today is attributable mainly to the circumstance that certain institutions have evolved and become predominant, especially private property, freedom of contract, contractual fidelity, freedom of commerce and trade, and the rule of law (Hayek 1988, p. 12). These institutions had made it possible for those groups that adopted them to expand more rapidly than others (they were more successful at procreating and at attracting outsiders). After the introduction of these institutions, it became apparent that productivity and the standard of living could be increased even more with greater numbers of individuals, because a growing population and a denser settlement structure made it possible to foster specialization and the division of labor. This, in turn, created a new basis for the further expansion of the population. According to Hayek (1988, p. 127), the process of population growth will slowly come to an end when all fertile regions of the earth are similarly densely occupied.

Hayek (1988, pp. 123–32) also maintains that the institutions of the free market economy are more useful to the poor than to the rich. The introduction of the market economy made it possible for poor people to survive and have children, which frequently would not have been possible without the earning opportunities made available to them by this economic system. Therefore, an increase in population as a result of the introduction of the market economy may initially lead to a reduction in average income per capita; only later will it rise. Hayek (1988, pp. 127–30) also stresses that the steepest increases in the population never occurred in the highly developed market economies, but in developing countries that were in the process of introducing market economy institutions. In these countries, people were already benefiting from the market economy (for example, in the form of better medical coverage), but had not yet fully adapted their behavior and traditions, especially their reproductive customs; these are customs that change only gradually.

Thus Hayek's argument is much more sophisticated than his critics claim. In a next step, we take a look at the empirical evidence. It does not contradict his theory at all, but is rather fully in conformity with it. The development of the population over the past several centuries can be explained very well by Hayek's theory. This becomes particularly clear when examining the rise of the Western world. In the course of this process, more and more countries and people adopted the system of individual liberty. After the system had become prevalent in England at the end of the seventeenth century, it was taken over on the West European continent and in North America (for example, by France, Germany, Canada and the USA) in the eighteenth century and during the first half of the nineteenth century. In the second half of the nineteenth century and in the twentieth century it gradually started to spread to Asia and Latin America (to Japan, for instance, as a consequence of the Meiji Revolution of 1868).[26] Additionally, millions of people emigrated to countries that offered more freedom than their home countries. The USA, for example, recorded net immigration of 15.8 million people between 1870 and 1913 alone (Maddison 1991, p. 240). During the settlement of North America by European immigrants, the native population, whose institutions were inferior to those of the West,[27] was displaced, in many cases through the use of force, which is evidence of Hayek's hypothesis of group selection (Reinhard 1985).

Those countries in which the system of individual liberty became prevalent experienced an enormous increase in their populations caused primarily not by immigration, but above all by a decline in child mortality and an increase in life expectancy. In the United Kingdom, for example, the population rose more than five-fold between 1700 and 1913 (see Table 1.3). In the USA, it rose 29-fold between 1820 and 2003. Before the system of individual liberty

*Table 1.3 Population (millions; mid-year)*

|  | UK | USA |
| --- | --- | --- |
| 1600 | 6.2 | 1.5 |
| 1700 | 8.6 | 1.0 |
| 1820 | 21.2 | 10.0 |
| 1913 | 45.6 | 97.6 |
| 2003 | 60.1 | 290.3 |

*Source*: Maddison (2003), pp. 35–41, 81–3

became prevalent, the population figures had been very low for centuries. For example, in all of Western Europe the population was only 25 million in the year 1000 – about as high as at the time of Christ's birth. In 2001 the figure was 392 million (Maddison 2003, p. 256).

In the wealthiest and most densely populated countries with free societies (for example, in Western Europe and Japan), the increase in population has since substantially flattened because the settlement density is now reaching a high level. In those wealthy, free countries that have not yet attained high settlement densities (for example, the USA), population growth is still continuing. However, as these countries are also slowly reaching high settlement densities, the population growth rate has meanwhile also started to decrease (see Table 1.4). In the developing countries, the rate of growth of the population is much higher, because people there also benefit from market economy institutions (for example, free trade), but their reproductive behavior is only gradually starting to adjust to the new overall conditions. In these countries as well, the population growth rate is declining as the standard of living rises

*Table 1.4 Population growth[a]*

|  | Japan | UK | USA |
| --- | --- | --- | --- |
| 1820–70 | 0.21 | 0.79 | 2.83 |
| 1870–1913 | 0.95 | 0.87 | 2.08 |
| 1913–50 | 1.32 | 0.25 | 1.21 |
| 1950–73 | 1.14 | 0.50 | 1.45 |
| 1973–2001 | 0.55 | 0.22 | 1.06 |

*Note*: [a] Annual average compound growth rates.

*Source*: Maddison (2003), p. 257

(Simon 1996, pp. 342–56). All of these empirical facts concur with Hayek's theory.

Simon's in-depth empirical study also corroborates Hayek's hypothesis that a higher settlement density leads to a higher standard of living. According to Simon (1996, pp. 357–98), an increase in population results in substantial improvements in the area of infrastructure (especially in transportation and communication), which is vital for long-term economic development. Moreover, population growth leads to faster technological progress, to an intensified division of labor and specialization, as well as to economies of scale and scope in production and distribution. In this manner, productivity increases and with it the standard of living. Finally, Simon's analysis also corroborates Hayek's hypothesis that average income per capita may initially decline at high population growth rates. According to Simon's calculations, average income per capita rises to levels higher than in countries with a low degree of population growth only after about 30 to 80 years (Simon 1996, pp. 471–85).

## The Socialist Countries of the Twentieth Century

Several of Hayek's critics confront him with the fact that many countries were governed by Communists for a long period of time in the twentieth century. This fact is said to contradict his theory. Paul (1988, p. 260) says that the 'success' of socialist regimes such as the Soviet Union cannot be explained by Hayek's theory because this type of 'retrogression' in cultural evolution is incompatible with his theory: '[O]n his evolutionary account the success of such status regimes as the Soviet Union are impossible to explain.' Miller (1989) and Steele (1987, pp. 181–2) hold that the rise in population and in the standard of living in the Soviet Union since the October Revolution falsifies Hayek's theory. 'Hayek's claim appears to be conclusively refuted' (Miller 1989, p. 315).

Paul's critique of Hayek is based on an erroneous understanding of his view of cultural evolution. As already set out in section 6, Hayek is well aware that in the course of development on the way to a Great Society, phases of retrogression may occur. Hayek himself always mentions socialism as a particularly significant example for this type of retrogression and explains in his theory of evolution why such movements that threaten the development towards a Great Society occur from time to time.

As regards the criticism of Miller and Steele, we must first of all clarify once more which are the hypotheses that Hayek formulated. Hayek ([1935a] 1948; [1935b] 1948; [1940] 1948) started early to prove theoretically that a socialist economic system must be much less efficient than a free market economy. Later on, his analyses on this topic became part of the theory of cultural evolution that he subsequently developed. They are now a central element and area of application of that theory. Hayek systematically pointed out the principal weaknesses of the socialist institutions. Due to these weaknesses, the standard of living in the socialist countries would be much lower than in market economies, according to Hayek. Based on this findings, he also held that it would be impossible to maintain today's global population if socialism were practiced throughout the world (1988, p. 9, 121). In 1988 he wrote: 'Communist countries such as Russia would be starving today if their populations were not kept alive by the Western world' (1988, p. 131).

The empirical facts are fully in line with these hypotheses. The socialist countries were only able to increase or maintain their populations because they participated in the numerous achievements of the Western world. For example, they conducted large-scale espionage on the technical inventions of the West and imitated them. Due to the low technological standard of their economic system, they were also forced to import many sophisticated goods from Western countries. Some socialist countries, such as the traditional agrarian export country of Russia, even had to start importing wheat and other foods in large quantities from the West to feed their populations (Merl 1995, p. 297). As they were able to finance these imports only partially by their own exports due to the low level of productivity of their economic system, they were forced to incur high debts in the West. Socialist countries that refused to import food from Western countries for ideological reasons (for example, Romania and North Korea) suffered severe famines time and again. Severe famines during which millions of people died also occurred as a result of the compulsory collectivization of agriculture and the deportation of entire ethnic groups. The total number of deaths due to socialism is estimated at almost 100 million (Courtois 1998, p. 16).

Hayek was also right in hypothesizing that the standard of living in the socialist countries would be much lower than in the West. In the USSR, for example, real GDP per capita was only approximately one-third of the US

*Table 1.5    Real GDP per capita (1990 international Geary-Khamis dollars)*

|        | China  | Japan   | USA     | USSR   |
|--------|--------|---------|---------|--------|
| 1969   | 722    | 8 874   | 15 179  | 5 225  |
| 1973   | 839    | 11 434  | 16 689  | 6 059  |
| 1977   | 895    | 12 064  | 17 567  | 6 454  |
| 1981   | 1 103  | 13 754  | 18 856  | 6 430  |
| 1985   | 1 522  | 15 331  | 20 717  | 6 701  |
| 1989   | 1 827  | 17 942  | 23 059  | 7 098  |

*Source*:    Maddison (2003), pp. 89, 101, 184

level (see Table 1.5). In China, before the start of the market economy reforms in 1978, real GDP per capita was only approximately 7 per cent of Japan's. Due to the low productivity of their economic system, the standard of living in the socialist countries dropped further and further below that of the West. For example, at the beginning of the 1950s, Poland's income per capita exceeded that of Spain, at the time which was also a largely agricultural country. By 1988, Poland's income per capita was only one-fourth of Spain's (Sachs 1993, pp. 22–6). Many other indicators – such as the number of durable consumer goods in a typical private household or the working time required to be able to purchase a unit of a specific consumer good – provide a good impression of the growing gap in the standard of living vis-à-vis the West as well (Kornai 1992, pp. 302–15). Please note that this development also impressively illustrates the mechanism of group selection.

As the author of this chapter has shown elsewhere, Hayek's theory can also be used to explain the collapse of the socialist systems at the end of the 1980s and their subsequent transformation into free market economies (Feldmann 1997). All institutions that had developed spontaneously in the course of cultural evolution and had made the economic rise of the Western world possible were radically condemned by the Communists and replaced by new institutions. Each of the institutions that the Communists created as a re-placement for the ones they eliminated (such as central planning instead of the market mechanism, state property instead of private property of the means of production) had serious functional deficiencies and thus contributed to the eventual collapse of socialism. Just as a side note, the criticism of Hayek's assessment of the productivity of the socialist systems was made before their collapse. The critics have since fallen silent.

## HAS HAYEK COMMITTED A NATURALISTIC FALLACY?

As already mentioned in section 7, a number of critics claim that, according to Hayek's theory, everything that survives in the course of cultural evolution is superior; by surviving, it proves its superiority. From the viewpoint of these critics, the theory lacks an independent benchmark for assessing the results of cultural evolution and for the assessment of political reform pro-posals. Neither does the theory, according to its critics, allow one to deduce any political reform proposals. Hayek is said to imply that what 'is', 'ought' to be. It is contended that he committed a naturalistic fallacy and supports an uncritical Panglossianism, namely, the belief that we live in the best of all possible worlds. To be consistent, socialist and other totalitarian regimes that have evolved in the course of cultural evolution would have to be accepted. Therefore, Hayek's theory is said to be fatalistic.[28]

Hayek (1988, p. 27) himself passionately refuted the charge of having committed a naturalistic fallacy:

> I have no intention to commit what is often called the genetic or naturalistic fallacy. I do not claim that the results of group selection of traditions are necessarily 'good' – any more than I claim that other things that have long survived in the course of evolution, such as cockroaches, have moral value. I do claim that, whether we like it or not, without the particular traditions I have mentioned, the extended order of civilization could not continue to exist ...; and that if we discard these traditions, out of ill-considered notions (which may indeed genuinely commit the naturalistic fallacy) of what is to be reasonable, we shall doom a large part of mankind to poverty and death.

If one accepts the preservation of today's mankind and its prosperity as a normative standard, then it is perfectly possible to deduce concrete political recommendations from Hayek's theory. First however, it must be recognized on the basis of Hayek's insights that cultural evolution cannot be directed by reason. Reason itself only emerged in the course of cultural evolution. Humans did not deliberately develop traditional institutions. Neither is their significance and interdependence fully understood by people, even today: '[M]an has not only never invented his most beneficial institutions, from language to morals and law, and even today does not yet understand why he should preserve them when they satisfy neither his instincts nor his reason' (Hayek [1978] 1979, p. 163). '[O]ur traditional institutions are not understood, and do not have their purposes or their effects, beneficial or otherwise, specified in advance' (Hayek 1988, p. 71). Moreover, the future conditions to which institutions must adapt cannot be predicted. This is another reason why cultural evolution cannot be steered or controlled.

Nonetheless, political reforms are of course possible and necessary because time and again the development towards a Great Society (or the continued existence of such a society) is being disrupted by diverse factors, as Hayek has shown. In section 6, the three most significant factors were already mentioned: powerful governments that corrupt traditional beneficial institutions by their power; inborn instincts that rebel against the discipline of learnt rules of conduct; reason that does not recognize the meaning of traditional institutions and desires to rise above these. Moreover, it could also happen that an entire society adopts moral values or other institutions that later on turn out to be harmful (Hayek 1960, p. 67). As Hayek has shown, these factors existed all at the same time in socialism. Therefore, it is only consistent that he called for the abolition of that system.

As Hayek has shown theoretically and empirically, the system of individual liberty is clearly superior to socialism; it has made the increase in human population and today's prosperity possible. No one has investigated the political implications of this insight in more depth than Hayek himself.[29] According to Hayek, all members of society must be given the largest scope of freedom possible to be able to pursue their own goals. Individual liberty must be guaranteed by general rules of law that treat all humans equally and do not constrict people's scope of action more than absolutely necessary. The private property of citizens must be effectively protected. Markets must be kept open. State interventions are to be ruled out because they distort and hinder the competitive process of continuous discovery of new knowledge, which allows people to continually increase productivity. Finally, the value of money must be kept stable in order for prices to fulfill their signaling and allocation functions. However, by designing the appropriate institutional framework, policy-makers will only be able to influence the general nature of the resultant order of actions. They will not be able to produce concrete results. Thus policy-makers should only 'cultivate a growth by providing the appropriate environment, in the manner in which the gardener does this for his plants' (Hayek [1975] 1978, p. 34).

According to Hayek, even within a free society, reforms will be possible and even necessary whenever developments go off track. However, since this order is founded on a tradition of learnt rules of conduct, the significance of which people cannot fully comprehend, one has to build on this very foundation of learnt traditions:

> [T]hough we must constantly re-examine our rules and be prepared to question every single one of them, we can always do so only in terms of their consistency or compatibility with the rest of the system from the angle of their effectiveness in contributing to the formation of the same kind of overall order of actions which all the other rules serve. There is thus certainly room for improvement, but we cannot redesign but only further evolve what we do not fully comprehend. (Hayek [1978] 1979, p. 167).

Hayek himself used the examples of law, private property, democracy and money to show in what respect and how in the course of cultural evolution each of these institutions' developments went wrong and which type of political reforms would be appropriate to solve the resulting problems.[30] All in all, the charge of committing a naturalistic fallacy is also obviously unjustified.[31]

## CONCLUSION

All major charges against Hayek's theory of cultural evolution are unfounded. The scope of applicability of the theory is not very narrow but rather covers the process of cultural evolution in its entire breadth, including deliberately created rules. Hayek's methodological individualism does not contradict his evolutionary approach but rather constitutes a necessary foundation for the explanation of social institutions and their evolution. Hayek's concept of rule following is not naturalistic but rather takes into account the scope within which individuals can reach decisions and act. Hayek's theory is not incomplete but explains the emergence, maintenance and spread of rules, and takes the significance of state power and historical accident into account. Hayek's theory is not teleological or ontogenctic but rather illustrates that the future of cultural evolution is unpredictable and that differentiation steadily increases in the course of evolution. Hayek's theory is falsifiable because it names the characteristics of beneficial institutions regardless of their success in the evolutionary process. The hypotheses that can be deduced from the theory are precise enough to explain the principles of cultural evolution and make pattern predictions. The concept of group selection does not contradict methodological individualism. On the contrary, Hayek explains the mechanism of group selection systematically based on the behavior of individuals. He also shows that the emergence and development of all major mechanisms through which behavior that is detrimental to groups can be largely prevented are a constituent part of the process of cultural evolution. Moreover, Hayek's theory has been impressively corroborated by a number of very different empirical studies. Finally, Hayek has not fallen prey to a naturalistic fallacy but rather himself derived many policy conclusions that can be deduced from his theory.

Still, all this of course by no means implies that Hayek's theory of cultural evolution has already been fully elaborated. Above all, the emergence, change and spread of social institutions require a more differentiated and methodically sophisticated examination. The same applies to the mechanism of group selection and to the mechanisms for the prevention of behavior that is detrimental to the group. Additionally, the theory has to be subjected to more specific and comprehensive empirical examination. Finally, its political implications should be elaborated more systematically and made more suitable for their practical application in politics. Nonetheless, the value of Hayek's theory and its possible future significance should not be underestimated. The theory explains the long-term development of human societies and their institutions comprehensively and in a uniform manner, uncovering deep-rooted causes and far-reaching effects. Its explanatory powers surpass all other attempts in this field to date and may even bring about a shift in the paradigms of the social sciences in the long run – a shift that may amount to nothing less than an evolutionist revolution.

# APPENDICES

## A1.1   List of Countries

Albania, Algeria, Argentina, Australia, Austria, Bahamas, Bangladesh, Barbados, Belgium, Belize, Benin, Bolivia, Botswana, Brazil, Bulgaria, Burundi, Cameroon, Canada, Central African Republic, Chad, Chile, China, Colombia, Costa Rica, Cote d'Ivoire, Cyprus, Democratic Republic of Congo, Denmark, Dominican Republic, Ecuador, Egypt, El Salvador, Fiji, Finland, France, Gabon, Germany, Ghana, Greece, Guatemala, Haiti, Honduras, Hong Kong, Hungary, Iceland, India, Indonesia, Ireland, Israel, Italy, Jamaica, Japan, Jordan, Kenya, Luxembourg, Madagascar, Malawi, Malaysia, Mali, Malta, Mauritius, Mexico, Morocco, Namibia, Netherlands, New Zealand, Nicaragua, Niger, Nigeria, Norway, Pakistan, Panama, Papua New Guinea, Paraguay, Peru, Philippines, Poland, Portugal, Republic of Congo, Romania, Senegal, Sierra Leone, Singapore, South Africa, South Korea, Spain, Sri Lanka, Sweden, Switzerland, Syria, Taiwan, Tanzania, Thailand, Togo, Trinidad and Tobago, Tunisia, Turkey, Uganda, United Arab Emirates, United Kingdom, United States, Uruguay, Venezuela, Zambia, Zimbabwe.

## A1.2   Data Description and Sources

### Economic freedom as defined by the 'Economic Freedom of the World (EFW)' summary index

The index measures the degree of economic freedom in the following five areas: (1) size of government: expenditures, taxes and enterprises, (2) legal structure and security of property rights, (3) access to sound money, (4) freedom to trade internationally, (5) regulation of credit, labor, and business. The summary rating of the index is the arithmetic mean of the five area ratings. The rating scale ranges from 0 to 10, with 0 representing the lowest and 10 the highest degree of economic freedom. Source: Gwartney and Lawson (2004).

### Economic growth

Annual percentage growth rate of real GDP. Source: Directorate-General of Budget, Accounting and Statistics (2003), International Monetary Fund (2004a), World Bank (2004).

### English language

The fraction of a country's population speaking English as a mother tongue. Source: Hall and Jones (1999).

**English legal origin**
Dummy variable that equals one if a country's Company Law or Commercial Code has an English common law tradition. Source: La Porta, Lopez-de-Silanes, Shleifer and Vishny (1999), World Bank (2003).

**Ethnolinguistic fractionalization**
Average value of five different indices of ethnolinguistic fractionalization. Its value ranges from 0 to 1. The five component indices are: (1) index of ethnolinguistic fractionalization in 1960, which measures the probability that two randomly selected individuals from a given country do not belong to the same ethnolinguistic group (the index is based on the number and size of population groups as distinguished by their ethnic and linguistic status); (2) probability of two randomly selected individuals speaking different languages; (3) probability that two randomly selected individuals do not speak the same language; (4) percent of population not speaking the official language; and (5) percent of population not speaking the most widely used language. Source: Easterly and Levine (1997).

**French legal origin**
Dummy variable that equals one if a country's Company Law or Commercial Code has a French civil law tradition. Source: La Porta, Lopez-de-Silanes, Shleifer and Vishny (1999), World Bank (2003).

**German legal origin**
Dummy variable that equals one if a country's Company Law or Commercial Code has a German civil law tradition. Source: La Porta, Lopez-de-Silanes, Shleifer and Vishny (1999), World Bank (2003).

**Investment share**
Gross capital formation as a percentage of GDP. Source: Directorate-General of Budget, Accounting and Statistics (2003), European Commission (2004), International Monetary Fund (2004b), International Monetary Fund (2004c), World Bank (2004).

**Latitude**
The absolute value of the latitude of the country, scaled to take values between 0 and 1. Source: La Porta, Lopez-de-Silanes, Shleifer and Vishny (1999).

**Log income per capita**
Natural logarithm of gross national income divided by mid-year population, converted into current international dollars using purchasing power parity

rates. Source: Directorate-General of Budget, Accounting and Statistics (2003), United Nations – Economic Commission for Latin America and the Caribbean (2003), World Bank (2004).

**Regional dummies**
Dummy variables for the following three regions: Africa, Asia, Latin America and the Caribbean.

**Secondary enrollment rate**
Students enrolled in secondary education, regardless of age, as a percentage of the population of the age group that officially corresponds to this level of education. Source: Directorate General of Budget, Accounting and Statistics (2003), United Nations – Economic Commission for Latin America and the Caribbean (2004), World Bank (2004).

**Transition country**
Dummy variable for countries in transition from centrally planned to market economy.

**War**
Dummy variable for interstate wars. Source: Ghosn and Palmer (2003).

**Western European languages**
The fraction of a country's population speaking one of five major languages of Western Europe as a mother tongue (English, French, German, Portuguese, and Spanish). Source: Hall and Jones (1999).

**Year dummies**
Dummy variables for each year except 2002.

## NOTES

1. See, for example, Radnitzky (1984), p. 9; Gray (1986), p. 135; Hodgson (1993), p. 153; Witt (1994), p. 178; Vanberg (1994a), p. 451; North (1999), pp. 81, 95–6.
2. In addition to discussing all relevant English publications, this chapter also makes use of important books and articles – written by Hayek as well as his critics – that up to now have only been published in German. All German quotations have been translated into English by the author of this chapter.
3. The following synopsis is based mainly on Hayek (1973); [1978] (1979); (1983) and (1988).
4. On organizations, see Hayek [1963a] (1969); (1973), pp. 46–54, and (1988), p. 37. On legislation and statute law, see especially Hayek (1973), ch. 4. On democracy, see Hayek (1960), ch. 7, and Hayek [1965] (1969); (1979).
5. See especially Hayek (1979), ch. 12 and 16.

6. Lange-von Kulessa (1997), pp. 271–6, and Caldwell (2001), pp. 548–51, also share this assessment.
7. Hayek himself stressed this point. See, for example, Hayek [1978] (1979), pp. 199–200.
8. For this reason, Hodgson's holistic perspective is not a useful complement to Hayek's approach as claimed by Lange-von Kulessa (1997), p. 283.
9. See also Hayek (1988), p. 63, and (1960). In the latter work mentioned, Hayek presents in great detail his arguments for the social desirability of individual liberty and what is required in the rules of conduct to secure individual liberty.
10. Vanberg (1984), pp. 104–6; (1994b), pp. 84–5, brings forth the allegation of functionalism, too.
11. Modern biology no longer considers ontogeny part of evolution. Today, biology defines evolution as only the development of species, that is, phylogeny.
12. Hayek makes statements of this kind in many other places. See Hayek (1960), pp. 40–1; (1967), p. 76; (1973), pp. 23–4; [1978] (1979), pp. 176, 198 and (1988), p. 26.
13. See Voigt (1992), p. 465; Vanberg (1994a), p. 460; O'Driscoll and Rizzo (1996), pp. 39–40.
14. See Bouillon (1991), p. 43; Voigt (1992), pp. 467, 470; De Vlieghere (1994), p. 299.
15. See Vanberg (1994b), pp. 84, 93–4. See also Steele (1987), p. 192; Paul (1988), pp. 259–60; Sugden (1993), p. 402.
16. This assessment is also shared by Radnitzky (1987), p. 66; Madison (1990), pp. 89–100; Vromen (1995), p. 173; Khalil (1996), p. 195; Lange-von Kulessa (1997), pp. 276–82; Whitman (1998), pp. 60–63.
17. See in particular Vanberg (1984), pp. 99–100; (1994b), pp. 85–93. Arnold (1980), pp. 350–1, Witt (1994), p. 185, and Denis (2002), pp. 276–8, express opinions in the same vein.
18. See Hayek (1967), pp. 78–80; [1978] (1979), pp. 155–61; (1988), pp. 21–2.
19. See Hayek (1967), p. 78; [1978] (1979), p. 160; (1988), pp. 11–12.
20. See Hayek (1967), p. 78; [1978] (1979), pp. 164–5, 170–1.
21. In later works, Axelrod and others studied these conditions in more depth. An overview of the relevant works is given in Axelrod and Dion (1988).
22. See Ostrom (1990); Ostrom et al. (1994).
23. Weede is not quite right in stating that England 'did not have any internal barriers to trade in the form of road tolls, river tolls or city gate tolls.' There were numerous tolls and other mercantilist restrictions on trade in early modern England as well. But the burden of these regulations was much lighter in England and the public authorities stopped enforcing them much earlier than in continental Europe (see Heckscher 1955).
24. On the 'Economic Freedom of the World (EFW)' index, see Walker (1988); Block (1991); Easton and Walker (1992); Gwartney et al. (1996); Gwartney and Lawson (1997), (1998); Gwartney et al. (2000); Gwartney et al. (2001); Gwartney et al. (2002); Gwartney et al. (2003); Gwartney and Lawson (2004). The Heritage Foundation regularly publishes an index of economic freedom as well (see, for example, Miles et al. 2005). However, this index only covers the years from 1995 on and is solely based on the assessments of in-house experts. The EFW index covers a much longer period of time and is largely based on objective data. Thus the latter is much more suitable to analyse the determinants of long-term economic development and is clearly superior from a methodological point of view.
25. Other researchers have obtained similar results in econometric studies before. See, for example, Scully (1992), (1997), (2002); Ali (1997); Easton and Walker (1997); Goldsmith (1997); Ayal and Karras (1998); Dawson (1998), (2003); Farr et al. (1998); Nelson and Singh (1998); Gwartney, et al. (1999); de Haan and Sturm (2000); Heckelman (2000); Wu and Davis (2000); Sturm and de Haan (2001); Carlsson and Lundström (2002); Green et al. (2002); Karabegovic et al. (2003).
26. For more on the emergence and spread of the system of individual liberty, see the volumes published in the series 'The Making of Modern Freedom', in particular Hexter (1992); Jones (1992); Wootton (1994); Van Kley (1994); Davis (1995); Konig (1995); Woloch (1996); Scheiber (1998); Eltis (2002). See also Birtsch (1981, 1987). On Germany, see also Krug (1995).

27. Although in most native American societies, the institutions of private property, law, the market economy and money were present, they were far less developed than in Western Europe. For example, there was no private property in land; the law was not characterized by general, abstract, certain and equal rules that secured individual liberty; there were neither flexible market prices nor an extended network of trade; the institutions of money and banking were still in their infancy.
28. See Buchanan (1975), p. 194, (1981), pp. 45–6; Brennan and Buchanan (1985), pp. 9–10; Gray (1986), p. 142; Miller (1989), p. 314; Voigt (1992), p. 465; De Vlieghere (1994), p. 293; Denis (2002), pp. 278–84.
29. See especially Hayek (1960), (1973), (1976a) and (1979).
30. On the institution of law, see especially Hayek (1960), ch. 10, 14 and 16, as well as (1973), ch. 3 to 6. On the institution of private property, see Hayek (1948) as well as (1988), pp. 35–7. On democracy, see Hayek (1960), ch. 7 and 17 as well as (1979). On the institution of money, see Hayek [1932] (1999) and [1976b] (1999).
31. Radnitzky (1984), Yeager (1989), Madison (1990), Schmidt and Moser (1992), Geue (1997), Geue (1998) and Whitman (1998) also share this assessment.

# REFERENCES

Acemoglu, Daron, Simon Johnson and James A. Robinson (2002), 'Reversal of fortune: geography and institutions in the making of the modern world income distribution', *Quarterly Journal of Economics*, **117** (4), 1231–94.

Ali, Abdiweli M. (1997), 'Economic freedom, democracy and growth', *Journal of Private Enterprise*, **13** (1), 1–20.

Arnold, Roger A. (1980), 'Hayek and institutional evolution', *Journal of Libertarian Studies*, **4**, 341–52.

Axelrod, Robert (1984), *The Evolution of Cooperation*, New York: Basic Books.

Axelrod, Robert and Douglas Dion (1988), 'The further evolution of cooperation', *Science*, **242**, 1385–9.

Ayal, Eliezer B. and Georgios Karras (1998), 'Components of economic freedom and growth: an empirical study', *Journal of Developing Areas*, **32** (3), 327–38.

Birtsch, Günter (ed.) (1981), *Grund- und Freiheitsrechte im Wandel von Gesellschaft und Geschichte. Beiträge zur Geschichte der Grund- und Freiheitsrechte vom Ausgang des Mittelalters bis zur Revolution von 1848*, Göttingen: Vandenhoeck & Ruprecht.

Birtsch, Günter (ed.) (1987), *Grund- und Freiheitsrechte von der ständischen zur spätbürgerlichen Gesellschaft*, Göttingen: Vandenhoeck & Ruprecht.

Block, Walter (ed.) (1991), *Economic Freedom: Toward a Theory of Measurement*, Vancouver BC: Fraser Institute.

Bouillon, Hardy (1991), *Ordnung, Evolution und Erkenntnis. Hayeks Sozialphilosophie und ihre erkenntnistheoretische Grundlage*, Tübingen: Mohr Siebeck.

Brennan, Geoffrey and James M. Buchanan (1985), *The Reason of Rules. Constitutional Political Economy*, Cambridge: Cambridge University Press.

Buchanan, James M. (1975), *The Limits of Liberty. Between Anarchy and Leviathan*, Chicago: University of Chicago Press.

Buchanan, James M. (1981), 'Möglichkeiten institutioneller Reformen im Rahmen kulturell geformter abstrakter Verhaltensregeln', in Viktor Vanberg (ed.), *Liberaler Evolutionismus oder vertragstheoretischer Konstitutionalismus? Zum Problem institutioneller Reformen bei F.A. von Hayek und J.M. Buchanan*, Tübingen: Mohr Siebeck, pp. 45–8.

Caldwell, Bruce (2001), 'Hodgson on Hayek: a critique', *Cambridge Journal of Economics*, **25** (4), pp. 539–53.

Carlsson, Fredrik and Susanna Lundström (2002), 'Economic freedom and growth: decomposing the effects', *Public Choice*, **112** (3–4), 335–44.

Courtois, Stéphane (1998), 'Die Verbrechen des Kommunismus', in Stéphane Courtois, Nicolas Werth, Jean-Louis Panné, Andrzej Paczkowski, Karel Bartosek and Jean-Louis Margolin (eds), *Das Schwarzbuch des Kommunismus. Unterdrückung, Verbrechen und Terror*, Munich and Zurich: Piper, pp. 11–43.

Davis, R.W. (ed.) (1995), *The Origins of Modern Freedom in the West*, Stanford, CA: Stanford University Press.

Dawson, John W. (1998), 'Institutions, investment, and growth: new cross-country and panel data evidence', *Economic Inquiry*, **36** (4), 603–19.

Dawson, John W. (2003), 'Causality in the freedom-growth relationship', *European Journal of Political Economy*, **19** (3), 479–95.

Denis, Andy (2002), 'Was Hayek a Panglossian evolutionary theorist? A reply to Whitman', *Constitutional Political Economy*, **13** (3), 275–85.

De Vlieghere, Martin (1994), 'A reappraisal of Friedrich A. Hayek's cultural evolutionism', *Economics and Philosophy*, **10** (2), 285–304.

Directorate-General of Budget, Accounting and Statistics (2003), *Statistical Yearbook of the Republic of China 2003*, Taipei: Directorate-General of Budget, Accounting and Statistics.

Easterly, William and Ross Levine (1997), 'Africa's growth tragedy: policies and ethnic divisions', *Quarterly Journal of Economics*, **112** (4), 1203–50.

Easterly, William and Ross Levine (2003), 'Tropics, germs, and crops: how endowments influence economic development', *Journal of Monetary Economics*, **50** (1), 3–39.

Easton, Stephen and Michael A. Walker (eds) (1992), *Rating Global Economic Freedom*, Vancouver BC: Fraser Institute.

Easton, Stephen and Michael A. Walker (1997), 'Income, growth, and economic freedom', *American Economic Review, Papers and Proceedings*, **87** (2), pp. 328–32.

Eltis, David (ed.) (2002), *Coerced and Free Migration: Global Perspectives*, Stanford, CA: Stanford University Press.

European Commission (2004), *Statistical Annex of European Economy. Spring 2004*, Brussels: European Commission.

Farr, W. Ken, Richard A. Lord and J. Larry Wolfenbarger (1998), 'Economic freedom, political freedom, and economic well-being: a causality analysis', *Cato Journal*, **18** (2), 247–62.

Feldmann, Horst (1997), 'Kulturelle Evolution und der Zusammenbruch des Sozialismus', *List Forum für Wirtschafts- und Finanzpolitik*, **23** (1), 82–101.

Geue, Heiko (1997), *Evolutionäre Institutionenökonomik. Ein Beitrag aus der Sicht der österreichischen Schule*, Stuttgart: Lucius & Lucius.

Geue, Heiko (1998), 'Sind ordnungspolitische Reformanstrengungen mit Hayeks Evolutionismus vereinbar?', *ORDO*, **49**, 141–63.

Ghosn, Faten and Glenn Palmer (2003), codebook for the Militarized Interstate Dispute data collection for the Correlates of War Project, version 3.0, accessed 28 November at www.cow2.la.psu.edu.

Goldsmith, Arthur A. (1997), 'Economic rights and government in developing countries: cross-national evidence on growth and development', *Studies in Comparative International Development*, **32** (2), 29–44.

Gray, John N. (1986), *Hayek on Liberty*, 2nd edn, Oxford: Basil Blackwell.

Green, Sam, Andrew Melnyk and Dennis Powers (2002), 'Is economic freedom necessary for technology diffusion?', *Applied Economics Letters*, **9** (14), 907–10.

Gwartney, James D. and Robert A. Lawson (1997), *Economic Freedom of the World. 1997 Annual Report*, Vancouver BC: Fraser Institute.

Gwartney, James D. and Robert A. Lawson (1998), *Economic Freedom of the World. 1998/1999 Interim Report*, Vancouver BC: Fraser Institute.

Gwartney, James D. and Robert A. Lawson (2004), *Economic Freedom of the World. 2004 Annual Report*, Vancouver BC: Fraser Institute.

Gwartney, James D., Robert A. Lawson and Walter Block (1996), *Economic Freedom of the World: 1975–1995*, Vancouver BC: Fraser Institute.

Gwartney, James D., Robert A. Lawson, Chris Edwards, Walter Park, Veronique de Rugy and Smita Wagh (2002), *Economic Freedom of the World. 2002 Annual Report*, Vancouver BC: Fraser Institute.

Gwartney, James D., Robert A. Lawson and Neil Emerick (2003), *Economic Freedom of the World. 2003 Annual Report*, Vancouver BC: Fraser Institute.

Gwartney, James D., Robert A. Lawson and Randall G. Holcombe (1999), 'Economic freedom and the environment for economic growth', *Journal of Institutional and Theoretical Economics*, **155** (4), 643–63.

Gwartney, James D., Robert A. Lawson, Walter Park and Charles Skipton (2001), *Economic Freedom of the World. 2001 Annual Report*, Vancouver BC: Fraser Institute.

Gwartney, James D., Robert A. Lawson and Dexter Samida (2000), *Economic Freedom of the World. 2000 Annual Report*, Vancouver BC: Fraser Institute.

Haan, Jakob de and Jan-Egbert Sturm (2000), 'On the relationship between economic freedom and economic growth', *European Journal of Political Economy*, **16** (2), 215–41.

Hall, Robert E. and Charles I. Jones (1999), 'Why do some countries produce so much more output per worker than others?', *Quarterly Journal of Economics*, **114** (1), 83–116.

Hayek, Friedrich A. von (1932), 'The fate of the gold standard', reprinted in Friedrich A. von Hayek (1999), *Good Money, Part I: The New World*, Chicago: University of Chicago Press, pp. 153–68.

Hayek, Friedrich A. von (1935a), 'Socialist calculation I: the nature and history of the problem', reprinted in Friedrich A. von Hayek (1948), *Individualism and Economic Order*, Chicago: University of Chicago Press, pp. 119–47.

Hayek, Friedrich A. von (1935b), 'Socialist calculation II: the state of the debate (1935)', reprinted in Friedrich A. von Hayek (1948), *Individualism and Economic Order*, Chicago: University of Chicago Press, pp. 148–80.

Hayek, Friedrich A. von (1937), 'Economics and knowledge', reprinted in Friedrich A. von Hayek (1948), *Individualism and Economic Order*, Chicago: University of Chicago Press, pp. 33–56.

Hayek, Friedrich A. von (1940), 'Socialist calculation III: the competitive "solution"', reprinted in Friedrich A. von Hayek (1948), *Individualism and Economic Order*, Chicago: University of Chicago Press, pp. 181–208.

Hayek, Friedrich A. von (1945), 'The use of knowledge in society', reprinted in Friedrich A. von Hayek (1948), *Individualism and Economic Order*, Chicago: University of Chicago Press, pp. 77–91.

Hayek, Friedrich A. von (1948), '"Free" enterprise and competitive order', in Friedrich

A. von Hayek, *Individualism and Economic Order*, Chicago: University of Chicago Press, pp. 107–18.

Hayek, Friedrich A. von (1952a), *The Counter-Revolution of Science. Studies on the Abuse of Reason*, 2nd edn (1979), Indianapolis, IN: Liberty Press.

Hayek, Friedrich A. von (1952b), *The Sensory Order. An Enquiry into the Foundations of Theoretical Psychology*, London: Routledge & Kegan Paul.

Hayek, Friedrich A. von (1955), 'Degrees of explanation', reprinted in Friedrich A. von Hayek (1967), *Studies in Philosophy, Politics and Economics*, Chicago: University of Chicago Press, pp. 3–21.

Hayek, Friedrich A. von (1960), *The Constitution of Liberty*, Chicago: University of Chicago Press.

Hayek, Friedrich A. von (1963a), 'Arten der Ordnung', reprinted in Friedrich A. von Hayek (1969), *Freiburger Studien. Gesammelte Aufsätze*, Tübingen: Mohr Siebeck, pp. 32–46.

Hayek, Friedrich A. von (1963b), 'Rules, perception and intelligibility', reprinted in Friedrich A. Hayek von (1967), *Studies in Philosophy, Politics and Economics*, Chicago: University of Chicago Press, pp. 43–65.

Hayek, Friedrich A. von (1964), 'The theory of complex phenomena', reprinted in Friedrich A. von Hayek (1967), *Studies in Philosophy, Politics and Economics*, Chicago: University of Chicago Press, pp. 22–42.

Hayek, Friedrich A. von (1965), 'Die Anschauungen der Mehrheit und die zeitgenössische Demokratie', reprinted in Friedrich A. von Hayek (1969), *Freiburger Studien. Gesammelte Aufsätze*, Tübingen: Mohr Siebeck, pp. 56–74.

Hayek, Friedrich A. von (1967), 'Notes on the evolution of systems of rules of conduct', in Friedrich A. von Hayek, *Studies in Philosophy, Politics and Economics*, Chicago: University of Chicago Press, pp. 66–81.

Hayek, Friedrich A. von (1969), 'The primacy of the abstract', reprinted in Friedrich A. von Hayek (1978), *New Studies in Philosophy, Politics, Economics and the History of Ideas*, Chicago: University of Chicago Press, pp. 35–49.

Hayek, Friedrich A. von (1973), *Law, Legislation and Liberty. A New Statement of the Liberal Principles of Justice and Political Economy, Vol. I: Rules and Order*, London: Routledge & Kegan Paul.

Hayek, Friedrich A. von (1975), 'The pretence of knowledge', reprinted in Friedrich A. von Hayek (1978), *New Studies in Philosophy, Politics, Economics and the History of Ideas*, Chicago: University of Chicago Press, pp. 23–34.

Hayek, Friedrich A. von (1976a), *Law, Legislation and Liberty. A New Statement of the Liberal Principles of Justice and Political Economy, Vol. II: The Mirage of Social Justice*, London: Routledge & Kegan Paul.

Hayek, Friedrich A. von (1976b), 'The denationalization of money: an analysis of the theory and practice of concurrent currencies', reprinted in Friedrich A. von Hayek (1999), *Good Money, Part II: The Standard*, Chicago: University of Chicago Press, pp. 128–229.

Hayek, Friedrich A. von (1978), 'The three sources of human values', reprinted in Friedrich A. von Hayek (1979), *Law, Legislation and Liberty. A New Statement of the Liberal Principles of Justice and Political Economy, Vol. III: The Political Order of a Free People*, London: Routledge & Kegan Paul, pp. 153–76 and 196–208.

Hayek, Friedrich A. von (1979), *Law, Legislation and Liberty. A New Statement of the Liberal Principles of Justice and Political Economy, Vol. III: The Political Order of a Free People*, London: Routledge & Kegan Paul.

Hayek, Friedrich A. von (1983), 'Die überschätzte Vernunft', in Rupert J. Riedl and Franz Kreuzer (eds), *Evolution und Menschenbild*, Hamburg: Hoffmann & Campe, pp. 164–92.

Hayek, Friedrich A. von (1988), *The Fatal Conceit. The Errors of Socialism*, Chicago: University of Chicago Press.

Heckelman, Jac C. (2000), 'Economic freedom and economic growth: a short-run causal investigation', *Journal of Applied Economics*, **3** (1), 71–91.

Heckscher, Eli F. (1955), *Mercantilism*, 2nd edn, 2 vols, London: George Allen and Unwin.

Heiner, Ronald A. (1983), 'The origin of predictable behavior', *American Economic Review*, **73** (4), 560–95.

Heiner, Ronald A. (1986), 'Imperfect decisions and the law: on the evolution of legal precedent and rules', *Journal of Legal Studies*, **15** (2), 227–61.

Heiner, Ronald A. (1989), 'The origin of predictable dynamic behavior', *Journal of Economic Behavior and Organization*, **12** (3), 233–57.

Hexter, J.H. (ed.) (1992), *Parliament and Liberty. From the Reign of Elizabeth to the English Civil War*, Stanford, CA: Stanford University Press.

Hodgson, Geoffrey M. (1993), *Economics and Evolution. Bringing Life Back into Economics*, Cambridge: Polity Press.

International Monetary Fund (2004a), *World Economic Outlook*, April, Washington, DC: IMF.

International Monetary Fund (2004b) *United Arab Emirates: Statistical Appendix*, Washington, DC: IMF.

International Monetary Fund (2004c) *Belize: Selected Issues and Statistical Appendix*, Washington, DC: IMF.

Jones, J.R. (ed.) (1992), *Liberty Secured? Britain before and after 1688*, Stanford, CA: Stanford University Press.

Karabegovic, Amela, Dexter Samida, Chris M. Schlegel and Fred McMahon (2003), 'North American economic freedom: an index of 10 Canadian provinces and 50 US states', *European Journal of Political Economy*, **19** (3), 431–52.

Khalil, Elias L. (1996), 'Friedrich Hayek's Darwinian theory of evolution of institutions: two problems', *Australian Economic Papers*, **35** (66), 183–201.

Kley, Roland (1992), 'F.A. Hayeks Idee einer spontanen sozialen Ordnung: Eine kritische Analyse', *Kölner Zeitschrift für Soziologie und Sozialpsychologie*, **44** (1), 12–34.

Konig, David Thomas (ed.) (1995), *Devising Liberty. Preserving and Creating Freedom in the New American Republic*, Stanford, CA: Stanford University Press.

Kornai, János (1992), *The Socialist System. The Political Economy of Communism*, Princeton, NJ: Princeton University Press.

Krug, Günter E. (1995), *Die Entwicklung ökonomischer Freiheitsrechte in Deutschland im Wandel von Staat, Wirtschaft und Gesellschaft vom Ancien Régime bis zur Reichsgründung (1776–1871)*, Frankfurt am Main: Peter Lang.

Landes, David S. (1998), *The Wealth and Poverty of Nations. Why Some Are So Rich and Some So Poor*, New York and London: W.W. Norton.

Lange-von Kulessa, Juergen (1997), 'Searching for a methodological synthesis – Hayek's individualism in the light of recent holistic criticism', *Journal of Economic Methodology*, **4** (2), 267–87.

La Porta, Rafael, Florencio Lopez-de-Silanes, Andrei Shleifer and Robert Vishny (1999), 'The quality of government', *Journal of Law, Economics, and Organization*, **15** (1), 222–79.

Maddison, Angus (1991), *Dynamic Forces in Capitalist Development. A Long-Run Comparative View*, Oxford, New York: Oxford University Press.

Maddison, Angus (2003), *The World Economy: Historical Statistics*, Paris: OECD.

Madison, G.B. (1990), 'Between theory and practice: Hayek on the logic of cultural dynamics', *Cultural Dynamics*, **3** (1), 84–112.

Merl, Stephan (1995), '"Jeder nach seinen Fähigkeiten, jedem nach seinen Bedürfnissen"? Über Anspruch und Realität von Lebensstandard und Wirtschaftssystem in Rußland und der Sowjetunion', in Wolfram Fischer (ed.), *Lebensstandard und Wirtschaftssysteme*, Frankfurt am Main: Fritz Knapp, pp. 259–306.

Miles, Marc A., Edwin J. Feulner and Mary Anastasia O'Grady (2005), *2005 Index of Economic Freedom*, Washington, DC: Heritage Foundation.

Miller, David (1989), 'The fatalistic conceit', *Critical Review*, **3** (2), 310–23.

Mises, Ludwig von (1963), *Human Action. A Treatise on Economics*, 3rd edn, Chicago: Henry Regnery Company.

Nelson, Michael A. and Ram D. Singh (1998), 'Democracy, economic freedom, fiscal policy, and growth in LDCs: a fresh look', *Economic Development & Cultural Change*, **46** (4), 677–96.

North, Douglass C. (1999), 'Hayek's contribution to understanding the process of economic change', in Viktor Vanberg (ed.), *Freiheit, Wettbewerb und Wirtschaftsordnung*, Freiburg im Breisgau: Haufe, pp. 79–96.

North, Douglass C. and Robert Paul Thomas (1973), *The Rise of the Western World. A New Economic History*, Cambridge: Cambridge University Press.

North, Douglass C. and Barry R. Weingast (1989), 'Constitutions and commitment: the evolution of institutions governing public choice in seventeenth-century England', *Journal of Economic History*, **49** (4), 803–32.

O'Driscoll, Gerald P. and Mario J. Rizzo (1996), *The Economics of Time and Ignorance*, 2nd edn, London, New York: Routledge.

Olson, Mancur (1965), *The Logic of Collective Action. Public Goods and the Theory of Groups*, Cambridge, MA: Harvard University Press.

Ostrom, Elinor (1990), *Governing the Commons. The Evolution of Institutions for Collective Action*, Cambridge: Cambridge University Press.

Ostrom, Elinor (2000), 'Collective action and the evolution of social norms', *Journal of Economic Perspectives*, **14** (3), 137–58.

Ostrom, Elinor, Roy Gardner and James Walker (1994), *Rules, Games, and Common-Pool Resources*, Ann Arbor, MI: University of Michigan Press.

Paul, Ellen Frankel (1988), 'Liberalism, unintended orders and evolutionism', *Political Studies*, **36** (2), 251–72.

Popper, Karl R. (1934), *The Logic of Scientific Discovery*, reprinted (1959), London: Hutchinson.

Radnitzky, Gerard (1984), 'Die ungeplante Gesellschaft. Friedrich von Hayeks Theorie der Evolution spontaner Ordnungen und selbstorganisierender Systeme', *Hamburger Jahrbuch für Wirtschafts- und Gesellschaftspolitik*, **29**, 9–33.

Radnitzky, Gerard (1987), 'An economic theory of the rise of civilisation and its policy implications: Hayek's account generalized', *ORDO*, **38**, 47–90.

Reinhard, Wolfgang (1985), *Geschichte der europäischen Expansion, Vol. II: Die Neue Welt*, Stuttgart: Kohlhammer.

Rosenberg, Nathan and Luther E. Birdzell (1986), *How the West Grew Rich. The Economic Transformation of the Industrial World*, London: I.B. Tauris & Co.

Sachs, Jeffrey D. (1993), *Poland's Jump to the Market Economy*, Cambridge, MA and London: MIT Press.

Scheiber, Harry N. (ed.) (1998), *The State and Freedom of Contract*, Stanford, CA: Stanford University Press.

Schmidt, Johannes and Peter Moser (1992), 'Unwissenheit und Regelevolution: Friedrich A. von Hayek vs. James M. Buchanan', *Zeitschrift für Wirtschaftspolitik*, **41** (2), 191–206.

Scully, Gerald W. (1992), *Constitutional Environments and Economic Growth*, Princeton, NJ: Princeton University Press.

Scully, Gerald W. (1997), 'Rule and policy spaces and economic progress: lessons for third world countries', *Public Choice*, **90** (1–4), 311–24.

Scully, Gerald W. (2002), 'Economic freedom, government policy and the trade-off between equity and economic growth', *Public Choice*, **113** (1–2), 77–96.

Simon, Julian L. (1996), *The Ultimate Resource 2*, Princeton, NJ: Princeton University Press.

Steele, David Ramsay (1987), 'Hayek's theory of cultural group selection', *Journal of Libertarian Studies*, **8** (2), 171–95.

Sturm, Jan-Egbert and Jakob de Haan (2001), 'How robust is the relationship between economic freedom and economic growth?', *Applied Economics*, **33** (7), 839–44.

Sugden, Robert (1986), *The Economics of Rights, Co-operation and Welfare*, Oxford and New York: Blackwell.

Sugden, Robert (1989), 'Spontaneous order', *Journal of Economic Perspectives*, **3** (4), 85–97.

Sugden, Robert (1993), 'Normative judgments and spontaneous order: the contractarian element in Hayek's thought', *Constitutional Political Economy*, **4** (3), 393–424.

United Nations – Economic Commission for Latin America and the Caribbean (2003), *Statistical Yearbook for Latin America and the Caribbean 2002*, Santiago, Chile: ECLAC.

United Nations – Economic Commission for Latin America and the Caribbean (2004), *Statistical Yearbook for Latin America and the Caribbean 2003*, Santiago, Chile: ECLAC.

Vanberg, Viktor (1984), 'Evolution und spontane Ordnung. Anmerkungen zu F. A. von Hayeks Theorie der kulturellen Evolution', in Hans Albert (ed.), *Ökonomisches Denken und soziale Ordnung*, Tübingen: Mohr Siebeck, pp. 83–112.

Vanberg, Viktor (1994a), 'Hayek's legacy and the future of liberal thought: rational liberalism vs. evolutionary agnosticism', *Journal des Economistes et des Etudes Humaines*, **5** (4), 451–81.

Vanberg, Viktor (1994b), 'Spontaneous market order and social rules. A critical examination of F.A. Hayek's theory of cultural evolution', in Viktor Vanberg (ed.), *Rules and Choice in Economics*, London, New York: Routledge, pp. 77–94 and pp. 252–60.

Van Kley, Dale (ed.) (1994), *The French Idea of Freedom. The Old Regime and the Declaration of Rights of 1789*, Stanford, CA: Stanford University Press.

Voigt, Stefan (1992), 'On the internal consistency of Hayek's evolutionary oriented constitutional economics – some general remarks', *Journal des Economistes et des Etudes Humaines*, **3** (4), 461–76.

Vromen, Jack J. (1995), *Economic Evolution. An Enquiry into the Foundations of New Institutional Economics*, London and New York: Routledge.

Walker, Michael A. (ed.) (1988), *Freedom, Democracy, and Economic Welfare*, Vancouver BC: Fraser Institute.

Weede, Erich (2000), *Asien und der Westen. Politische und kulturelle Determinanten der wirtschaftlichen Entwicklung*, Baden-Baden: Nomos.

Whitman, Douglas Glen (1998), 'Hayek contra Pangloss on evolutionary systems', *Constitutional Political Economy*, **9** (1), 45–66.

Witt, Ulrich (1994), 'The theory of societal evolution. Hayek's unfinished legacy', in Jack Birner and Rudy van Zijp (eds), *Hayek, Co-ordination and Evolution. His Legacy in Philosophy, Politics, Economics and the History of Ideas*, London and New York: Routledge, pp. 178–89.

Woloch, Isser (ed.) (1996), *Revolution and the Meanings of Freedom in the Nineteenth Century*, Stanford, CA: Stanford University Press.

Wootton, David (ed.) (1994), *Republicanism, Liberty, and Commercial Society, 1649–1776*, Stanford, CA: Stanford University Press.

World Bank (2003), *Doing Business in 2004: Understanding Regulation*, Washington DC: World Bank.

World Bank (2004), WDI online database, accessed 20 July at www.worldbank.org.

Wu, Wenbo and Otto A. Davis (2000), 'Two freedoms, economic growth and development: an empirical study', *Public Choice*, **100** (1–2), 39–64.

Yeager, Leland B. (1989), 'Reason and cultural evolution', *Critical Review*, 3 (2), 324–35.

# 2.  Hayek's theory of the mind[1]

## Brian J. Loasby

### INTRODUCTION

The theory of the mind presented by Hayek in *The Sensory Order* (1952) is an elaboration of ideas set down in a paper written in 1919, before he had committed himself to the study of economics. Hayek's theory invites comparison with earlier attempts by Adam Smith and Alfred Marshall to explain how human minds work, which were also produced before they turned their attention to economics. Like Hayek, both were confronted as young men by the problematic status of supposedly-objective knowledge, and like Hayek both responded by developing a theory in which human beings create knowledge by forming connections within particular domains. All three recognise the impossibility of demonstrating that any such process can deliver proven truth, and envisage sequences of trial and error within particular contexts, leading to the preservation of what seems to work – until it no longer does, when a new sequence of trial and error begins. In other words, they all offer what we would now call evolutionary theories, in the broad sense of variation, selection, and the preservation – which is always provisional – of selected variants. It would not be appropriate in this chapter to undertake an extensive comparison between the three (and still less appropriate, though tempting, to explore the relationships between their psychological theories and the content and methods of their work in economics); but selective references to similarities and complementarities will be used to illustrate or extend aspects of Hayek's theory.

### HAYEK'S *SENSORY ORDER*

The problem which attracted Hayek's attention was this. 'In order to be able to give a satisfactory account of the regularities existing in the physical world the physical sciences have been forced to define the objects of which this world exists increasingly in terms of the observed relations between these objects, and at the same time more and more to disregard the way in which these objects appear to us' (Hayek 1952, pp. 2–3). Not only have sensory qualities been progressively discarded from this scientific account; the scientific categories neither encompass the sensory categories nor provide a sufficient basis for reinterpreting them, but constitute a distinctive ordering which overlaps but does not supersede the sensory order. Thus 'objects which appear alike to us do not always prove to behave in the same way towards other objects, ... objects which phenomenally resemble each other need not be physically similar to each other, and ... sometimes objects which appear to be altogether different may prove to be physically very similar' (Hayek 1952, pp. 5–6). Hayek accepts the superiority of the physical order as a representation of relationships within the physical world, including the physical properties of human brains, but he does not raise the question why the human species should have first developed what, from the perspective of the physical sciences, appears to be an inferior classification system – but on which we still rely for everyday living; instead he asks how this sensory order came into existence. 'How' may be thought a more 'scientific' question than 'why', and in this instance it may also be thought to have logical priority: indeed Hayek's analysis provides a basis for explaining why, as we shall see later. However, the primary concern of this chapter is the value of Hayek's analysis as a general theory of the creation of mental orders – an explanation of how the mind works.

Since the disparity to be explained is that between a classification based on the effects produced by external events on our senses and a classification based on their effects on other external events, the focus of enquiry is on systems of relationships, and the key to Hayek's analysis is the hypothesis that each set of 'causal connexions' is linked to a set of 'structural connexions' within the human brain. It follows that the sensory and physical orders are linked to different neurological networks developed independently. The essential point to note here is that connections within the brain are selective, and so connections between human perceptions and the physical world (including the physical world of the brain) are also selective; moreover, being selected within the human brain, which as a physical system is capable of sustaining alternative connections, they are 'subjective' rather than 'objective'. The characteristic Austrian emphasis on subjectivity therefore has a psychological, indeed biological, basis. Moreover, the subjectivity of the human mind is not just a 'veil' which conceals but does not influence the operation of physical laws; it has real effects. It allows great scope for error (connections may be false or incomplete) and for sheer ignorance as defined by Israel Kirzner (1973) in his theory of entrepreneurship (connections may never have been made); it also allows great scope for imagination and novelty, as emphasised by Shackle (1979) in his examination of human choice (through the making of new connections).

These possibilities are all examples of the potential for diversity of inter-pretation between individuals resulting from the cumulative interaction between differing environments and different patterns of connections within the brain, which between them constitute distinctive 'experiences'. Because of the nor-mal connotations of the word 'experience' it may be more appropriate to speak of 'construing the replication of events', a terminology employed by the American psychologist George Kelly (1963), whose ideas have some striking affinities with Hayek's, as we shall see. This is indeed an accurate definition of the process that is analysed in Hayek's neuropsychological theory, for what events are deemed to constitute a replication is determined by the interpretative framework that is applied to them, as in Kelly's own account of human mental processes. For both Hayek and Kelly, this frame-work is both prior to any particular interpretation and subject to modification in the process of interpretation. The influences on the formation of connec-tions, and on the possibilities of aligning them with the external world and of mutual understanding between people who are using different frameworks, then become an important field of study, within which cultural institutions have a significant role.

Because its conceptual basis is that of a selectively-connected system, Hayek's theory is to be sharply distinguished from general equilibrium mod-els, in which every element is connected to every other. The completeness of these connections in general equilibrium models (the equivalent of a 'field theory') is the basis both for analyses of the existence and stability of general equilibrium allocations and for claims about their welfare properties, which are therefore vulnerable to Hayek's criticisms. Potts (2000) has produced an incisive argument that the incompleteness of their connections is the crucial fact about all economic systems; the incompleteness of all cognitive systems is the foundation of Simon's work on human decision-making and organisa-tional design, and Simon, like Hayek, insists on the importance of interactions between the external environment and the 'internal environment' (Hayek 1952, p. 109) of the human brain. The incompleteness of connections is compatible with a unitary order, on which Hayek (1952, p. 19) insists, but it is also compatible with the development of alternative unitary orders as mutually inconsistent representations of a set of phenomena. It is an essential feature of Hayek's criticism of 'scientism' that the physical order, like the sensory order, exists in the space of representations.

Hayek's hypothesis of connectivity also naturally suggests the need for a process-theoretic explanation of the development of selective and systematic connections, and this is what he provides. Suggesting a topological isomor-phism between the neural and phenomenological orders (Hayek 1952, p. 40), he argues that instead of direct connections between particular stimuli and particular sensory qualities, the effect that is produced by any stimulus depends, first, on how (or indeed whether) it is translated into an impulse in some nerve fibre (Hayek 1952, p. 10) and, second, on the location of this impulse in relation to other impulses within the network of connections that has already been established within the brain (Hayek 1952, p. 53). 'The transmission of impulses from neuron to neuron within the central nervous system ... is thus conceived as the apparatus of classification' (Hayek 1952, p. 52). De Vecchi explores the influence on Hayek's thinking of gestalt psychology, to which Hayek makes approving references. Gestalt perceptions are derived not from the parts but from the relationships between them; these relationships are 'the result of a process of organization ... performed by the nervous system' (De Vecchi 2003, p. 144).

Thus 'the qualities which we attribute to the experienced objects are strictly speaking not properties of that object at all, but a set of relations by which our nervous system classifies them' (Hayek 1952, p. 143); and this set of relations is located in the space of representations, which corresponds to Popper's World 3. Hayek immediately and explicitly draws on Popper's language to emphasise that '*all* we know about the world is of the nature of theories and all "experience" can do is to change these theories'; in other words, we create a different set of connections within the space of representations. All knowledge, including 'knowledge how' as well as 'knowledge that' (Ryle 1949), is constituted by connections; it is a particular set of relationships among many other sets which are technically possible, and any such set is always potentially subject to replacement – though major changes are not easily achieved, as has often been demonstrated.

Every theory is the outcome of a trial and error process in which theories, and the patterns of neural connections which embody them, are tested by the effectiveness of the actions to which they lead or of their success in interpreting phenomena. The test is of sufficiency, not optimality, in relation to what Hayek (1952, p. 19) calls 'the discriminations that we perform', which he associates with Ryle's (1949) category of 'knowing how'. These discriminations may be of very many kinds and of very many degrees of precision (Hayek 1952, p. 71) and so, therefore, may be their ranges of sufficiency (as Kelly also notes). The perception that a theory is no longer adequate, as a basis for action or understanding, stimulates a search for a better theory; and it is such a process, Hayek argues, that has gradually led to the supersession, for some important purposes, of sensory theories by physical theories. As Hayek points out, this gives us some reason (though not, as we shall see, a conclusive reason) to expect a closer fit between these physical theories and the physical environment, provided that this environment does not change at a faster rate than the revision of theories – a point to which we shall return when we come to consider alternative versions of this evolutionary process.

However, because we must always use theories to interpret experience before we can use experience to modify theories, existing theories provide the conditions which stimulate, or fail to stimulate, the revision of theories and the starting point for any such revision; thus history matters, for the physical as well as the sensory order, though we need not assume that it determines unique paths or unique outcomes. Moreover, since all of these theories 'are generalizations about certain kinds of events, and since no number of particular instances can ever prove such a generalization, knowledge based entirely on experience may yet be entirely false' (Hayek 1952, p. 168). This, we should note, is a restatement of David Hume's objection to induction as a means of demonstrating empirical truth, and also an endorsement of Popper's position. It is also a powerful argument in favour of basing knowledge on a variety of experience, in Kelly's sense: knowledge will be greater if the production and testing of knowledge is dispersed.

## NEODARWINISM AND NEOCONSTRUCTIVISM

Hayek's theory of the formation and modification of mental orders is explicitly designed to encompass two distinct processes, one of which 'takes place in the course of the development of the single individual' and one 'in the course of the development of the species and the results of which will be embedded in the structure of the individual organism when it commences its independent life (or when it reaches maturity ...)' (Hayek 1952, p. 102). The idea of an embedded framework of the human mind which (correctly) controls human knowledge of such basic and universal concepts as space and time was developed, in a non-evolutionary fashion, by Kant in response to Hume, and it was Herbert Spencer (now so out of favour) who proposed an evolutionary interpretation of such embedding which would preserve Kant's conception of the mind's power of structuring perceptions against the claims of extreme empiricists (Raffaelli 2003, pp. 31–4), while abandoning Kant's claim that these structures embodied true knowledge, thus preparing the way for Hayek's two processes. Hayek (1952, p. 166) extends this interpretation by arguing that 'experience does not begin with sensations or perceptions, but necessarily precedes them ... and the distinction between sensory qualities, in terms of which alone the conscious mind can learn about anything in the external world, is the result of such pre-sensory experience'. It seems natural to ascribe this evolutionary sequence to the species rather than the individual.

Since Hayek's specific objective was to explain how the sensory order could differ from the physical order, it was reasonable for him to leave open the application of his unifying principle to the distinctive systems of individual and species development; but it is now difficult to ignore the important differences between them. Hayek (1952, pp. 102–03) very carefully avoids any discussion of these differences, and his presentation in terms of individual development, which was – and for many of us still is – easier to connect with our own established schemes of ordering, presumably explains why Hayek's theory of species development is so often overlooked. Some neoDarwinians, however, are very sensitive to the implications of proposing two distinctive evolutionary processes. They would argue that Hayek's theory of development within the lifetime of an individual gives no reason why any order developed in this way should be transmitted across generations, whereas the neoDarwinian transmission mechanism of genetic inheritance can be comfortably fitted to a theory of the development of species-specific patterns of behaviour.

Hayek's account of development within the individual may be interpreted as driven by experience in Kelly's sense of the constructions that are imposed on a sequence of events in the course of interaction between an individual brain and a specific environment; but in species development the role of 'experience' is not to stimulate experimental changes in mental ordering but to select among changes which have occurred by random mutations. The double helix is a device for accurate reproduction, and so all mutations must be technically regarded as mistakes in copying; and although environmental factors may be allowed to influence the frequency of mistakes it is a fundamental principle of neoDarwinism that it cannot influence the kind of mistakes that are made. If we apply this principle, 'experience' can make no contribution to the generation of interpretative systems, but is strictly confined to selecting among modifications that are unrelated to experience; those modifications which enhance fitness are preserved by accurate copying to succeeding generations. Experience-led learning by individuals is regarded with suspicion by neoDarwinians, and it cannot be inherited; our mental orders are genetically adapted to some past environment, with the era of hunter-gatherers being a current favourite (see Cosmides and Tooby 1994).

Indeed we may now observe an emerging conflict for supremacy in the social sciences between the rival unifying theories of rational choice equilibrium and neoDarwinian evolution. The two stand in a curious relationship. Both are theories about selection between alternatives and the preservation of what is selected; and in both, selection is based on the consequences of those alternatives which are presented for selection. However, rational choosers, being equipped with rational expectations, know these consequences in advance, and having made the correct choices they naturally have no wish to change them, but remain in their equilibrium state until there is some shock to the economic system. (Their cognitive system, being already fully connected and therefore perfect, never changes.) In the neoDarwinian model, by contrast, no-one knows the consequences of the available alternatives, and any attempt to design alternatives in order to produce desirable consequences is a pretence that is unworthy of science; but if neoDarwinian processes can discover the best answer that is currently available only after trying all existing (though not all possible) alternatives, the best currently available answer will nevertheless be discovered, and once discovered it will be conserved in the genetic code, which may then be indistinguishable from an equilibrium allocation. By appropriate allowance for the costs of this process one may even be able to claim that the outcomes are optimal, along similar lines to the claims for optimality, subject to information and transaction costs, that are sometimes put forward in economics. Thus assumptions which appear to be polar opposites can, with a little sleight of thought, support identical outcomes.

Now deriving equilibria from the initial data is analytically simpler than tracing processes, because the stages of these processes are not full equilibria and are therefore difficult for the modeller to control in a non-arbitrary fashion. Partial equilibria can be devised, but any particular partial equilibrium is always open to objection – particularly by those who believe either in rationality or in the long-term power of neoDarwinian processes. (The standard isolation of game theoretic models from the wider environment raises dual questions about the appropriateness of this assumption of environmental irrelevance and their applicability in a wider domain, which modellers do not always address.) So we should not be surprised that some evolutionary theorists are attracted to equilibrium modelling; and one particularly attractive application is the attribution of particular medical conditions or behaviour to specific genes. The explanation of performance by structure is a favourite theoretical principle across the disciplines, and a direct link between final outcomes and the initial data has the dual appeal of simplicity and plausibility, especially when the initial data can be identified as a specific gene sequence.

However, the dominance of this strategy has encountered some resistance among neuropsychologists; and the combination of argument and evidence which they have produced should have particular resonance among social scientists of an evolutionary inclination, especially those who are impressed with Hayek's reasoning. The following account is based on a series of papers, some jointly-authored, by Professor Annette Karmiloff-Smith, Head of the Neurocognitive Development Unit at University College London and an acknowledged leader in her field. Her assessment of the importance of this issue is indicated by her decision to use it as the topic of a lecture to mark the Centenary of the British Psychological Society (Karmiloff-Smith 2002), in which she argues for the significance of individual development in shaping the outcomes of human genetic endowment. She begins by outlining the use by neoDarwinian geneticists of evidence from adult neuropsychological patients and children with genetic disorders to support claims that the human brain is organised into specialised modules each of which functions in ways that are directly determined by specialised genes. She offers a fundamental methodological criticism that will appeal to all Austrians (and to many other economists who have reservations about orthodox practices in relating theory and evidence): an exclusive focus on the relationship between initial conditions and end-states may lead us astray, and a better understanding of causation requires attention to the processes by which these end-states are produced.

Her central example is a genetic disorder, the Williams Syndrome, which is clearly associated both with the deletion of 17 specific genes and with a specific set of physical consequences in adults, including a smaller brain volume, an abnormal size, orientation and density of neurons, and atypical proportions of several regions of the brain, together with psychological consequences of low IQ and low spatial skills, with the notable exception of unimpaired proficiency in facial recognition. This combination appears to supply strong *prima facie* evidence for an exclusively genetic explanation, and has been cited (e.g. by Pinker 1997, 1999) in support of a theory of the direct determination of behaviour, including altruism, aggression, intelligence, spatial cognition and language, by specific genes or specific sets of genes (Karmiloff-Smith 2002, p. 526).

This exclusive explanation is then confronted with further evidence. First, patients who lack a subset of these 17 genes do not exhibit corresponding subsets of the symptoms: there is no simple mapping from specific genes to specific outcomes. (Though the sample size is small, universal claims, such as that for exclusive and specific genetic determination of particular end-states, may logically be refuted by a single counter-example; questions about the sample must be questions about the experimental procedure which has generated an apparent counter-example, not about its logical status.) Second, the claim that the apparently unimpaired proficiency of people with Williams Syndrome in facial recognition demonstrates an intact face-processing module is undermined by careful experimentation, which revealed that these people were processing faces feature by feature, whereas the supposed 'face-processing module' relies on overall configuration. (Of particular interest is the observation that control subjects are equally reliant on processing by feature when presented with inverted faces; the wider implications of this will be considered later.) Differences between the experimental subjects and the control subjects were also found in the means of producing some other supposedly-intact skills. Thus the 'pattern of intact versus impaired modules formed from intact versus mutated genes', which the theory of purely genetic determination requires, is removed by '[d]ifferentiating between superficial behavioural scores and underlying cognitive processes' (Karmiloff-Smith 2002, p. 536). Third, experimentation with infants revealed substantial differences from the results with adults, while the use of infants with Down's Syndrome as controls had the incidental effect of demonstrating notable differences between the infant and adult states of those affected by this syndrome also; such changes in response during the course of development, implying a reconfiguration of neural networks, are not consistent with nativist claims that directly link impaired modules with adult states (Karmiloff-Smith 2002, p. 538).

These results do not, of course, overthrow the conception of a genetically driven evolutionary process, or indeed the argument that many human physical and behavioural characteristics are genetically determined; but the modified theory that is offered by Professor Karmiloff-Smith, in conjunction with other cognitive neuropsychologists, allows scope for 'complex pathways from gene-to-brain-to-cognitive-processes-to-behaviour' (Karmiloff-Smith 2002, p. 526). Genetics, and the neoDarwinian model of which they are the focus, retain a major role, both directly and by providing frameworks and bases for development; but there is nevertheless considerable space for social scientists to develop evolutionary explanations of a somewhat different kind, for which genetic constraints may provide an appropriate baseline, such as all evolutionary explanations need. This kind of permissive linkage between disciplines appears to correspond to Ziman's view of science. Though commending 'weak' reductionism – the search for underlying commonalities – as a research strategy, Ziman (2000, pp. 323, 326) objects to 'strong' reductionism – the unification of knowledge by the universal application of fundamental principles, precisely because no such principles can explain 'the spontaneous emergence of novel modes of order in complex systems'; and these selective connections produce 'a *simplification* of nature, and of human cognition as naturally evolved, that actually makes scientific research possible'.

Explanations of the emergence of order, in human brains and in human societies, are not confined to random mutations and natural selection, though neither is excluded, but can incorporate the search for novelty, though making new connections, and choices that are made for what appear to be good reasons, because they embody plausible connections. Choices are never purely deductive nor entirely programmed, but we may be able to suggest why particular reasons may be thought to be good and why searches may be undertaken in particular circumstances and may proceed in particular directions. Our theories are not therefore restricted to explaining how people may get things right, but may also help to understand how they may go astray – and an understanding of the reasons for failure may have practical uses. The drastic simplifications of assuming all economic agents to be hard-wired optimisers who are extremely well-informed (and if confronted with asymmetric information know precisely what are the implications of what they do not know), which excludes the need for any process other than Bayesian updating, will, however, not suffice. The kind of psychology-based social science developed by Hayek, however, is highly congenial.

In fact, the final sentence of Karmiloff-Smith's lecture would serve as a present-day introduction to Hayek's *Sensory Order*: 'The contrasting view [to the static model of genetic determination of adult states] presented in this lecture is that our aim should be to understand how genes are expressed *through development*, because the major clue to genotype-phenotype relations is not simply in the genes, or simply in the interaction between genes and environment, but in the very process of development itself' (Karmiloff-Smith 2002, p. 540). In other papers she argues that 'on the gene side, the interaction lies in the outcome of the interacting, cascading effects of interacting genes and their environments and, on the environment side, the interaction comes from the infant's *progressive* selection and processing of different kinds of input. ... The child's way of processing environmental stimuli is likely to change repeatedly as a function of development, leading to the progressive formation of domain-specific representations' (Karmiloff-Smith 1998, p. 390).

In a jointly written paper advocating 'an emergentist solution to the Nature–Nurture controversy', she and her colleagues emphasise 'the extraordinarily plastic and activity-dependent nature of cortical specialisation'. Because 'cortical regions are likely to differ from the outset in style of computation, which means that they will also differ in the variety of tasks they can perform best', there may be widespread dispositions to convert domain-relevance into domain-specificity; nevertheless any particular pattern of domain-specificity is a consequence of development – a particular organisation of the genetic endowment (Bates et al. 1998). The argument that localisation of mental functions does not imply localisation in any particular part of the cortex, and that alternative pathways may be developed in response to specific damage, had already been made by Hayek (1952, pp. 147–8), citing Lashley's (1929) account of 'vicarious functioning' and 'equipotentiality'. Though much is genetically determined and the remainder is genetically constrained, nevertheless in important respects 'the brain progressively sculpts itself, slowly becoming specialised over developmental time' (Karmiloff-Smith 2002, p. 527).

'The expression of genes through development', rather than entirely by programming, may itself be given an evolutionary explanation, as Karmiloff-Smith notes:

> although evolution has pre-specified many constraints on development, it has made the human neocortex increasingly flexible and open to learning during postnatal development. In other words, evolution is argued to have selected for adaptive outcomes and a strong capacity to learn, rather than prior knowledge. Within such a perspective, it is more plausible to think in terms of what we might

call domain-relevant mechanisms that might gradually *become* domain-specific as a result of processing different kinds of input. (1998, p. 390)

There has been some evolution away from genetically specified domain-specificity towards a genetically enabled multi-specific capability for creating domain-specific skills through development. Domain-specificity is a general characteristic, but some domains may be genetically specified and others may become specified during the course of development.

Present-day humans therefore embody a partial shift from 'evolution in the course of the development of the species' towards 'evolution in the course of the development of the single individual' – a shift which has been confirmed by natural selection, but which entails other forms of selection (for a discussion of some of these, see Loasby 2001). This process of learning works through the creation and modification of connections within the brain, for selective connections are the key to human cognition. If two stimuli are experienced differently, 'this difference must be reflected somewhere in the brain. Every new piece of learning changes the structure of the brain in some fashion, however minor' (Bates et al. 1998). This is precisely how learning is modelled by Hayek. The development of a new system of connections that constitutes a physical order, and which at first supplements and then increasingly supersedes our sensory order in many contexts, may be seen as a consequence of this major trend in selection within the human species. We should not be surprised that evolutionary processes are themselves subject to evolution; this is the source of Hayek's problem of the discrepancy between the sensory and physical orders.

The greater brain size of emerging primate species allowed for an increasing range of behaviour by members of each species; but what appears to have been a crucial change resulted from a very rapid increase in brain size in the proto-human species between 500 000 and 100 000 years ago. Because it followed the change to an upright stance, which inhibited enlargement of the birth canal, this increase could be accommodated only by the birth of infants at a very early stage of brain development; this made them extremely vulnerable to both accident and predation for an exceptionally long period, and could therefore have been selected for only if it was associated with some great advantage. This advantage, we may now conjecture, seems to have been precisely the ability of this new genetically endowed cognitive capacity to form better representations of each individual's local environment by construing the replication of events within that environment, and to develop more appropriate skills to deal with it – which is the kind of adaptation cited by Karmiloff-Smith. For this purpose 'the unusually slow period of human postnatal brain development' (Karmiloff-Smith 1998, p. 394) is actually an advantage, for the connections in the brain are being formed while the child is interacting with the environment. With an appropriate genetic endowment of programmable rather than programmed capacity, domain-specific skills can now be developed within individuals as well as through the development of the species; and this new variant of evolution can cope with faster environmental change than reliance on the selection and diffusion of fortuitous genetic mutations, and also with movement into an environment that has not previously been experienced by that individual.

This interaction between the growing brain and the environment could not have happened if the development, as well as the potential, of this larger brain were strictly genetically determined; but the extraordinary increase in the size of the brain entailed a far greater proportionate increase in the number of potential connections, and it is very hard for a non-specialist to see how the programming capacity of the genome could have increased sufficiently to cope with this increase. Specialists appear to share this view. 'On mathematical grounds, it is difficult to understand how $10^{14}$ synaptic connections in the human brain could be controlled by a genome with approximately $10^8$ genes, particularly when ... humans share approximately 98 per cent of their genes with their nearest primate neighbours' (Bates et al. 1998). Hayek's (1952, p. 185) proposition that 'the capacity of any explaining agent must be limited to objects with a structure possessing a degree of complexity lower than its own' was applied to the limitations of the human brain; it is no less applicable to the programming capacity of the human genome.

This diminution of genetic control has allowed cognitive development to be shaped by interaction with particular environments at the level of the individual, on evolutionary principles of variation and selective preservation. Thus the evolutionary process has itself evolved, as genetic determination has been supplemented by a genetically enabled potential for adaptation on a much shorter timescale than genetic evolution. The principle that greater diversity requires a relaxation of central control is familiar in studies of organisational design and innovation; and it is, of course, a central principle of Austrian economics. (It is not good news for economists who rely on general equilibrium modelling.) That this diversity within the human species should apparently be an unintended consequence of the increase in brain size (even though to a neoDarwinian all consequences are unintended) should also appeal to an Austrian mindset.

## SMITH AND MARSHALL

The evolution of the evolutionary process may be used to extend Hayek's theory of the mind by explaining why the physical order should have developed later than the sensory order, and why it should have developed on different principles. It is a remarkable fact (and rather more than a double coincidence) that this explanation can draw on the theories of the human mind that, as noted in the Introduction, were constructed by Adam Smith and Alfred Marshall.

Whereas Hayek's primary focus, as his title indicates, was on the sensory order, in his exposition of 'the principles which lead and direct philosophical enquiries' Adam Smith ([1795a and 1795b] 1980a and 1980b) had sought to account for the development of mental representations of the physical order, taking as his principal illustration the succession of astronomical theories. Smith was familiar with Hume's simple demonstration that there could be no observational or experimental procedure for demonstrating the truth of any universal empirical law, and consequently no impregnable basis for deductive reasoning about phenomena. He accepted Hume's recommendation that we should seek to understand the psychological processes by which people come to believe in certain empirical laws, and developed an explanation which drew on the interaction between basic human emotions and the innovative human mind – or what we might now describe as the interaction between the consequences of species development and development within the individual.

Smith argued that among the fundamental human characteristics are discomfort when unable to make sense of phenomena, which becomes severe if these phenomena are repeatedly encountered, balanced by relief and pleasure at an apparently satisfactory explanation, especially when the explanation is aesthetically pleasing. These characteristics impel people to seek comfort by the invention of 'connecting principles' that can be satisfactorily imposed on events and to adopt plausible or ingenious connecting principles that have been developed by others; the discomfort occasioned by the failure to accommodate some new phenomenon within an established pattern provides the stimulus to create a new interpretative system by a rearrangement of connections, which may also require a rearrangement of categories (for example the set of 'planets'). From the perspective of Hayek's analysis, Smith may be interpreted as explaining how a physical order emerges – and diverges – from a sensory order, and showing how sensations guide this process. Because Hayek does not attempt any specific explanation of the development of the physical order it is not surprising that he does not discuss the role of sensory elements as motivators or selection criteria in that development, which is such a notable feature of Smith's theory.

That Smith, like Hayek, had a conception of knowledge as a set of replaceable theories is most strikingly demonstrated by his insistence that Newton's theory was the product of Newton's imagination, not a direct perception of the truth. As Smith noticed, its general acceptance is to be explained by the rhetorical appeal of its unifying principle, which unites terrestrial and cosmological phenomena; this appeal is also discussed in his *Lectures on*

*Rhetoric* (Smith 1983, pp. 145-6). Smith's analysis also explains the popularity in many disciplines of theoretical schemes which relate performance to structure. Smith ([1795a] 1980a, p. 77) even noticed that the desire for theoretical comfort could be powerful enough to override the evidence of the senses, such as the overwhelming sensory evidence of a stationary earth, in order 'to preserve the coherence of the ideas of their imagination'. This difference in selection criteria between the sensory and physical orders helps to explain how development at the level of the individual may override some of the results of development at the level of the species.

Because psychology was then closely associated with philosophy, it is not surprising that Smith did not attempt to provide a physiological underpinning for what we may now call his evolutionary theory of cognition. Instead he used it to explain how the division of labour promotes the growth of knowledge. First, science emerges as an identifiable category of knowledge, and then, as scientific knowledge expands, specialisation between the sciences simultaneously increases the range of study within the scientific community and the attention to detail within each sector; this attention to detail accelerates the perception of anomalies which, by causing intellectual discomfort even when they appear to have no practical significance, stimulate the invention of new 'connecting principles' that may accommodate them. This is the first appearance of Smith's great theme, from which he derived his fundamental proposition that the division of labour, by encouraging a focus on detail which generates problems and stimulates the development of new connections within particular domains, is the primary instrument of economic growth (Smith [1776] 1976b) – a theory of growth that is truly endogenous (for an extended account, see Loasby 2002).

Marshall's early encounter with the problems of knowledge has been explored by Butler (1991), Groenewegen (1995) and Raffaelli (2003). It may be sufficient here to note that it was partially prompted by a major intellectual controversy about the possibility of demonstrating religious truths, which coincided with Marshall's own doubts; and it led him, like Smith, to consider the psychological processes by which people acquire what is deemed to be knowledge. His response was clearly shaped by Alexander Bain's (1864, 1865) major reorientation of psychology from philosophy towards physiology, which had the unintended effect of making it readily accessible to Darwin's ideas, as Marshall quickly realised; he had read *The Origin of Species* by 1867 (Groenewegen 1995, p. 119). Perhaps prompted by his mathematical training, and consciously following the example of Charles Babbage, he wondered how adequately these psychological processes could be represented by a mechanical system, and devised the most elaborate model of his whole life in order to investigate the possibilities. It seems that he was unaware that Darwin and Babbage were both indirectly influenced by Smith's ideas: the Belgian biologist Milne-Edwards (1827, p. 534) had recognised that the differences between species could be explained as a consequence of the division of labour, and had thereby given Darwin a major clue to the adaptive consequences of Malthusian competition; and the French mathematician Prony's decision to organise the production of mathematical tables according to Smith's example of pin-making had inspired Babbage (see Raffaelli 2003, pp. 52-3). Smith (e.g. [1795a] 1980a, p. 66) had also drawn attention to the resemblances between mechanisms and systems of thought.

Marshall (1994) envisages a 'machine' comprising a 'body' that can receive 'sensations' from its environment and perform actions in response, and a 'brain' that controls this body but has no direct contact with the environment. This brain must therefore operate, as in Smith's and Hayek's theories, by making selective connections, collecting 'ideas of sensations' and 'ideas of actions' into categories and forming links between them. The suggested mechanism is of wheels connected by bands, which may become tighter or looser, according to the 'ideas of sensations' that become associated with the consequences of actions. Marshall shows how such a machine could develop complex patterns of relationships, which would differ between machines, even of identical design, because of differences in their environments and in the initial formation of connections.

Marshall then postulates the emergence of a new species of machine that incorporates a second level of control within the brain. In this level similar mechanisms are used for different purposes, in an early example of exaptation as an evolutionary mechanism. Ideas of sensations received which have not been linked to any idea of satisfactory action at the lower level can now be referred to this higher level, which may generate the idea of a novel action and associate it with the idea of a sensation produced by its effects. Expectations appear; but they appear as conjectures, which are subject to a mental selection process before the survivors are exposed to selection in the environment. Since both the conjectures generated at this level and the internal selection processes applied to them are not random but oriented to problems, the course of development is now influenced by purposive behaviour. This does not conform to modern neoDarwinian principles of variety generation; but since purpose does not imply an ability to make correct predictions it is consistent with general evolutionary principles, as is illustrated by Darwin's own example of selective breeding.

Marshall's model is an evolutionary mechanism that respects basic economic principles and illustrates the effectiveness of the division of labour in promoting the growth of knowledge. The second level of the brain, which is much more energy intensive, requires the prior development of the first as an effective survival mechanism and subsequently as a problem-generator; with this precondition it becomes an important source of potential improvement in the machine's performance, achieved at low overall cost in mental energy by the separation of levels and specialisation between them. The additional effort of generating and checking ideas is undertaken only when the existing set of routines has proved inadequate, and does not disturb those elements in the set which appear to work well; any improvements in performance are stored at the lower level, and thus cease to require active supervision. It is an efficient mechanism for making local adjustments, a precursor of Marshall's partial equilibrium analysis.

Hayek was content to have demonstrated the nature of the sensory and physical orders as selective connections and the process by which these orders are formed, and to have shown that this process readily accommodated differences between the two. The ideas of Marshall and Smith may be invoked to extend his argument. Marshall clearly distinguishes between the evolution of 'machines' as a species and development at the level of the individual within the range of possibilities inherent in each stage of species development. This range is significantly enhanced by introducing imagination as a generator of ideas and an internal selection process which is somewhat differently oriented; we should not therefore be surprised if some of the patterns originating at the second level fail to correspond with those generated at the lower level. Smith's account of the motivation that led to the development of the physical order, illustrated in some detail for astronomy and summarily for 'the ancient physics' (Smith [1795a and 1795b] 1980a and 1980b), takes us a little further by emphasising the fundamental desire for the 'tranquillity and composure' of the imagination (Smith [1795a] 1980a, p. 46). Smith is dealing with 'knowledge that' which, as Ryle (who is cited by Hayek) observed, may not be at all closely matched to 'knowledge how'; and so we should not be surprised if success in comforting the imagination is sometimes achieved at the expense of conformity with the evidence of the senses. A distinctive set of selection criteria, operating during the course of development of the individual (which is how Smith presents the story, with an inherited set of motives and cognitive capabilities) is likely to produce a distinctive order. This view is perfectly consistent with Hayek's theory, and indeed may be interpreted as supporting it.

Smith, Marshall and Hayek all built their systems on the fundamental economic principle of scarcity; but what is scarce in their systems is human cognitive capacity and the energy that is necessary to drive it. These are precisely the only resources that are assumed to be freely available in most formal models in present-day economics, which thus ignore the most fundamental of all allocation problems that human beings face. The psychological systems of Smith, Marshall and Hayek rely on routines and institutions which economise on cognition, and so do the economic systems that they later considered and which are populated by human beings who are equipped with such systems. The economising properties of ecological rationality provide the theme of Vernon Smith's (2003) Nobel Lecture, in which Hayek is appropriately cited; and for him as for these earlier authors the preservation of established structures is an important economising principle. (The practice of mainstream economists naturally exemplifies these features rather than the principles that are apparently embedded in their models.) These routines and institutions have the additional economising merit of focusing attention on the issues for which they are inadequate at any particular time; consequently they are systems in which the evolutionary sequence of variety generation, selection, and the preservation of selected variants in the form of modified or novel routines and institutions is a natural occurrence. Indeed, one can say that there can be no evolution without routines. This evolutionary sequence may be handled, in somewhat different ways, at several levels; these may include, for example, genetic and neurophysiological structures, ideas, and organisations, formal and informal, which link together clusters of routines and institutions and provide both the framework and the problems for continuing innovation.

## SOME IMPLICATIONS

Hayek's principal application of his proposition about the limits of any apparatus of classification is to show that 'no explaining agent can ever explain objects of its own kind, or of its own degree of complexity, and, therefore, that the human brain can never fully explain its own operations' (Hayek 1952, p. 185); thus, although we can hope to understand the principles underlying our own mental processes, 'mind must remain forever a realm of its own which we can know only through directly experiencing it, but which we shall never be able fully to explain or to "reduce" to something else' (Hayek 1952, p. 194). This is his conclusion to his investigation into the problem of psychological explanation; human cognition is inevitably bounded, as Simon also insisted. He also draws attention to the impossibility of achieving a full explanation of the world around us, while simultaneously supplying a principle of organisation for the human brain and for human societies; and this is the starting-point for the following discussion.

Hayek's impossibility theorem warns us that our knowledge is necessarily fallible and incomplete, but it also suggests how it may be improved and tested, and what kinds of opportunity costs are likely to be incurred along different pathways of attempted improvement. Knowledge is created by selecting connections which will constitute domain-specific modules; and we may identify two general principles on which to base this selection, which apply both to everyday cognitive operations and to those special cases –

which are not so very special – in which we are consciously attempting to construct interpretative frameworks, some of which we may choose to call theories. One directs us towards fine discrimination in our definition of categories, at the expense of reducing the breadth of our view and ignoring interactions with the rest of the universe, thus restricting our pattern-making to a narrow domain which we may be able to explore in some depth. The second principle points towards the strategy of aggregating the elements of our universe into invented categories on the basis of similarities that we suppose are significant for our particular purpose, while ignoring the differences within each category which we assume are of little relevance for that purpose (or which we simply fail to notice), thus creating a domain which is broad but almost empty. In discussing the forms taken by the division of labour, Smith ([1776] 1976b, pp. 17–21) recognised the complementarity between closely focused attention and the possibility of 'combining the powers of the most distant and dissimilar objects'. Though each has a physical counterpart in the human brain, all categories are located in the space of representations, and may be manipulated without further reference to what they are deemed to represent. Such manipulations may be enlightening, or misleading; much depends on how they are used (Loasby 2003).

As Hayek (1952, p. 176) pointed out, nothing can be recognised unless it can be assigned to some existing category; and all such categories are based on conjectural principles of selection. Perhaps the clearest, and prior, statement of this necessary principle of contextual similarity as the basis of human thought and action, and the implicit dangers of ignoring apparently irrelevant differences in favour of salient resemblances, was provided by Frank Knight (1921, p. 206). Vernon Smith (2003) and the contributors to *Bounded Rationality: The Adaptive Toolbox* (Gigerenzer and Selten 2001) are similarly aware of the advantages of domain-limited interpretations and procedures, but tend to underplay the dangers – which is understandable in the context of their own purposes. Hayek (1952, pp. 145-6) emphasises that all classification must be based on selected elements, so that the resulting 'system of acquired connexions ... will give only a very distorted reproduction of the relationships' which it purports to represent, and 'will often prove to be false', generating misleading expectations. Simon (1982, II, pp. 306–07) similarly observes that because of the active filtering involved in both direct perception and the handling of information, 'the perceived world is fantastically different from the "real" world'.

Domain-related classifications, and the procedures associated with them, are always susceptible to changes in the environment to which they are applied. Hence the importance of a procedure for revising, or even replacing, classifications which no longer seem to work, and of a strong intrinsic (and therefore genetic) motivation to do so; such revisions are of course the means by which the physical order began to emerge from the sensory order. The possibility of revision implies the ability to conceive of alternative principles of classification on which to construct representations – and to accept them. As a clinical psychologist, Kelly was particularly concerned with the difficulties that some people experience in preserving the internal coherence of their interpretative system while making the revisions necessary to maintain an adequate correspondence with a changing environment; and Smith and Marshall both recognised the tendency for the domain-limited systems used by each individual to become more firmly rooted over time.

However, the human species may escape such individual limitations. The multifarious forms of the division of labour among its members have produced an extraordinary variety of representations and so have enormously increased the total of human knowledge. Hayek's account of the functioning of the human brain, the ideas and neurocognitive theory of Smith and Marshall, all support the conclusion that human knowledge is dispersed and incomplete; furthermore, the particular potential and limitations of the human brain imply that knowledge can be less incomplete only if it is more dispersed. The division of labour exploits the ability of individuals to create domain-specific networks – if they are given the freedom to so. In currently-fashionable terminology that implies delegation and empowerment, or in economic language, imperfectly specified contracts; but the obverse of such discretion is loss of control, which to those concerned with the overall efficiency of allocation, either as analysts or policy-makers, is a serious deficiency. Efficient allocation is not a concept favoured by Austrian economics, because it is interpreted in a way that denies subjectivity, uncertainty, process, and innovation.

The incentive problems of dispersed knowledge, under the title of asymmetric information, have become a major focus of attention in economics, and that in itself is no bad thing; but because full specification (at least of all contingencies and their implications) is necessary for the calculation of system optima, it is inevitable, though unfortunate, that such problems are treated as some kind of 'organisational failure', rather than being inherent in the conditions for success. Kirzner (1973), by contrast, has rightly insisted on differential alertness to opportunities (which may be explained by differential pattern formation across individuals) as an essential contributor to economic progress. One important consequence of this prevalent attitude is an implicit assumption that the co-ordination of dispersed knowledge is simple if incentives are entirely compatible, whereas there is abundant evidence of the major contribution of well-intentioned misunderstandings to many failures: for those of a generous disposition, economists' recommendations to the transition economies of eastern Europe may be so classified. The apparently analysable problems of information have diverted attention from the more fundamental issue of interpretation; asymmetric interpretation is at once a threat to co-ordination, a basis for opportunism and a route to innovation.

It is no accident that the principles and compromises that are inherent in the use of human mental capabilities are to be found in the organisation of social, economic and political systems, for the operation of these systems entails equivalent cognitive problems, which cause us to rely on abstract systems of rules for the selection and classification of relevant phenomena. As De Vecchi (2003) points out, Hayek used this equivalence in his later work, and advocated the dispersion of both political power and economic decision-making; Kirzner has pursued the theme of domain-specific entrepreneurial alertness and Marshall (1919, pp. 647-8), though describing the state as 'the most precious of human possessions', insisted on the importance of confining it to 'its special work', and applied his cognitive model of conjectured linkages to industrial organisation (Raffaelli 2003). Marshall recognised the connection between the management of co-ordination problems in the economy and the management of co-ordination problems within the brain: both require combinations of routines and novelty, and these combinations are themselves modified by evolutionary processes of trial and error.

Economic growth and the growth of knowledge both entail the division of labour in order to achieve an effective allocation of resources to the development of domain-limited cognitive modules within the economy and within society – indeed within many kinds of 'space'. These are the advantages of the division of labour that have led biological evolution towards the variety of species; they have led human societies towards the variety of knowledge. The genetic specification of life forms has created many short-lived inefficient allocations of resources along the way, for only a very small proportion of all possible genetically induced specialisations produce any advantages; but as Smith saw, the most important advantage of the division of labour is not its effective application of the differentiated knowledge and capabilities that are already available but the effects of specialisation on the generation of new knowledge and new capabilities, which also create many short-lived inefficient allocations of resources to unsuccessful novelties along the way to significant improvements. The economy is an evolving system which is continually creating and modifying domain-specific modules of knowledge, and of productive organisations that are based on particular combinations of knowledge.

It is important that the resulting knowledge-domains should be imperfectly specified. In Nelson and Winter's (1982) evolutionary theory, the primary units of evolution are skills, including skills of organisation, which are treated as cognitive programmes of limited scope; but Nelson and Winter take care to emphasise and to illustrate how ambiguous this scope may be, and use this ambiguity within their theory. Imperfect specification is also a condition of those experiments at the margin, inspired by differences of temperament and interpreted experience, on which Marshall relied for the variations that were 'a chief cause of progress' (Marshall 1920, p. 355), and it is essential for Penrose's (1959, 1995) central notion of the imagination of new services to be obtained from resources and of new productive opportunities to which these services may be directed. Discretion is important in two ways: it allows the development of substantially different cognitive structures for different specialisms, and it also allows local variation, and therefore localised progress within each specialism. Both major and minor differences in the environment make their distinctive contributions; and these environments include the size and structure of organisations, which were of especial interest to Marshall. The merits of the imperfectly specified brain structure are realised within the imperfectly specified contracts of the Coasean firm and the imperfectly-specified activities of a Hayekian economy.

Since increasing attention is being paid to the knowledge content of capital, it may be helpful to apply to structures of knowledge, Lachmann's (1978) analysis of capital goods: they are substitutable between uses but within each use they are complementary to a particular set of other capital goods when combined in a specific way; in other words they are multi-specific. Lachmann's warning also applies: just as the value of capital cannot be maintained simply by maintaining the current set of combinations, so the value of knowledge cannot be maintained simply by perpetuating its current uses. It is indeed an important characteristic of knowledge that it can be reused, but what is most important is that it can be reused in ways that are not simply deducible from current uses – a consideration which is not prominent in endogenous growth theory, because it is not easily accommodated within the system of thought to which that theory belongs. Imagination (which Lachmann rated almost as highly as Shackle) is the genetically derived device by which genetic evolution allows the human species to exceed the limits of genetic evolution.

The digital revolution in information processing has diverted attention from the structural nature of knowledge. The evidence on facial recognition presented earlier is particularly relevant at this point. The motivation to recognise faces is, we may presume, a shared genetic endowment – its advantages in the formation of human society (including its importance in controlling opportunism) are obvious; but it is not linked to a unique facial module. Recalling that recognition by feature is always employed by those affected by the Williams Syndrome, but also by those not so affected when they are presented with inverted faces, we may identify recognition by feature as the default mode; configural recognition is employed by those who have both the capability to do so and have also been presented with the material that is necessary to build patterns. Pattern-making is an inherited capability, which may therefore be impaired by a genetic disorder; but how that capacity is used depends on the environment and individual attempts to make sense of it. The use of different procedures for upright and inverted faces is also a demonstration that domains may become very specific through development at the level of the individual; few people encounter inverted faces frequently enough to build appropriate patterns by which to identify them, but experiments with inverting spectacles have shown that it can be done. (There is also a familiar economic principle at work here; investment in developing the skill of configural recognition within a specific domain is not justified if this skill is very rarely used.) Developed capabilities are configurations that economise on cognition; Marshall (1920, p. 251) explains how someone who has learnt to skate can employ that knowledge as a unit in constructing more elaborate figures. Ziman (2000, p. 120) points out that 'pattern recognition is deeply embedded in scientific practice', and that the construction, use and modification of such patterns within each scientific field is a particular (we may say domain-limited) application of a universal and inter-subjective human capability.

Patterns provide a basis for extending similarities by physical and mental experimentation at the margin; and since cognitive patterns differ somewhat between people there will be different margins at which to experiment. There will also be different margins at which knowledge may be most readily absorbed from other people or from written or electronic sources, for absorption requires incorporation into or amendment of some existing configuration; and what is absorbed is likely to differ slightly even between those who have undergone standardised training. Creativity also starts from existing configurations; for every individual, creative and absorptive capacity both depend on the ability to make new connections, and are therefore limited by the connections that are already established; this ability and its potential domain, we may suppose, are genetically determined, but its use is not. The particular knowledge of the circumstances of time and place on which Hayek placed such emphasis is itself the product of connections that define particular relationships.

A characteristic of this cognitive theory, as of all evolutionary theories, that is often overlooked is the intimate dependence of change on the absence of change. Systematic development is impossible unless there is a stable baseline from which to begin and a stable environment against which options may be assessed – and which, in theories such as Hayek's that allow for deliberate attempts to generate conjectures, may give direction to these attempts. Routines stabilise evolved patterns, thus releasing mental energy and providing a basis for experiment; this interplay between routine and innovation, within an individual, a firm, an industry, and an economy, is a pervasive theme in Marshall's economics (Raffaelli 2003). A natural consequence of this dependence of innovation on stability (which is also essential to neoDarwinian theory) is a substantial degree of path-dependency within each cognitive domain – including that of a whole economy, as is indicated by Marshall's (1919) surveys of national systems; but this tendency is partially offset by the variety and the quasi-independence of domains – another consequence of the combined effects of cognitive limitations and the division of labour.

The counterpart of this quasi-independence is the problem of co-ordination, which arises in two forms: the compatability of separately produced knowledge, and its comprehensibility to those who have not participated in its production. The division of labour offers to the innovator the protection of cognitive distance; the integration of what has been divided requires cognitive proximity, though perhaps only at the points of contact. We should not overlook the effects of our shared genetic inheritance, which extends beyond the substantial component of programmed behaviour to the shared procedures by which our interpretative frameworks are formed (Ziman 2000, p. 121). Smith's (1976a) hopes for a civil society rested substantially on his argument that most people could both understand and appraise the behaviour of others in situations that were different from their own; and Hayek's view of human institutions was similar to Smith's. Since then, social and economic evolution, based on an inherited capacity to create differentiated patterns, has increased the variety of situations and increased the possibilities of juxtaposing interpretative frameworks that have few elements or connections in common. Development within the individual dilutes the shared genetic inheritance of domain-specific behaviours. The problems of balancing internal and external coherence analysed by Kelly applies to groups, and to relations between groups as well as individuals; and cultural evolution, in particular, may serve either to reinforce or to override the similarities of attitudes and behaviour embedded in humans on which both Smith and Hayek relied. Neither the emergence of spontaneous order nor the maintenance of an order spontaneously created is guaranteed.

## CONCLUSION

As Potts (2000) has reminded us, a system consists of elements (which may themselves be systems) and the connections between them; changes in systems may therefore be traced to changes in either elements or connections, or to interactions between these two kinds of change. Structures matter. Marshall's (1920, p. 139) suggestion that organisation should be reckoned as a distinct agent of production is not an idiosyncratic idea, especially as he defined organisation very broadly. Hayek's theory of the mind is a theory of connection-building: at the level of the species, it is part of a general theory of genetic evolution; at the level of the individual it is a theory of the innovative mind; and if one combines the two we have a theory of the evolution of the evolutionary process itself, along the lines suggested by Karmiloff-Smith and her co-authors.

Domain-specificity (more accurately domain-limitation) is a key concept. The genome appears to be inherently a method of constructing a system of domain-specific elements, embodying Smith's principle of the division of labour; but with the remarkable enlargement of the human brain we seem to have a partial but significant supplementation of genetically determined domain-specificity (which seems likely to include at least a major part of the sensory order) by genetically enabled development of domain-relevant capabilities towards domain-specificity at the level of the individual – which may include some differentiation between the domains of 'knowledge how' and 'knowledge that'. As Hayek argues, this requires novel – and additional – patterns of connections within the brain; and these patterns are produced, as Smith and Shackle notably emphasised, by the human imagination. Though the results of genetic evolution are still pervasive, there are now significant possibilities for development at the level of the individual to modify, and even sometimes to override, development at the level of the human species.

The mental orders that are created by our imagination and tested in specific domains are themselves forms of organisation, for all knowledge is a structure of selected connections. Now although much of our 'life-world knowledge ... is coded organically into our behaviour, genetic make-up and bodily form' (Ziman 2000, p. 299), these created mental orders vary greatly across individuals. Consequently the knowledge that can be made available in any human society depends on organisation – which means on particular patterns of connections – that exploit the advantages of similarity (local variation within imperfectly specified patterns) and of differentiation (different patterns), and so can produce new species of knowledge incomparably faster than genetic evolution. The creation, distribution and selective connection of domain-specific modules within the economy is a central issue for explaining economic development and for effective policy at the level of firms and governments.

## NOTE

1. This chapter is adapted from an article published under the same title in *Evolutionary Economics and Economic Theory*, edited by Roger Koppl; *Advances in Austrian Economics*, Volume 7, pp. 101–34, published by Elsevier.

# REFERENCES

Bain, Alexander (1864), *The Senses and the Intellect*, 2nd edn, London: Longmans Green and Co.

Bain, Alexander (1865), *The Emotions and the Will*, 2nd edn, London: Longmans Green and Co.

Bates, Elizabeth, Jeffrey Elman, Mark Johnson, Annette Karmiloff-Smith, Domenico Parisi and Kim Plunkett (1998), 'Innateness and emergentism', in William Bechtel and George Graham (eds), *A Companion to Cognitive Science*, Oxford: Basil Blackwell, pp. 590–601.

Butler, Robert W. (1991), 'The historical context of the early Marshallian work', *Quaderni di Storia dell'Economia Politica*, **92** (2–3), 269–88.

Cosmides, Lena and John Tooby (1994), 'Origins of domain specificity: the evolution of functional organization', in Lawrence A. Hirschfeld and Susan A. Gelman (eds), *Mapping the Mind*, Cambridge: Cambridge University Press.

De Vecchi, Nicolò (2003), 'The place of gestalt psychology in the making of Hayek's thought', *History of Political Economy*, **35** (1), 135–62.

Gigerenzer, Gerd and Reinhard Selten (eds) (2001), *Bounded Rationality: the Adaptive Toolbox*, Cambridge, MA and London: MIT Press.

Groenewegen, Peter D. (1995), *A Soaring Eagle: Alfred Marshall 1842–1924*, Aldershot, UK and Brookfield, USA: Edward Elgar.

Hayek, Friedrich A. von (1952), *The Sensory Order: An Enquiry into the Foundations of Theoretical Psychology*, Chicago: University of Chicago Press.

Karmiloff-Smith, Annette (1998), 'Development itself is the key to understanding developmental disorders', *Trends in Cognitive Sciences*, **2**, 389–98.

Karmiloff-Smith, Annette (2002), 'Elementary, my dear Watson, the clue is in the genes ... or is it?', *Proceedings of the British Academy*, **117**, 525–43. Oxford: Oxford University Press for the British Academy.

Kelly, George A. (1963), *A Theory of Personality*, New York: W.W. Norton.

Kirzner, Israel M. (1973), *Competition and Entrepreneurship*, London and Chicago: University of Chicago Press.

Knight, Frank H. (1921), *Risk, Uncertainty and Profit*, Boston, MA: Houghton Mifflin. Reprinted Chicago: University of Chicago Press, 1971.

Lachmann, Ludwig M. (1978), *Capital and its Structure*, Kansas City: Sheed Andrews and McMeel.

Lashley, K.S. (1929), *Brain Mechanisms and Intelligence*, Chicago: University of Chicago Press.

Loasby, Brian J. (2001), 'Selection processes in economics', in Kurt Dopfer (ed.), *Evolutionary Economics: Program and Scope*, Boston, MA, Dordrecht and London: Kluwer Academic Publishers, pp. 253–76.

Loasby, Brian J. (2002), 'The evolution of knowledge: beyond the biological model', *Research Policy*, **37** (8–9), 1227–39.

Loasby, Brian J. (2003), 'Closed models and open systems', *Journal of Economic Methodology*, **10** (3), 285–306.

Marshall, Alfred (1919), *Industry and Trade*, London: Macmillan.

Marshall, Alfred (1920), *Principles of Economics*, 8th edn, London: Macmillan.

Marshall, Alfred (1994), 'Ye machine', *Research in the History of Economic Thought and Methodology*, Archival Supplement 4, 116–32, Greenwich, CT: JAI Press.

Milne-Edwards, Henri (1827), 'Nerf', in M. Bory de Saint-Vincent (ed.), *Dictionnaire Classique de l'Histoire Naturelle*, 17 vols, Paris: Rey et Gravier.

Nelson, Richard R. and Sidney G. Winter (1982), *An Evolutionary Theory of Economic Change*, Cambridge, MA and London: Belknap Press.

Penrose, Edith T. (1959, 1995), *The Theory of the Growth of the Firm*, Oxford: Basil Blackwell (1959); 3rd edn, 1995, Oxford: Oxford University Press.

Pinker, Steven (1997), *How the Mind Works*, New York: W.W. Norton.

Pinker, Steven (1999), *Words and Rules: The Ingredients of Language*, New York: Basic Books.

Potts, Jason (2000), *The New Evolutionary Microeconomics: Complexity, Competence and Adaptive Behaviour*, Cheltenham, UK and Northampton, MA, USA: Edward Elgar.

Raffaelli, Tiziano (2003), *Marshall's Evolutionary Economics*, London and New York: Routledge.

Ryle, Gilbert (1949), *The Concept of Mind*, London: Hutchinson.

Shackle, George L.S. (1979), *Imagination and the Nature of Choice*, Edinburgh: Edinburgh University Press.

Simon, Herbert A. (1982), *Models of Bounded Rationality*, 2 vols, Cambridge, MA: MIT Press.

Smith, Adam (1759), *The Theory of Moral Sentiments*, reprinted in David D. Raphael, and Alec L. Macfie (eds) (1976), *Glasgow Edition of the Works and Correspondence of Adam Smith*, vol. I, Oxford: Oxford University Press.

Smith, Adam (1776), *An Inquiry into the Nature and Causes of the Wealth of Nations*, reprinted in Roy H. Campbell, Andrew S. Skinner, and W.B. Todd (eds) (1976), *Glasgow Edition of the Works and Correspondence of Adam Smith*, vol. II: Oxford: Oxford University Press.

Smith, Adam (1795a), 'The principles which lead and direct philosophical enquiries; illustrated by the history of astronomy', in *Essays on Philosophical Subjects,* in W.P.D. Wightman (ed.) (1980), *Glasgow Edition of the Works and Correspondence of Adam Smith*, vol. III, Oxford: Oxford University Press, pp. 33–105.

Smith, Adam (1795b), 'The principles which lead and direct philosophical enquiries; illustrated by the ancient physics', in *Essays on Philosophical Subjects*, in W.P.D. Wightman (ed.) (1980), *Glasgow Edition of the Works and Correspondence of Adam Smith*, vol. IV, Oxford: Oxford University Press, pp. 106–17.

Smith, Adam (1983), *Lectures on Rhetoric and Belles Lettres*, ed. J.C Bryce, Oxford: Oxford University Press.

Smith, Vernon L. (2003), 'Constructivist and ecological rationality in economics', *American Economic Review*, **93** (3), 465–508.

Ziman, John M. (2000), *Real Science: What It Is, and What It Means*, Cambridge: Cambridge University Press.

# 3. Evolution of legal rules: Hayek's contribution reconsidered

## Jürgen G. Backhaus

### INTRODUCTION: THE PRODUCTION OF LEGAL INSTITUTIONS

It has been known for long, but since Paul Samuelson's elegant (1954) formulation, it is commonplace in economics and some of the neighbouring social sciences that a useful distinction can be made between private goods and public goods. The major policy implication of this analytical distinction is that the production and allocation of private goods can be left to de-centralised forms of decision making, such as the market; whereas the production of a public or collective good cannot generally be entrusted to private initiative, since individual free-riding behaviour may thwart attainment of the allocational optimum. For this reason, production of a public good requires some collective actions, not necessarily on the part of the State, but at least on the basis of some club-like arrangement (Buchanan 1965) which may be forthcoming as a consequence of private initiative.

This is all very well known and could be left for further elaboration to specialists in public economics or else classroom discussion if public goods were exclusively a matter of economic concern. This is, however, not at all the case. It is well known that the law itself is a public good (Buchanan 1975, ch. 7), and so are legal institutions, such as property, contracts, tort rights and remedies, the legal forms of business organisation, etc. What really is involved may be gleaned from this statement found in Douglass North's book, (*Structure and Change in Economic History*, 1981, p. 68) where at the end of the part on historical economic theory, he lists the following as one of five shortcomings of his otherwise rather encompassing and ambitious approach:

> While most of the elements of a theory of institutional change are developed ..., there is no neat supply function of new institutional arrangements specified in the framework. What determines the menu of organizational forms that a society devises in response to changing relative prices? Institutional innovation is a

public good, with all the characteristics of such goods, including the free rider problem.

This disclaimer describes the topic of the present chapter very well. The treatment, however, takes the perspective of economic policy rather than economic history. Hence, the discussion also goes beyond North in not just picturing a ruler who wants to reap as large as possible a profit from the economy of his State. Substitute 'social welfare' for 'profit', and you have the approach to economic policy taken by earlier theorists, such as Tinbergen (1959). A more institutions-oriented approach is clearly warranted for both the sake of relevance and realism. In modern times, economic policy is not reduced to maximising the rulers' wealth.

In what follows, by legal economic policy we shall understand that type of economic policy which is designed to shape legal institutions in the interest of economic activity. Legal economic policy is nowadays formulated within a context of rather more complex institutions, which define incentives and constraints to which policy-makers respond. It is for this reason that a public choice perspective was adopted for the analysis presented in this section. Such a perspective is particularly necessary in the context of transitional economies.

There are basically two different ways in which legal institutions are being produced. They may decentrally evolve through long chains of judicial rule making, as in the common-law tradition, or they may be promulgated by central legislative authorities. The latter is commonly referred to as codification. This language suggests an economic approach to a problem, which has a long intellectual tradition in legal theory. On the continent, we recall the dispute between Thibaut and Savigny (see Savigny 1814, 1815), and in the United States we are reminded of Jeremy Bentham's letters, such as the one to President Madison in 1811,[1] or of David Douglas Fields's code. Resisting, however, the considerable temptation to take off for an excursion into the history of legal doctrines, we prefer to tackle the problem in purely economic terms; all the while being well aware of some of the often noted limitations of this approach, for example, that economic efficiency may not be the only concern that propels the development (i.e. the production) of legal institutions. As we have cast the problem now, it appears to be a perfectly general one, inviting little but lofty speculation and a lengthy regurgitation of settled ideas. Let us therefore clearly state the objective of the analysis, against which the performance may be judged.

The general problem is readily identified: what determines the efficiency and effectiveness of economic policy with respect to the creation and development of legal institutions? Can we identify conditions which policies must meet in order to be efficient? With respect to legislated changes in company law, the argument can be made that legal rules *imposed* by either the legislature or the supreme court cannot by virtue of this very imposition be claimed to be efficient in the sense of containing Pareto superior moves; since, if that were indeed the case, they should have come about as a consequence of voluntary agreement. The proposition is certainly puzzling. Wouldn't it appear that those countries which habitually resort to codification as their method of producing legal institutions are systematically forgoing the benefit of efficient rules? This contrasts squarely with yet another notion, which is at least as widely held to be self-evident within the economics profession.

A considerable part of the economic analysis of the law is built on and around the proposition that features and structures of the law can be explained in terms of their efficiency.[2] Hence, the process of their creation and development must have consisted of at least some Pareto improvements.[3] Sometimes, the notion of the efficiency of the law is extended only to the common law, the implication being that codification is an inefficient way of legal rule formation. Should we therefore rush to the conclusion that the State would be well advised to refrain from legal economic policy? That the State would be better not trying to shape legal institutions and leave attainments at efficiency in legal matters to processes of gradual development instead of conscious design (Hayek 1968)? Such conclusions, although they are often explicitly made or at least insinuated,[4] are really not very compelling from the point of view of the political economist.

It is well known that many a political system uses codification as the foremost technique for producing legal institutions. It would seem that the use of an obviously inefficient technique would run up against widespread opposition and could only be maintained if its use bestowed considerable benefits on those who exercise the choice between different techniques of legal rule making.

A similar discussion has previously taken place in the economics literature when scholars began to analyse the economic consequences of co-determination in Germany. Co-determination, which entails worker participation in the supervision of enterprise decision taking,[5] requires a profound change in the legal structure of the modern corporation. Typically, under co-determination, several seats on a board of directors are reserved for labour or its representatives.

The production of legal institutions is to be seen as just one of several tasks of economic policy. Therefore, introducing the problem in the light of the theory of economic policy helps to clarify some otherwise fairly muddled issues. The first part elaborates on those criticisms of the law and legal change, which take the Pareto principle as their point of reference. This type of criticism is advanced in the context of a particular school of thought, the Austrian school, although a property rights approach could also be taken.[6]

This approach is dealt with in the second subsection. Furthermore, an overview is given of the efficiency-oriented approach to studying the law. This approach is related to the preceding one, but separate in the focus of the analysis, the participating scholars and the media of publication preferred. It turns out that there is an overlapping area where both techniques of legal rule making can be efficiently employed. That is, the efficiency-oriented approach to studying the law cannot, as it usually is, be turned into an argument against codification as a suitable technique of efficient legal rule making. The explanation of these propositions is the main point of section 3. The fourth part, entitled 'The status quo', is devoted to an analysis of the production of the law itself. The analysis is intended to be positive throughout. At first glance, it would therefore seem to have to follow the efficiency-oriented approach quite narrowly. This is, however, neither true nor our exclusive concern. Rather, the Austrian approach, apart from its obvious normative contentions and implications, has several positive interpretations too. Although, in the long run, only efficient legal institutions can be expected to prevail, the production of the law can still be dominated by short-run interests to redistribute wealth for example, in a rent-seeking environment. An economic approach postulating rational behaviour of individuals is consistent with efficient as well as inefficient outcomes. As a matter of fact, economic analysis would be at odds with efficient outcomes under some circumstances that generate inefficiency. The issue hinges on the institutional constraints with which individuals are confronted. Hence, in section 5 a public choice approach is taken in an attempt to analyse some salient features of the production of the law; all the while keeping in mind that the process of producing legal institutions is seen as an integral part of economic policy. Finally, the main conclusions cast these results into the economic policy context: What can we learn from the analysis for a theoretical understanding of legal economic policy?

In particular, the question is: what we can get by way of a theoretical understanding of the issues underlying mass privatisations. The questions used to provide the comparative analysis in section 3 builds on this theoretical understanding.

## ECONOMIC POLICY AND THE INSTITUTIONAL FRAMEWORK

Economic policy came into being as a scholarly discipline when it was discovered that wealth could be acquired by other than war-like activity and governments increased their efforts to control its flow (Bonn 1980). Ever since, two completely different issues have remained intrinsically intertwined in the theory of economic policy: the allocational issue of how to further the generation of wealth and the distributional problem of how to divide the social dividend. While epistemologically these issues have a differing status and require different analytical treatment, in the area of economic policy they cannot be completely separated one from the other. Allocational considerations have distributional implications, and vice versa. This state of affairs involves a comparative lack of elegance, which the sub-discipline of economic policy suffers against, for example, pure economic theory. This is reason enough for theorists of economic policy to be more acutely aware of methodological issues (Robbins 1976; Myrdal 1932).

The distinction between positive economics and political economy[7] is a matter of methodological clarity, not of practical relevance. Nobody has probably made this clearer than Lionel Robbins, to whom the opposite position was often though falsely ascribed:

> Economics as a positive science has no status as ethical or political prescription. But no one in his senses would contend that it is reasonable to prescribe what is desirable in this respect without a knowledge of what is possible – of what effects are likely to follow from what specific type of political or individual action – any more than it would be reasonable to proceed to architectural design without prior knowledge of materials and their potentialities. (Robbins 1976, p. 2)

Thus, the scope of political economy is equally large as the scope of positive economics, encompassing any problem on which the economist can hope to provide useful knowledge for the potential benefit of some political actor. Usually, however, economic policy (as a scholarly discipline) tends to be more narrowly conceived in terms of what a government in a Western-type political economic system is apt to define as its task in the field of economic policy. Here, Jan Tinbergen (see Schiller 1962, 1964) has distinguished between quantitative economic policy, qualitative economic policy, and reform policy. Political economy of legal institutions would deal with the latter two of these three aspects.

A different and somewhat more complex classification scheme was employed by Kirschen et al. (1964) for their ambitious empirical investigation. They combined the objectives of economic policies and the instruments with which they might be attained and thus produced a huge matrix of different types of economic policies. For our purposes it is sufficient to note that legal economic policy, i.e. those types of economic policy which use variations of the legal order in order to attain economic policy results, is widely used. Kirschen et al. divide economic policy, as far as instrument use is concerned, into four categories, of which legal economic policy, which is defined as inducing changes in the institutional framework, is one. It is interesting that in their empirical research this type of economic policy was often found to be present, but rarely considered the most important instrument with respect to any particular policy objective. This is hardly surprising. Policy objectives tend to be conceived for the short run, while legal economic policy is often most important in terms of its long-run implications.

Another distinction, which is frequently made, refers to economic policy affecting

- the economic process and its stabilisation;
- the structure of an economy and its even development; and
- the order of an economic system and attempts at developing rules and institutions compatible with this order, basic structure or general character (Schiller 1962, s. 210 passim; 1964).

The third aspect in this sequence is that area of political economy which systematically involves a discussion of legal institutions and their compatibility with the economic system, which the legal framework is expected to sustain in its operation.

One important subset of this aspect of political economy is an analysis of corporate legal structures and their impact on the behaviour of collective economic agents, such as firms. In this branch of political economy, we need to be particularly aware of the difference between scientific value judgements and an assessment of the likely effects of institutional changes or variations on individual or collective behaviour. The economist, qua economist, is in no position to discuss the legality of or constitutionality of proposed changes; he or she can only discuss the likely consequences of (effective) policies on the legal environment.

This statement is as obvious as it is a relevant reminder to be kept in mind when looking at the writings of members of both the Austrian school and the Chicago school. Professor von Hayek as well as Judge Posner tend to underemphasise the distinction between economic analysis and legal reasoning.

This is reason enough to note six guidelines for the political economist, which an eminent teacher of the subject has written up by way of introducing a collection of readings in economic policy (Gaefgen 1966).

These six admonitions should be kept in mind by the political economist:

- There should be a sharp distinction between judgements of value and judgements of facts.
- The analysis should be systematically based on economic theory.
- The perspective should encompass general interdependencies in the economic system and not be confined to a partial analysis.

- The analysis should be empirically based, wherever possible.
- We should be institutionally relevant in considering the conditions and constraints, under which actors, and political actors in particular, are taking their decisions, and
- The analysis should systematically take into account the extent to which information is accessible to both policy-makers and economic agents.

There is no doubt that the first of these rules is the most difficult to follow. Although ever since Max Weber's influential methodological writings in 1904, scientific results and personal convictions are to be as clearly distinguished as possible as a matter of scholarly ethics and principle, in practice the political economist may often not be able to disentangle facts and values.

The political economist cannot be reduced to the role of a technician of economic policy – as the quote from Lord Robbins might suggest – who takes political ends as given and designs the most effective means accordingly. This conception is simply untenable, since first, economic theories can hardly be ideologically neutral,[8] the analyst must take a conscious choice of aspects, relationships, and data to be considered with his theory; second, because the mere selection of economic problems reflect value judgements; and third, because means and ends cannot be sharply distinguished (Smithies 1955). Since these political matters can hardly be felt to be the volitional choices and idiosyncratic beliefs of the political economist who happens to address a politically relevant economic problem, there is a long tradition in political economy of basing the analysis on the prevalent ideological beliefs or national ideologies of the society for which political economic analysis is being undertaken. For example, Smithies defends the use of national income as an indicator of social welfare with reference to the prevailing 'national ideology' although he feels that economic theory could not support such a position. To quote directly:

> Whatever the theoretical justifications, which we believe to be slight, the national income has become firmly implanted in the national ideology as a measure of welfare. (Smithies 1955, p. 11)

This renders an interesting example illustrating the temporary nature of such popular convictions. The normative basis of political economic analysis is a function of both time and of place. Today, about 40 years after Smithies delivered his lecture in the Brookings Institution, it has become obvious that the national ideology would no longer support this choice of a suitable indicator of social welfare. The methodological position outlined by Smithies

is, by the way, perfectly pragmatic and by all means individually less demanding than Weber's more stringent ethical standards. Smithies is probably
correct in assuming that the political economist has no desire to be esoteric.
A political economist who bases his analysis on normative assumptions which
are not borne out by the national consensus 'would scarcely get a political
hearing' (Smithies 1955, p. 4), which is likely what he most dearly wants.[9] A
political economist, in all probability, would therefore try to assess the national consensus as carefully and accurately as possible, in the interest of his
own effectiveness. Guided by nothing but his own interests he would fulfil a
function which:[28]

> is not to attempt to create a Utopia that conforms to his own predilections. His
> task is to determine the economic conditions whereby society can realise its
> aspirations, to recognize that there is continual interaction between the eco-
> nomic means employed and the objectives that a society sets for itself, and to
> propose changes in those objectives when economic analysis reveals that soci-
> ety may be frustrated through the pursuit of contradictory ends. (Smithies 1955,
> p. 5)

The approach is not, of course, at all new with Smithies. The first economist who consciously employed what only later became to be called the
contractarian approach seems to have been Knut Wicksell with his 'New
principle for just taxation' (see Wicksell 1896). The approach consisted in
first trying to distill a kind of national consensus, second, formulating a
corresponding principle which captures the essence of the agreement, and
third, designing an institutional arrangement under which the principle
would be translated into an improved practice. In Wicksell's classical treatment, he first analysed in painstaking detail the history of financial
institutions of the Swedish kingdom in order to arrive at his New Principle.
Essentially, this principle incorporated the idea of *quid pro quo* relationships in the public economy. Essentially, this New Principle was very much
in line indeed with then recent (marginalist) developments in public finance
theory.[10] But this coincidence should not tempt us to mistake Wicksell's
New Principle as an eager application of fashionable theory to an old and
thorny problem. Rather, Wicksell followed an inductive approach. The New
Principle was indeed nothing more, and nothing less, than an abstraction
from the old rationale which had always underlain the Swedish system of
taxation; and which he had discovered in the course of his historical studies. It is precisely this historical persistence in the face of numerous
opportunities for change, which justifies invoking the notion of a national
consensus or *social contract*, which was found to have been embodied in
the Swedish institutions Wicksell had studied. Likewise, the persistence of
the consensus justified its generalisation into a Principle with possible

applications beyond the national context where it had originally been found to have evolved. Wicksell's approach amounts to consensual (not unanimous) decisions governing the provision of public services as well as the concomitant taxation by which these services are being financed. Unlike his disciple Lindahl ([1919] 1958), who used the principle as an analytical device, Wicksell designed an institutional arrangement for the socio-political conditions of his time. These conditions were a constitutional monarchy, a heterogeneous citizenry to which corresponded a system of heterogeneous political parties, a parliament vested with the budgetary prerogative and an executive branch of government fitting Leviathan assumptions (see Brennan and Buchanan 1980), i.e. eager to grow and to tax.

This historical example is the prototype of political economic analysis in the contractarian tradition, which was later fervently popularised in numerous writings by James M. Buchanan[11] and found a very neat and concise expression in an article (1979) and textbook (1981) by Bruno S. Frey. The predominant characteristic of this approach and comparative advantage as contrasted with other, and at times competing, versions of political economy consists in its *crystal clear criterion for analytical success*. If the theoretical analysis is correct and if the national consensus has been properly and perceptively appreciated, and if the institutional design is realistic, inherently logical and behaviourally sound and robust, chances are that (some version of) the political economic proposal will become reality. Political implementation is the ultimate success criterion for contractarian political economic analysis. While it is quite true that democratic societies experience the continued and unchallenged persistence of inefficient institutions which benefit some powerful interests, a contractarian approach which reflects the interests predominant in a particular society will, if the economic analysis embodied in a particular proposal is correct, invariably produce the optimal institutional solution which cannot be any further Pareto improved. Accordingly, the basic tenets of the contractarian approach to political economy are the attainment of Pareto-efficient solutions (consequent to an informational input into the system), improvements that are generated by the work of the political economist. The whole approach is obviously consensus based. Likewise, using a contractarian approach requires an analysis which takes the interdependence between policy and economy systematically into account. We note that Professor Gaefgen's criteria are indeed met by the contractarian approach.

1. A clear distinction between judgements of value and judgements of facts is maintained. However, for the contractarian, societal values are facts and inputs into his analysis.
2. Contractarian analysis is systematically based on economic theory.

3. The contractarian perspective encompasses general interdependencies in the economic system and is not confined to a partial analysis.
4. The analysis is empirically based, because otherwise it would be unlikely to succeed.
5. It is institutionally relevant in considering the conditions and constraints, under which actors, and political actors in particular, are taking their decisions.
   And
6. The analysis systematically takes into account the extent to which information is accessible to both policy-makers and economic agents.

The last two points deserve a couple of further remarks. The adviser's task is then seen in the arrangement of *constitutional contracts* (Frey 1979, p. 310). A constitutional contract meets the following conditions:

- It applies to fundamental and long-range decisions.
- It is formed in a natural state, i.e. behind a veil of ignorance.
- It must have the (unanimous) consent of all individuals and/or groups concerned.
- It is the result of a Pareto-superior improvement which may be due to new information or social innovation (ibid., pp. 308–09).

The constitutional contract is like a blueprint for institutional reform, designed on the basis of political economic analysis. Since the entire approach in its efficiency orientation is tied to the Pareto principle, one may wonder why any such improvement is held to be at all possible. Why should the improvement not already have come about as the consequence of some spontaneous development, instigated by benefit-seeking agents?

There are several reasons why new possibilities for social improvements may not have come about spontaneously. They may exist because of:

- a lack of information on the part of the relevant agents;
- high transactions costs in the market, where a political solution can be more efficiently rendered;
- strategic behaviour on the part of individual or groups, especially in the 'small numbers' case, which can leave the participants in a Prisoners' Dilemma-type situation (Frey 1979, p. 310).

The political economist can find himself in a position of being able to overcome these obstacles and bring about consensus either by generating uncertainty in order to induce interest groups and other participants to take a long-run perspective, or by proposing compensation schemes – always a possibility if efficiency gains can indeed be claimed for the proposal – or by pointing out convincingly that non-cooperation is not in the best interest of the party trying to free ride.

Obviously, the mere scheme of a proposal for a constitutional contract is not yet sufficient. The proposal for a constitutional contract must be accompanied by provisions for the post-constitutional period. A scheme for implementation is required which ensures compliance in order to avoid free-riding behaviour on the part of some or all economic agents who rely on the constitutional contract being enforced. Free-riding behaviour would invariably result in a breakdown of the entire reform and, consequently, prevent the constitutional contract from being adopted in the first place.

What can we learn form this discussion for the political economy of legal institutions? Before proceeding in the agenda to the contributions of the Austrian school, let us give an intermediate summary.

There are six conclusions that we should like to draw at this point.

1.  The law is a crucial component of any economic system. Its features determine the overall efficiency of the economy.
2.  In that the law is a public good, its production cannot be completely entrusted to the market. Rather, ensuring the production of the proper legal institutions is an important task of economic policy.
3.  It follows that a theory of legal economic policy cannot but be an important subset of any theory of economic policy.
4.  Economic policy as a theoretical endeavour is plagued by the problem of value judgements. This is even more crucial in legal economic policy than it may be in such areas as quantitative economic policy because of the inherent normative implications of legal problems.
5.  Two approaches to the theory of economic policy may be usefully distinguished; they deal with the problem of value judgements in different ways. The pragmatic approach lists a number of guidelines for the theorist of economic policy to observe. The contractarian approach aims at embodying empirically relevant value judgements held in a particular society into political economic analysis. Its specifically economic significance lies in the systematic reliance on the Pareto criterion. The two approaches are neither mutually exclusive, nor are they equally applicable under the same conditions. Both approaches, in this study, are frequently incorporated into the analysis.

## THE AUSTRIAN SCHOOL

Legal institutions and the change of the law occupy central positions in Austrian thought on economic policy. The Austrian school is not, of course, a homogenous intellectual unit. We shall therefore focus on the contributions of only two of their leading protagonists, notably Friedrich von Hayek and Ludwig M. Lachmann. The former is undoubtedly the most prominent and widely honoured of the Austrian economic and social scientists. He has succeeded in developing a coherent interdisciplinary conception of the interdependence between economics, the law, the economy, legal institutions, and economic policy. Ludwig Lachmann, on the contrary, has taken these and earlier Austrian contributions and applied them to the problem of legal change in corporate structure. This is important, because the value of a theory can best be determined in specific applications.

### Hayek's approach to economic policy

Before introducing the slightly bewildering taxonomy of the Hayek system, this part will first deal with the Austrian approach to economic policy in general. Other subsections try to synthesise the Austrian view on what makes for good legal institutions and to suggest what an economic analysis of legal institutions in accordance with this approach can accomplish for a better understanding of economic policy as it affects legal institutions.

The most succinct statements on economic policy in the Austrian tradition we probably find in the condensed treatment in Hayek's inaugural lecture which he delivered, more than forty years ago, in the University of Freiburg in Germany. (The lecture was given on 19 June 1962.)

As compared to most theories of economic policy, Hayek's approach is quite particular. This uniqueness involves at least two respects:

- as regards the limitations of economic policy and the knowledge thereof;
- as well as concerning normative conclusions.

While the approaches to economic policy described above, i.e. the pragmatic approach and the contractarian approach, presuppose the existence of an art which enables policy-makers to achieve desired results by applying available means, von Hayek denies this basic presupposition almost entirely. There are, according to him, two basic limitations to economic policy as a scientific discipline. The first limitation has been well recognised ever since Max Weber issued his intense warnings.

It is a matter of intellectual honesty to distinguish between 'ought' and 'is', value judgements and analytical insights; it is equally important to make this distinction patently obvious to anyone who otherwise might be misled to take value judgements for fruits of scientific labours. (Hayek 1969, p. 163. Significantly, Hayek adds that some societies make it more difficult for the researcher to be honest than others.)

This point, however, does not carry as far as some have suggested it does. In particular, it cannot serve to justify the complete elimination of normatively-based, applied economic analysis, a point forcefully brought home by the contractarians. It is also interesting to note that Lord Robbins, to whom this argument has often been attributed, literally turns the point around into a plea for political economy, as a pursuit separate from but by no means less important than theoretical or empirical economics (Robbins 1935).

Hayek, again, takes a more radical position. In his view, honesty and sincerity in the social sciences require an attitude which questions widely held beliefs and may thus easily be mistaken for a political statement (Hayek 1962, 1969, p. 164)

Avoiding politically delicate issues is obviously as much a manifestation of a political choice as is explicitly taking them up. Consequently, theoretical purists who avoid politically debated issues cannot be said to be any less political in their research attitudes than political economists who take a critical posture vis-à-vis contemporary politics. In Hayek's view, then, the political element in the theory of economic policy is more apparent than real. For him, the more important limitation of a scientific approach to economic policy lies elsewhere.

The economy in the Austrian view (Hayek 1969, pp. 162) is interpreted as a self-regulating spontaneous order, a catallaxy, which governs itself through the use of knowledge; this knowledge is unavailable to any one agent who is part of the catallactic game. Consequently, any one political measure will lead to multiple repercussions and reactions on the part of the single agents in the economy, who react to impulses and economic incentives unknown to the policy-maker and do so in the light of a stock of decentralised knowledge (information) and individual experience equally unknown and inaccessible to the politician. Thus, the political economist can only hope to offer meaningful predictions of a very general kind. He can discuss the behaviour and change of general patterns or orders, while at the same time ignoring particular manifestations compatible with the general pattern. This methodological insight has immediate consequences for practical economic policy. To the extent that economic scientists ignore the precise consequences of measures of economic policy vis-à-vis the economy, all other agents will share the same ignorance, and so will policy-makers.

One would be wrong to expect Hayek to be led, by this reasoning, to an agnostic liberalist attitude towards economic policy. Far from decrying any kind of economic policy as interventionist and potentially harmful or disruptive, he tries to formulate general criteria which economic policies have to meet in order to be successful. As we recall, the contractarian view had an exogenous success criterion, the final adoption of a policy proposal. Hayek tries to arrive at criteria, which would be (necessary) conditions for success, but more specific than the Pareto criterion on which the contractarians rely. While single incoherent economic measures should generally be avoided, even if a partial application of economic theory suggested that they might be beneficial, policies should be discussed in terms of their general character and approach and underlying (ideological) principles. (Hayek 1969, p. 163. Compare this with Eucken's *'Systemgerechtigkeit'* und *'Funktionsfähigkeit'*[12] in the jurisdiction of the German Constitutional Court (BVerfG).)

This seems to fly in the face of a positive approach to economics. Again, the suggestion follows straightforwardly from Hayek's theory of knowledge. Any social system is built around certain basic values on which agents rely in forming their expectations. As long as policies are solidly based on these same values held in a particular society, individuals are likely to be better equipped to deal with the intended and unintended consequences of economic policy and less likely to circumvent or avoid the political norm. Hence, in the Austrian view, economic policies should be evaluated in terms of their general character, not with respect to particular effects they have on certain individuals or groups (ibid.).

This is a standard of policy effectiveness with a minimum of normative implications. Value judgements are taken as societal realities, which economic policy has to take into account. And the status quo, as far as it has evolved over time, is taken as the point of departure for pragmatic reasons. There are no normative qualities attached to it. Finally, the value judgements held by the individual researcher or professional group of researchers, such as economists, are again societal realities and, as such, subject to economic analysis and scrutiny. (See for example, his 'The intellectuals and socialism', *University of Chicago Law Review* **16**, 1949. Also witness Hayek's long-standing interest and steady contribution to the history of economic analysis.)

It is indeed surprising how close Hayek comes to the contractarian tradition, which has developed in Wicksell's footsteps. This proximity shows up in his insistence on coherent economic policy programmes, broadly based on a historically stable ('constitutional') national consensus. Still, implementation of such policies involving particular individuals or groups, each individually and in turn, have to be persuaded to co-operate in the economic policy effort.

It almost goes without saying that Hayek's theory of economic policy suggests a very cautious approach. But as far as economic policy is concerned, Hayek is certainly not an abstentionist. As a matter of fact, a number of his policy proposals, such as the one concerning a denationalisation of money (Hayek 1978) would involve major reconstructions of the Western monetary system and, in consequence, would leave strong marks on the entire Western world. Hayek's approach to economic policy, favouring, as it does, restraint on the part of government in pursuit of particular objectives and interests, suggests a strong role of government as maker of economic policy with respect to the development of legal institutions which further economic development. He finds himself firmly entrenched in the German tradition to economic policy, which dates back to the cameralists[13] in suggesting as the basic guideline of economic *policy maximisation of the social product* as opposed to, for example, the maximisation of individual net present values.

This is the vantage point from which Buchanan tries to unfavourably compare the Hayek system with his own contractarian approach; he writes:

> I have no faith in the efficacy of social evolutionary process. The institutions that survive and prosper need not be those that maximise man's potential. Evolution may produce social dilemma as readily as social paradise. (Buchanan 1975, p. 176)

Likewise:

> The forces of social evolution alone contain within their workings no guarantee that socially efficient results will emerge over time. (Buchanan 1977, p. 31)

It is precisely because Hayek shares this view that he envisions a broad scope for economic policy.

The approach suggests, then, three basic postures. First, economic policy is predominantly legal-economic policy. Second, there are two different sources of the law: social evolution and legal economic policy. Very often legal institutions, which have evolved over time, may be efficient. (Of course, there is no guarantee that they will be.) From this it follows that one should avoid the constructivist trap of an overzealous design of new legal institutions. Third, there are a number of basic guidelines, which should be observed when new legal institutions are being suggested. These guidelines may be summarised as follows:

1. Efficient economic activity relies on the unquestioned acceptance of three basic legal institutions, namely, property, contract and tort (Hayek 1969, pp. 179). These should not be questioned or otherwise made uncertain.
2. New legal arrangements should be scrutinised with respect to the incentive structures they determine (Hayek 1969, p. 181).

3. Legal rules need be mutually consistent one with the other. Hence, new rules have to fit into the dogmatics or 'system' of the existing legal order (ibid.).
4. In general, new legal structures should be made so as to favour the development of the market economy (Hayek 1969, p. 183).
5. In particular, they should be so designed that a maximum use of existing information ('knowledge' in his earlier writings) is possible.

He writes:

> Also, 'information' is clearly often preferable to where I usually spoke of 'knowledge', since the former clearly refers to the knowledge of particular facts rather than theoretical knowledge to which plain 'knowledge' might be thought to refer. (Hayek 1979, xii)[14]

All this implies that there should be restraint with respect to policy-makers' desire to achieve particular ends as compared to the more broadly conceived goal of maximising the social dividend. More technically it implies that the legislative procedure should not be used when enforcement of the legislative act cannot be expected in the long run and remain generally applicable, but only one isolated instance or problem is to be regulated (1969, p. 191).

As is well known, Friedrich von Hayek subsequently worked out these conceptions in greater detail. In 1971 appeared *The Constitution of Liberty* (with respect to the problem of codification, see in particular ch. 13) and in 1973 through 1979 his work of three volumes *Law, Legislation, and Liberty*. Here he proposed a detailed methodological framework in volume I, his criticism of the interventionist welfare state, which he sees as marred by blurred distinctions between the difference functions of government (i.e. policy-making and rule making) in the second volume, and the proposal of a bicameral system of government (reflecting the aforementioned distinction) along with several other desirable features of 'the political order of a free people' in the third volume. Obviously, for the task at hand, the first volume is the most important of this set of three.

At the heart of his conceptual framework, we find several important distinctions. In particular, there are two types of order.

By 'order' we shall throughout describe *a state of affairs in which a multiplicity of elements of various kinds are so related to each other that we may learn from our acquaintance with some expectations concerning the rest, or at least expectations which have a good chance of proving correct.* (Hayek 1973, p. 36 original emphasis)

One type of social order, namely what is commonly referred to as an organisation, Hayek terms 'taxis' which he defines as a man-made or:

... exogenous order or an arrangement (that) may again be described as a construction, an artificial order or, especially where we have to deal with a directed social order, as an *organisation*. (Hayek 1973, p. 37)

The other type of order has evolved over time, and he terms it 'cosmos'. It is self-generating or endogenous, a spontaneous order which has gradually incorporated the reactions of individuals to different social states as well as the adaptations to these reactions (Hayek 1973, p. 37).

One salient implication of this distinction concerns the *purposes* of orders. Organisations typically are intended by their founder or architect to serve a purpose, whereas order, having evolved over time, is not readily identified as such unless an intellectual effort is made to uncover its patterns, for it does not serve any single purpose. They may serve a multitude of purposes, and being aware of their existence and the way in which they function will greatly facilitate one's furthering of different purposes within the 'cosmos' (Hayek 1973, p. 39).

Hence, again, ignoring order may cause a policy-maker to pursue economic policies which may not only not achieve the desired end, but also conflict with the unrecognised order and in due course produce all manner of unintended consequences which, in turn, can be attributed to the initiated policy only by identifying the order with which these naïve economic policies have conflicted. This demonstrates the important place which economic policy occupies in Hayek's system. He places great emphasis on the necessity of intellectual work in order to help pursue effective economic policies. The next quote shows how economic policy can properly be achieved and when it will fail:

While it is sensible to supplement the commands determining an organisation by subsidiary rules and to use organisations as elements of a spontaneous order, it can never be advantageous to supplement the rules governing a spontaneous order by isolated and subsidiary commands concerning those activities where the actions are guided by the general rules of conduct. This is the gist of the argument against interference or 'intervention' in the market order. The reason why such isolated commands requiring specific actions by members of the spontaneous order can never improve but must disrupt that order is that they will refer to part of a system of interdependent actions determined by information and guided by purposes known only to the several acting persons but not to the directing authority. (Hayek 1973, p. 51)

Hence, economic policy can indeed even aim at particular objectives. But achievement of these objectives cannot be legislated. Rather it is necessary to set up some type of order, such as an organisation or 'taxis', as an element of the overall spontaneous order. Where the success of the taxis or organisation depends upon achievement of this goal or policy objective, and hence, members of the organisation will strive towards attaining it. On the other hand, achieving a particular policy objective may also be tried by singling out an order that has historically evolved over time, a 'cosmos', implementing the policy objective as one of the several purposes which the cosmos may serve, and, towards that end, defining incentives compatible with the order of that cosmos. For example, instead of intervening in the market by decree, the State may set up organisations that operate within the market framework and under the market rule, but achieve objectives different from those other firms may try to attain. In the sphere of social policy, not-for-profit organisations which have a well-defined and sensible mission may serve as a convenient example.

It is important that both criteria be met. For example, in the social services, the success of a charitable organisation should not be made dependent upon the plight the organisation can show to exist, but upon achievement of a positive goal of reducing a pre-existing ill or providing a general level of welfare. Organisations that care for the blind should receive allocations in keeping with the number of blind persons they make independent, not on the number of people they claim to care for. The latter incentive system locks the easy-to-care-for blind into continuous care, while neglecting for example, the blind and mentally handicapped whose care and schooling is expensive and labour-intensive. When combating cancer is the goal, a cancer research foundation would put itself out of business if it ever found a cure for cancer, provided such a cure exists, unless the prize were set in terms of finding that cure. If a civil service based on merit promotions and honorary distinctions is to regulate a business, it is wrong to offer money bonuses to the civil servants, instead of promotions and honorary distinctions at the appropriate time, which serve to set the civil service apart from the business world. In each single case, uniform, across-the-board provisions are apt to either fail or be inefficient.

The legal design of such elemental parts of the larger cosmos of which they form a part is, then, one of the central concerns of economic policy. It is this context which makes the common law such a noteworthy subject of economic study. Hayek explains this well:

> The important insight to which an understanding of the process of evolution of law leads is that the rules which will emerge from it will of necessity possess certain attributes which laws invented or designed by a ruler may, but need not possess, and are likely to possess only if they are modelled after the kinds of rules which spring from the articulation of previously existing practices. (Hayek 1973, p. 85)

It would, of course, be absurd to infer from this quote that a particular legislative proposal is doomed to be inefficient and will upset the existing legal order unless we can point to some precedent in the common law. There is no trans-cultural pre-eminence of the common law, from an economic policy point of view. For example, if a new legal form for a publicly held corporation is debated in a legislature, Hayek's argument suggests that it would be wise to look for parallels in similar legal-economic systems. The search is for parallel legal institutions, which have already withstood the test of practical experience and judicial review. Imitating these parallels may be preferable to legislating new legal designs, provided the relevant traits of the legal cultures under review are at all comparable.

This is exactly what has always happened in preparing grand legislative successes (e.g. the *BGB* – Civil Code – in Germany)

Far from belittling the importance of legislation as a source of the law, Hayek explicitly stresses the complementarity of common law and legislation as well as the importance of legislative corrections in the development of common law. There are several reasons why corrections are required. The first, of course, is the familiar 'social dilemma', into which spontaneous developments may lead:

> For a variety of reasons, the spontaneous process of growth may lead into an impasse from which it cannot extricate itself by its own forces or which it will at least not correct quickly enough. (Hayek 1973, p. 88)

Second, 'wholly new circumstances' (Hayek 1973, p. 88) may arise which require a reversal of the law, a task for which courts are ill-suited.

> [It] is not only difficult but also undesirable for judicial decisions to reverse a development, which has already taken place and is then seen to have undesirable consequences or to be downright wrong. The judge is not performing his function if he disappoints reasonable expectations created by earlier decisions. (Hayek 1973, p. 88)

A related reason is that legislation can look into the future, while judicial decisions necessarily look into the past. That is, judges decide cases about matters past, and their decisions rendered on cases past will reflect on cases in the future, while legislation can, without affecting the proper adjudication of past cases, promulgate different rules for future cases, new rules to which individuals can readily adapt (Hayek 1973, p. 89).

He adds that often the perception of what is just undergoes a change which, in turn, may require new legislation:

> The necessity of such radical changes of particular rules may be due to various causes. It may be due simply to the recognition that some past development was based on error, or that it produced consequences later recognised as unjust. But the most frequent case is probably that the development of the law has lain in the

hands of members of a particular class whose traditional views made them regard as just what could not meet the more general requirements of justice. There can be no doubt that in such fields as the law and the relations between master and servant, landlord and tenant, creditor and debtor, and in modern times between organised business and its customers, the rules have been shaped largely by the views of one of the parties and their particular interests – especially where, as used to be true in the first two of the instances give, it was one of the groups concerned which almost exclusively supplied judges. (Hayek 1973, p. 89, fn. omitted)

We might add that the same reasons would probably apply to the relationship between the corporation and its employees.

Another important terminological distinction, which corresponds to the differentiation between the different types of orders, cosmos and taxis, parts 'nomos', the lawyers' law, from 'thesis' i.e. those rules of organisation of government with which legislatures have been chiefly concerned (Hayek 1973, p. 94).

Hayek makes the surprising remark that nomos is actually the more abstract type of law. This is surprising as one should think that legislation concerns the general, while adjudication deals with the particular. But it should be kept in mind that in distinguishing nomos and thesis, Hayek is not interested in addressing the question 'common law vs. codification', that, for example, Jeremy Bentham had concerned himself with. Codification tries to cast nomos into one readily accessible document. It is not an ad hoc attempt to organise a concern with a particular end in mind. And therefore, the judge-made law revolves around general principles that the judges have tried to develop over time – and on which, it might be added, codification typically builds.

It seems that the constant necessity of articulating rules in order to distinguish between the relevant and the accidental in the precedents which guide him, produces in the common-law judge a capacity for discovering general principles rarely acquired by a judge who operates with a supposedly complete catalogue of applicable rules before him. When the generalisations are not supplied ready-made a capacity for formulating abstractions is apparently kept alive, which the mechanical use of verbal formula tends to kill. The common-law judge is bound to be very much aware that words are always but an imperfect expression of what his predecessors struggled to articulate (Hayek 1973, p. 87).

The same would certainly apply to the judges sitting on the benches of supreme courts in the continental system, and to the judges appointed to constitutional courts in particular who, in trying to resolve particular cases, have nothing to apply but the general principles laid down in the constitutional document.

This document, incidentally, often uses unduly vague language, designed at the time of its drafting to patch up rather diverse political intentions of the 'founding fathers'.

Since Hayek views judge-made law and legislation as mutually symbiotic, the decisions of supreme courts and constitutional courts in continental legal cultures which rely on codification as their prime source of the law must be expected to be a particularly fertile depository of nomos, the law of the spontaneous order.

The rules on nomos:

> are *discovered* either in the sense that they merely articulate already observed practices or in the sense that they are found to be required complements of the already established rules if the order which rests on them is to operate smoothly and efficiently. They would never have been discovered if the existence of the spontaneous order of actions had not set the judges their peculiar task, therefore rightly considered as something existing independently of a particular result will be free inventions of the designing mind of the organiser. (Hayek 1973, p. 123, emphasis in original)

All this implies that legal economic policy should be firmly based on these general rules of nomos, which have developed in a particular society. There is, hence, a much more complicated interdependency between the legal order on the one hand and economic policy on the other. While the legal order certainly constrains economic policy, this should be read to imply that legal economic policy is constrained by the rules of nomos while thesis is constrained by the rules under which the economy operates and economic policy is a scientific attempt at uncovering existing orders and the regularities and requirements of their performance in order to fit political purposes into existing systems.

It is clear that the collapse of the state socialist system provided the new circumstances Hayek talks about. These require extensive legislation on the part of the state in order to make the formation of market forces possible. The in-depth analysis of deficiencies of mass privatisations in the five countries studied, that the questionnaire method makes possible, can effectively build on the Austrian approach in spotting chances for improvement.

Hayek introduces a fifth neologism after taxis and thesis, cosmos and nomos. Catallaxy refers to the economy as a whole, but Hayek suggested, and most scholars writing in the Austrian tradition pay heed to this advice, not using the word 'economy', which originally referred to the micro unit or household economy, the economy as a whole is but a network of many interlaced economies (Hayek 1976, p. 108).

The distinction is significant and corresponds to what has been previously said about taxis and cosmos. Economies, i.e. households and firms, in the

Austrian view are organisations which have been deliberately set up and which serve a limited number of goals. Their operations are consciously planned, and they dispose of idiosyncratic information, which is not generally available, or of interest to other economies. A catallaxy, on the other hand, is the special kind of spontaneous order produced by the market through people acting within the rules of the law of property, tort and contract (Hayek 1976, p. 109).

In a catallaxy, an unknown variety of different goals and aspirations is being pursued, and there is no one conscious will directing the operation of the whole. Would this imply that Austrian economics holds economic policy to be something impossible, a contradiction in terms? The answer must be a resounding no.

There is room for catallactic economic policy. Although there can be no substitution of one political will for the multitude of ends pursued by the different economic units in a catallaxy, the State may very well pursue political ends within this order. This may be either by means of influencing the legal environment of economic activity, or it may be through economic pursuit within this legal environment, which is when the State operates as one economic entity among many equals, pursuing economic goals under the rules of the market.

## THE STATUS QUO

Hayek's approach to economic policy has often been charged among other things, with being ultra-conservative, because of the importance attached to the status quo. In this respect, by the way, the approach is in no way different from the other approaches to economic policy discussed. Both the pragmatic and the contractarian approach take the status quo as the point of departure from which policy proceeds and as the reference point of the analysis. Whenever the Pareto principle is used as the benchmark of economic analysis, the status quo assumes a particular importance (see the Backhaus, Samuels interchange published in *Analyse und Kritik*, 1980, 1981).

But Hayek gives a particular justification for this reliance on the status quo which is proper to the Austrian view. This reasoning revolves around the notion of uncertainty.

Since any established system of rules of conduct will be based on experiences which we are only partly knowledgeable of, and will serve an order of action in a manner which we only partly understand, we cannot hope to improve it by reconstructing anew the whole system. If we are to make full use of the experience which has been transmitted only in the form of traditional rules, all criticisms and efforts at improvement of particular rules must proceed within a framework of given rules which for the purpose in hand must be accepted as not requiring justification (Hayek 1976, p. 24).

This does not mean that any particular legitimacy is attributed to the status quo. This (latter) statement is correct even though the status quo is emphasised as being singular in embodying past and present and, in most cases, relevant information not embodied in any other system of rules or, for that matter, social states.

> When we say that all criticism of rules must be immanent criticism, we mean that the test by which we can judge the appropriateness of a particular rule will always be some other rule which for the purpose in hand we regard as unquestioned. ... The ultimate test is that not consistency of the rules but compatibility of the actions of different persons which they permit are required. It may at first seem puzzling that something that is the product of tradition should be capable of both being the object and the standard of criticism. But we do not maintain that all tradition as such is sacred and exempt from criticism, but merely that the basis of criticism of any one product of tradition must always be other products of tradition which we either cannot or do not want to question; in other words that particular aspects of a culture can be critically examined only within the context of that culture. (Hayek 1976, p. 25)

Hence, which aspects are to be taken as given and which are to be variable is up to the volitional choices of the political economist. This choice is *not* predetermined by the approach to the analysis, rather by the purposes of the enquiry.

We are forced to conclude that the Austrian approach is really not very conservative at all, at least in so far as economic policy is concerned. Any aspect of the reality accessible to the political economist may be questioned; only provided that the question is well defined, including a proper delineation of what is not going to be addressed and hence taken as given.

## THE SEPARATION OF RULE-MAKING AND POLICY-MAKING

In concluding this section, let us note one important institutional recommendation which follows from Hayek's legal theory. As the reader will recall, Hayek distinguishes between two processes, which create order. The first involves the spontaneous order or cosmos resulting from the many different and mutually interdependent actions of the agents in a social system. Second, the equally spontaneous order produces rules governing the first process. Both the spontaneous orders and the rules, which govern their evolution, are the unintended social product of a continuous chain of mutual adaptations. It is in this sense that nomos, the evolved law, embodies lasting principles of jurisprudence pertinent to a particular culture in which it reigns. Nomos should indeed not be confused with natural law of which Martin Luther said: 'De iure naturae multa fabulamur.' (Werke. Kritische Gesamtausgabe in 58 Bänden. Weimar 1883 Vol. 56, p. 355)

One reviewer of Hayek's political economy (Scott Gordon 1981) who equated nomos with natural law which, since the middle ages, many an authoritarian ideology has used to justify all kinds of grave injustices and infringements upon the conduct of people, rather lost for words, in view of this grave inconsistency, exclaimed:

> In view of the political history of natural law doctrine, it is astonishing that Hayek, whose dedication to individual freedom is sincere beyond question, would engage in the slightest flirtation with, much less embrace, such a diseased and meretricious old drab. (Gordon 1981, p. 479, fn. omitted)

It is not 'the old drab' which Hayek embraces. Hayek's nomos is character-ised and singled out by the openness of the process through which it develops, it is not pronounced ex cathedra but has, instead developed through a chain of many interlaced and mutually interdependent but *decentrally* taken decisions. Nomos is thus the product of a self-organising structure, after the elements that constitute an order have gone through many interactions and reached a certain consensus, and it is the independence from outside interference which ensures that nomos, the law of liberty, cannot degenerate into a natural law of the scholastic tradition, which, after all, was conceived to serve a hierarchical world committed to the single end of praising the lords in words and deeds.

How can we judge a particular piece of legislation, e.g., in order to decide whether it is good law or bad?

Hayek says that overall order does not necessarily result from individuals following rules: 'Individual responses to particular circumstances will re-sult in overall order only if the individuals obey such rules as will produce an order.' But we can never know in advance what rules will produce order. Hayek says that those groups that survive and adapt to their environment better than others have done so precisely because they have adopted the most appropriate set of rules. It would appear that we are conducive to survival by looking at those groups that have survived. But we cannot know which particular rules are most conduced to survival, and which may be copied by others, because clearly some rules survive in any system even though they serve no useful purpose (Barry 1979, p. 82, footnote and italics omitted).

Hence, there is no philosophers' stone which can help us tell the good law from the bad, beforehand. But this is not a limitation of Hayek's philosophy, as Barry claims (ibid.).

It rather has to do with the uncertainty about future states to which individuals respond, for instance, by taking precautions. This implies that requirements for good law can never be substantive, they have to be procedural, for example, in ensuring that individuals are left free enough to develop new ways of reacting to the law and unforeseen events.

Therefore, in passing a law, the legislature has to make sure that, while binding, it leaves individuals (and firms) enough flexibility to react to it differently, to opt for legal ways not to be bound by the law. The law must offer alternatives to individuals, to take either one choice or the other, depending on their particular circumstances. The procedure of implementing the law must be such that adverse (and unforeseen) consequences, not intended by the legislature, can be avoided by the citizen.

There is one procedural principle on which Hayek places particular importance. We are referring to what has become the cornerstone on which resides his proposal for 'the political order of a free people'. The principle requires that in a social organisation, the rule-making body be distinct from the policy-making body.

> We want, and I believe rightly, that both the laying down of general rules of conduct binding upon all and the administration government be guided by the wishes of the majority of the citizens. This need not mean, however, that these two tasks should be placed into the hands of the same body, nor that every resolution of such a democratically elected body must have the validity and dignity that we attach to the appropriately sanctioned general rules of conduct. (Hayek 1979, p. 22)

> Though, if we want democratic government, there is evidently need for a representative body in which people can express their wishes on all the issues which concern the actions of government, a body concerned chiefly with these problems is little suited for the task of legislation proper. To expect it to do both means asking it to deprive itself of some of the means by which it can most conveniently and expeditiously achieve the immediate goals of government. In its performance of governmental functions, it will in fact not be bound by any general rules, for it can at any moment make the rules which enable it to do what the momentary task seems to require. Indeed, any particular decision it would make on a specific issue will automatically abrogate any previously existing rule it infringes. Such a combination of governmental and rule making power in the hands of one representative body is evidently irreconcilable, not only with the principle of the separation of powers, but also with the ideals of government under the law and the rule of law. (Hayek 1979, p. 25)

It should be fairly obvious that this principle has numerous applications well beyond the range of government proper, i.e. whenever a social organisation has achieved a certain size and conforms to rules that guide decision taking, and where, hence, rule-making and policy-making need to be separated. The modern corporation is just one of many examples that come to mind.

Hayek's political economy in the Austrian tradition bears on the science of economic policy with respect to economic rule-making, i.e. with respect to economic legislation. Hayek's contribution to economic policy is immense, but it is concentrated on an area, which is typically not the focus of economic policy research. While most of what is written in the area of economic policy is concerned with policy proper, Hayek's political economy addresses the question of what legislation will best suit catallactic orders.

## EFFICIENT LAW

Having discussed (1) the pragmatic approach to economic policy, (2) the contractarian method, (3) the Austrian school, it remains to be decided whether any of them, and if so, which one(s), will likely provide incentives for efficient economic decisions. How is it that an efficient company law may at all come about? Although this question goes to the roots of the law as such, and has concerned legal scholars for millennia, in economics it has only recently attracted wider attention.[15] Not surprisingly, the problem remains somewhat elusive. For example, Douglass North (1981) regrets that while most of the elements of a theory of institutional change have been developed, there is no neat supply function of new institutional arrangements that might enter the neoclassical framework. What determines, he asks, the menu of organisational forms that society devises in response to changing relative prices? And his answer suggests a difficulty, not a solution: institutional innovation is a public good, with all the characteristics of such goods, including the free-rider problem (ibid., p. 68).

This, however, already provides a first hint. The free-rider problem in economics is the more relevant, the more an individual is able to rely on others for the provision of a good while withholding his own contribution towards the provision. That is, free riding occurs when the free rider faces only minimal or no consequences of his behaviour. To take an example: if in a community of a thousand there were one thousand legal solutions to provide, and each issue were to be decided by a different individual randomly assigned to the case, anyone in this society would be a free rider with respect to providing efficient law. The incentive to decide efficiently would be minimal, the resulting decisions pitiful. And this is why North suggests that institutional innovation will come from rulers rather than constituents, as the rulers may be able to reap some of the benefits from efficient institutional innovations and hence will be personally interested in providing efficient law. Rulers who provide efficient legal institutions would be attractive to constituents, and would therefore also be able to levy a tax in reaping a reward for providing efficient legal institutions. The reverse would hold when a service deteriorates or the tax price increases. With respect to the decline of Rome, North is explicit:

> The gains to individual constituents of being members of the world wide empire called Rome had significantly declined, enjoyed and ended. More and more individual parts of the empire found that local units provided them with more protection than they could get from the bickering, internally agonised Roman state. Thus, they came to the conviction that their well being depended on local autonomy. (ibid., p. 167)

And with respect to the modern state after the second industrial revolution, the explanation of structural change relies on the provision of new property rights that protected innovators and inventors. The emphasis is, indeed, not on technological developments, but rather on positive government action (ibid., p. 187) in the development of more efficient markets and the better peaceful definition and enforcement of property rights over goods and services. Likewise, he notes an activist government approach to cope with some repercussions of the newly created property rights structures.

The development of intellectual property rights posed complex issues in the measurement of the dimensions of ideas as well as complex problems over the trade-off between raising the private rates of return and innovation and monopoly-restraints of trade as a result of the grant of exclusive rights over time. While the private rate of return has been raised by better specified property rights over invention and innovation, a good part of the basic research has been financed by government and takes place in universities – reflecting the growing public awareness of the high social rate of return of scientific advances (ibid., p. 173).

Hence, the production of property rights posed some unanticipated consequences that the property rights producer, i.e. the legislature, sought to tackle as well. Note that the perspective is one in which the legislature, i.e. the ruler, sets out to maximise wealth. This highlights well the basic themes of the approach taken by North: It is important to combine incentives for legislative efficiency with the power to legislate.

We summarise the argument by saying that efficient institutional change will come about when the institutional innovator, notably the powers in charge of the state, will benefit from efficient institutional change while suffering considerably from inefficient legal institutions.

While the economic theory of efficient legal institutions has served some economic historians well in explaining the rise and decline of states, the notion that a particular type of law, i.e. the common law, reflects a concern for efficiency was suggested both as a yardstick for legal doctrine and as a basic principle to generate hypotheses on legal economic research. Posner and Landes formulated a model which asserts that the common law is economically efficient while statutory law is not. The basis of this theory turns on the respective forum in which the judicial, i.e. the common law, and the legislated, i.e. the statutory law are decided. Posner et al. claim that judicial cases are settled in a forum where the lawmaker is isolated from elections, special interests, etc.; it is seen to be necessarily more efficient than legislated law which is formed in a less objective arena. The efficiency of the judicial system is further fuelled by the positive motivation of the judges. Posner initially asserted that a judge's aspiration for higher offices, promotion, etc. was the driving force behind his positive motivation. He later amended this reason to the idea that the judges' more general desire to impose their adjudicated preferences on society was one of the causes. Although Posner's common-law theory is an evolutionary one, subscribing to the theory that inefficient rules impose greater costs on society and are therefore more likely to be relitigated and overturned than efficient rules, it differs from other evolutionary theories in that it uses the positive motivation of judges as a major force in driving common law toward efficiency.

While Posner tends to see the cause of the efficiency of the common law in the motivation of its judges, Paul Rubin, for example, focuses on litigants' motivation as the key to understanding the forces that drive the common law towards efficiency. His evolutionary common-law model depends on relitigation of inefficient rules until they become efficient, and according to Rubin, this relitigation depends on parties with an interest in precedent, taking their cases against inefficient rules to court. Rubin identifies three types of situations that are possible in involving parties to a dispute. These three situations are:

1.  Both parties are interested in a particular precedent;
2.  Only one party is interested in a given precedent, while the other is not; and
3.  Neither party is interested.

In the first case, where both parties are interested in precedent, Rubin believes that the precedents will eventually evolve towards efficiency. The reason for this is that if the rule or rules are inefficient, the party held liable will have an incentive to force litigation. If, however, the rule or rules involved are efficient, then the liable party will meet resistance against shifting the burden and the efficient rule will prevail over time. In the second case, where just one person is interested in the precedent, there is a tendency for the precedent to evolve in favour of that party, whether the precedent is efficiently decided or not. This is because the party with a stake in future cases will find it worthwhile to litigate the case as long as liability rests with him and the party with no stake would not find the litigation worthwhile.

In the third case involving no interested party, there would be no change of the rule. The present rule would stay in effect regardless of its efficiency, because neither party cares enough to litigate the matter. All three scenarios imply, of course, that there are powerful incentives in the common-law tradition which encourage efficiency.

A third approach was taken by George L. Priest, who in contrast to both Posner and Rubin states that efficient rules are more likely to endure as controlling precedent regardless of the motivation of the individual judges or of the interests in precedent of the litigants in the allocative effects of the rules. Priest goes on to point out that this drive is also present in judicial interpretations of constitutions and statutes. Instead of relying on the motivation of judges and litigants, Priest's theory depends on people treating a legal rule as a commodity.

A change in relative prices (as between efficient and inefficient rules) will change the distribution of consumption choices towards relatively cheaper and away from more expensive commodities (Priest 1977).

Since the costs of rules imposed are always higher than the costs of efficient rules, it follows that disputes arising under inefficient rules will be more likely to lead to litigation than those arising under efficient rules.

And to further contradict Posner, Priest states that a random pick or even a bias against efficiency by a judge, because a judge can only preside on a case brought before him, would still not change the judicial system's propensity towards efficiency. How would this compare with the formation of statute law? Along with their previously mentioned differences regarding the motivation of judges and litigants, Posner and Rubin also disagree on the relative efficiency of statutory law. Although they both seem to agree that the common law is more efficient than statutory law, they do so for different reasons. Posner states that statutory law is not very efficient because it is not decided in an objective forum. It is more often than not just a means for redistributing income or wealth. Rubin holds that statutory law is generally less efficient than the common law because of the time period in which the respective law was drawn up. According to Rubin, most of the law written before the 1930s was generally efficient and most law drawn up after that time, which coincides with an increase in statutory law, tends to be less efficient.

Rubin sees the major reason for this peculiar chronological phenomenon in the ease with which interest groups can form effective political organisations in contrast to earlier times. He is careful, though, to point out that although up to the present day the inefficiency effects of the formation of interest groups have probably outweighed the efficient ones, it is not necessarily true that this will always be the case. Rubin says that there are some aspects of interest groups driving statutory law towards efficiency, too. As an example he draws an analogy between litigants who spend resources on influencing judicial law making, and interest groups who do it to statutory law making. He believes both of these types of spending contribute towards efficiency.

One of the fiercest critics of legislation and staunchest defender of judge-made law was the late Bruno Leoni who felt that the relationship between the market economy and a legal system centred on judges and/or lawyers instead of on legislation tends to be much less clearly realized than it should be, although the equally strict relationship between a planned economy and legislation is too obvious to be ignored in its turn by scholars and people at large. As a yardstick, he advanced the following three principles:

> It seems to be unquestionable that we should, on this basis, reject the resort to legislation whenever it is used merely as a means of subjecting minorities in order to treat them as losers in the field. It seems also unquestionable that we should reject the legislative process whenever it is possible for the individuals involved to attain their objectives without depending upon the decision of the group and without actually constraining any other people to do what they should never do without constraint. Finally, it seems simply obvious that whenever any doubt arises about the advisability of the legislative process compared with some other kind of process having for its object the determination of rules or behaviour, the adoption of the legislative process ought to be the result of a very accurate assessment.

Again, the whole argument hinges on the possibility of legislation being an instrument for the distribution of income or wealth from the constituents to the legislators. Where this is not feasible or imminent, the criticism would not seem to apply.

## CONCLUSION

In conclusion we can note that despite many interpretations to the contrary, Hayek provides for a wide scope for economic policy, in particular if conducted through a process here called legal economic policy – as opposed to an approach linking policy objectives and particular measures case by case.

## NOTES

1. 'Madison replied in 1816, after an interval of five years, courteously refusing and understandably softening the blow with a number of vague phrases. To this reply Bentham replied, subjecting to microscopic examination every evasive word used by Madison. In 1817, he published a circular to all the governors of all the states in the Union and finally a vast collection of eight letters addressed to the citizens of the

American United States. In these, at enormous length and with remorseless detail, he defined and expounded the cardinal virtues of a properly drafted code of law. These were "aptitude for *notoriety*", "*completeness*" and "*justifiedness*" or support by adequate reasons' (Hart 1982, pp. 76–7).

2. See the symposion issues of the *Journal of Legal Studies*, 'Change in the common law: legal and economic perspectives', **9**, 1980; and *Hofstra Law Review*, 'Symposium on efficiency as a legal concern', **8** (3&4), 1980.

3. See the symposion on 'Evolutionary models in economics and law', *Research in Law and Economics*, **4**, 1982.

4. See in particular the contributions by Pejovich and Posner cited in this chapter.

5. A description of the legal provisions of the 1976 co-determination act as well earlier legislation is available in English: Der Bundesminister für Arbeit und Sozialordnung, Mass privatisation in the Federal Republic of Germany. Bonn 1978

6. We are in particular referring to the contributions by Hayek, and Lachmann; Furubotn, Pejovich, and North.

7. We use the term 'political economy' synonymously with 'theory of economic policy' as opposed to economic policy practice or the art thereof. When referring to that aspect of economic policy which involves the legal order we use the term 'legal economic policy'. This has always been a concern of political economy, so there is no need for a distinctive term for the theory of this type of economic policy.

8. And ideological elements may even be a driving force in their development (see J. Schumpeter 1949, pp. 345–59).

9. Even if he remains politically without influence, the economic contributions made in seeking political influence may be long lasting, as Walras's example can teach us.

10. Notably Cossa 1876, Ricca-Salerno 1888, Antonio de Vitti de Marco 1890, Ugo Mazzola 1890, 1895, Maffeo Pantaleoni 1882, 1886, Flora 1893, Graziani 1897. See a survey in Einaudi (1932).

11. Notably in the *Limits of Liberty* (1975).

12. These can roughly be translated as system compatibility and functionality.

13. This refers to the approach to political economy developed in continental Europe during the 17th and 18th centuries.

14. For his earlier writings, see his classical article on 'The Use of Knowledge in Society' in the *American Economic Review*, 1945.

15. Of course, the topic is not new to economics, as the writings of, among others, Wagner, Veblen and Sombart demonstrate.

## SELECT BIBLIOGRAPHY

Alchian, A. and H. Demsetz (1972), 'Production, information costs and economic organisation', *American Economic Review*, **62** (5), 777–95.

Barry, Norman P. (1979), *Hayek's Social and Economic Philosophy*, London: Macmillan.

Baums, Th. (1994), 'Corporate governance in Germany: system and recent developments', Universität Osnabrück, Institut für Handels- und Wirtschaftsrecht, Working Paper, 1/94.

Bonn, Moritz Julius (1931), 'Economic policy', in *Encyclopedia of the Social Sciences*, vol. 5, 333–40.

Brennan, Geoffrey and James M. Buchanan (1980), *The Power to Tax: Analytical Foundations of a Fiscal Constitution*, Cambridge: Cambridge University Press.

Buchanan, James M. (1965), 'An economic theory of clubs', *Economica* **32**, 1–14.

Buchanan, James M. (1975), *The Limits of Liberty: Between Anarchy and Leviathan*, Chicago: University of Chicago Press.

Buchanan, James M. (1977), *Freedom in Constitutional Contract: Perspectives of a Political Economist*, College Station, London: Texas A&M University Press.

BverfGE 50, 1979, 290 'Mitbestimmungsgesetz 1976'.

Coase, R. (1937), 'The nature of the firm', *Economica*, **4**, 386–405.

Coffee, J.C. (1996), 'Institutional investors in transitional economies:lessons from the Czech experience', in R. Frydman, C.W. Gray and A.Rapaczynski (eds), *Corporate Governance in Central Europe and Russia*, vol. 1, CEU Press.

Corbet, Jenny and Colin Mayer (1991), 'Financial reform in Eastern Europe: progress with the wrong model', *Oxford Review of Economic Policy*, **7** (4), 57–75.

De Alessi, L. (1980), 'The economics of property rights: a review of the evidence', *Research in Law and Economics*, **2**, 1–47

Einaudi, L. (1932), 'Preface', in *Antonio de Vitti de Marco, Grundlagen der Finanzwissenschaft*, Tübingen: Mohr/Siebeck.

Fama, E. and M. Jensen (1983a), 'Separation of ownership and control', *Journal of Law and Economics*, **26**.

Fama, E. and M. Jensen (1983b), 'Agency problems and residual claims', *Journal of Law and Economics*, **26**.

Frey, Bruno S. (1979), 'Economic policy by constitutional contract', *Kyklos* **32**, 307–19.

Frey, Bruno S. (1981), *Theorie demokratischer Wirtschaftspolitik*, Munich: Vahlen.

Furubotn, E. and S.Pejovich (1972), 'Property rights and economic theory: a survey of the literature', *Journal of Economic Literature*, **10**, 1137–62

Gaefgen, Gerard (1966), 'Einleitung des Herausgebers', in Gerard Gaefgen (ed.), *Grundlagen der Wirtschaftspolitik*. Cologne/Berlin: Kiepenhauer & Witsch, pp. 11–21 (12–14).

Gordon, Scott (1981), 'The political economy of F.A. Hayek', *Canadian Journal of Economics/Revue Canadienne d'Economique*, **14** (3), 470–87, 1993.

Gorton, G. and F. Schmid (1994), 'Universal banking and the performance of German firms', Wharton School working paper, October.

Hart, H.L.A. (1982), *Essays on Bentham: Studies in Jurisprudence and Political Theory*, Oxford: Clarendon Press 1982, pp. 76–7.

Hayek, Friedrik A. von (1949), 'The intellectuals and socialism', *University of Chicago Law Review*, **16**.

Hayek, Friedrich A. von (1968), 'A self generating order for society', in John Nef (ed.), *Towards World Community*, The Hague.

Hayek, Friedrich A. von (1969), 'Rechtsordnung und Handelsordnung', in *Freiburger Studien*, Tübingen: Mohr/Siebeck, pp. 161–98 (167)

Hayek, Friedrich A. von (1971), *The Constitution of Liberty*, Chicago: University of Chicago Press.

Hayek, Friedrich A. von, *Law, Legislation, and Liberty*, Chicago: University of Chicago Press, I (1973), II (1976), III (1979).

Jensen, M. (1983), 'Organisation theory and methodology', *The Accounting Review*, **LVII** (2).

Jensen, M. and W. Meckling (1976), 'Theory of the firm, managerial behaviour, agency cost and ownership structure', *Journal of Financial Economics*, **3**, 305–60.

Kaplan, S. (1994), 'Top executives, turnover and firm performance in Germany', *Journal of Law, Economics and Organisation*, **10**, 142–59.

Kirschen, Etienne *et al.* (1964), *Economic Policy in our Time*, Amsterdam: North Holland.

Lindahl, Erik [1919] (1958), Positive Lösung: Die Gerechtigkeit der Besteuerung. Lund ['Just taxation: a positive solution'], in R.A. Musgrave and A.T. Peacock (eds), *Classics in the Theory of Public Finance*, London: Macmillan 1958, 168–76.

Moore, Thomas G. (1983), 'Introduction: corporations and private property', *Journal of Law and Economics* **26**, 236.

Myrdal, Gunnar (1932), *Das politische Element in der nationalökonomischen Doktrinbildung*, Berlin, American translation by Paul Streeten under the title *The Political Element in the Development of Economic Theory*, Cambridge, MA: Harvard University Press, 1934.

North, Douglass C. (1981), *Structure and Change in Economic History*, New York: Norton. (There is a long review in the *Wall Street Review of Books* **11** (3), 1983.)

Nunnenkamp, Peter (1995), 'The German model of corporate governance: basic features, critical issues, and applicability to transition economies', Kiel Institute of World Economics working paper, no. 713.

Pejovich, S. (1972), 'Towards an economic theory of the creation and specification of property rights', *Review of Social Economy*, **30**.

Prodhan, Bimal (1990), 'Ownership and control: an international perspective', management research papers, Templeton College, University of Oxford.

Prodhan, Bimal (1993), 'Corporate governance and long term performance', management research papers, Templeton College, University of Oxford.

Robbins, Lionel (1935), *An Essay on the Nature and Significance of Economic Science*, 2nd edn, London: Macmillan & Co.

Robbins, Lionel (1976), *Political Economy: Past and Present. A Review of Leading Theories of Economic Policy*, London: Macmillan.

Samuelson, Paul A. (1954), 'The pure theory of public expenditure', *Review of Economics and Statistics* **36**, 387–9.

Savigny, Friedrich Carl von (1814), *Vom Beruf unserer Zeit für Gesetzgebung und Rechtswissenschaft*, Heidelberg: Mohr & Zimmer.

Savigny, Friedrich Carl von (1815), 'Über den Zweck dieser Zeitschrift', *Zeitschrift für geschichtliche Rechtswissenschaft* **1** (1), 1–17.

Schiller, Karl (1962), 'Wirtschaftspolitik', in *Handwörterbuch der Sozialwissenschaften*, 12, Stuttgart-Tübingen-Göttingen: Fischer-Mohr/Siebeck-Vandenhoeck & Ruprecht, pp. 210.

Schiller, Karl (1964), *Der Ökonom und die Gesellschaft: Das freiheitliche und das soziale Element in der modernen Wirtschaftspolitik*, Stuttgart: Gustav Fischer, pp. 63–90.

Schleifer, A. and R.W.Vishney (1997), 'A survey of corporate governance', *Journal of Finance*, **LII**, 737–83.

Schumpeter, Joseph Alois (1949), 'Science and ideology', *American Economic Review* **39**, 345–59.

Simon, H. (1957), *Models of Man: Social and Rational*, New York: Macmillan.

Smithies, Arthur (1955), 'Economic welfare and policy', in *Economics and Public Policy: Brookings Lectures 1954*, Washington, DC: Brookings Institution, pp. 2–3.

Tinbergen, Jan (1959), 'The theory of the optimal regime', in his *Collected Papers*, Klassen, Koyck & Witteveen (eds), Amsterdam.

Weber, Max (1904), 'Die Objektivität sozialwissenschaftlicher und sozialpolitischer Erkenntnis', *Archiv für Sozialwissenschaften und Sozialpolitik*, 22–87.

Weber, Max (1951), 'Wissenschaft als Beruf', in *Gesammelte Aufsätze zur Wissenschaftslehre*, Tübingen: Mohr/Siebeck, 1951(2).

Wicksell, Knut (1896), 'Über ein neues Prinzip der gerechten Besteuerung', in *Finanztheoretische Untersuchungen*, Jena: Gustav Fischer.
Williamson, O.E. (1975), *Markets and Hierarchies*, New York: Collier Macmillan.
Williamson, O.E. (1985), *The Economic Institutions of Capitalism*, New York: Free Press.

# 4. Hayek and the evolution of designed institutions: a critical assessment

**Christian Schubert**

## INTRODUCTION

Friedrich A. v. Hayek's cognitively based theory of cultural evolution continues to be an important source of inspiration for the attempts of economists to explain processes of institutional development.[1] The research is however by and large focused on the evolution of *informal* institutions that are 'results of human action but not of human design' (Ferguson). This is in line with an influential strand of thinking – represented by, in particular, Hume, Smith, and Menger – that views institutions as the spontaneous, undesigned and mostly unforeseen macro products of the dynamic interplay of myriads of individual interactions (Witt 1994).

This well-established research focus neglects, however, the fact that at least in modern democratic societies that are governed by a multi-layered political, administrative and judicial governance system, many institutions which play a key role in coordinating economic behavior are a product of conscious and purposeful *design*. At least within the evolutionary economics camp, the development of these institutions has largely been overlooked. Instead, approaches based on a neoclassical methodology (such as, for example, public choice, public finance, and law and economics) dominate the field. In what follows, designed institutions are defined as those rules of the market game that are (1) intentionally created by a specialized agent or small group of agents, and (2) enforced by the same or a different specialized agent or small group of agents.[2] Thus, both legislative and judge-made legal rules fall into this category. While strictly speaking, a large subset of the (genuinely 'economic') rules governing interactions within firm organizations should also be considered as designed institutions, they will not play a role in this chapter.

This chapter examines the question: in what way Hayek's theory of cultural evolution can contribute to a – yet to be elaborated – evolutionary theory of the development of designed institutions. Put differently, can there be an 'Evolutionary political economy', inspired by Hayek's approach? What could the latter look like? Arguably, it will include (1) a *positive* theory of the evolution of legislative and judge-made legal rules; (2) an *instrumental* theory of the working properties and comparative effects of alternative sets of rules, given some pre-specified performance criterion (this entails some conception of the appropriate institutional underpinnings of a spontaneous or 'catallactic' social order); (3) an instrumental theory concerning the economic function of democratic institutions; and (4) a *normative* theory about the adequacy and legitimization of alternative evaluation criteria.[3] In other words, the following research questions are to be examined:

1. How do designed institutions evolve over time?
2. How do alternative rules affect the working properties of an 'extended order'?
3. What is the economic function of democratic collective decision-making procedures?
4. According to which criteria should designed institutions be evaluated, given our insights into the working properties of spontaneous orders?

To be sure, Hayek's work covers all four aspects of an evolutionary theory of designed institutions. What appear to be most promising however are his contributions to the second and third (i.e., the instrumental or 'functional') aspect. Concerning the former, Hayek has established the basis for a re-orientation of applied political economy, which had traditionally been grounded, at least implicitly, on a static model of the market order, thereby neglecting the dynamic and epistemic features of economic systems.

Concerning the third question, Hayek proposes a fruitful paradigmatic shift in analysing collective decision-making procedures not as mechanisms to aggregate given and fixed individual preferences (the 'Arrovian' way), but rather as social learning and deliberation mechanisms that allow the processing and productive use of decentralized positive and normative knowledge. This 'epistemic' turn could well turn out to be a sound foundation for an evolutionary approach to Public Choice topics. As regards the fourth (normative) question, Hayek develops a theory about the actual 'welfare contribution' of spontaneous social orders: It is not allocative efficiency but rather the capability to process decentralized, mostly tacit, knowledge about the 'local circumstances of time and space' that makes a catallactic order (*cosmos*) superior relative to any consciously arranged 'economy' (*taxis*). In light of this welfare goal, Hayek has however only given scattered clues as to (1) under which conditions the (as a rule, epistemically superior) spontaneously evolved institutions (*nomoi*) should be corrected by consciously designed rules (*theseis*), and (2) how the latter can be designed in such a way that they do not affect the knowledge-processing capacities of the spontaneous order.

In this context, developing a Hayekian political economy also requires one to clarify the relationship between Hayek's approach and the *contractarian* tradition within constitutional economics (Vanberg 1999); more precisely, it will be argued that the latter can be made compatible with a Hayekian perspective on policy issues if the traditional Hobbesian paradigm (so strongly rejected by, for example, Hayek 1973, pp. 91–3) is replaced with a Humean orientation (so fervently praised by, for example, Hayek 1991).

The chapter is organized as follows. Section 2 discusses the Hayekian perspective on the positive explanation of the development of designed institutions, with a special focus on Hayek's theory of judge-made law. To be sure, *instrumental* questions cannot be strictly isolated from this positive account, since they strongly affect Hayek's concept of designed institutions. Section 3 discusses Hayek's normativity, while section 4 briefly overviews the Hayekian approach to the epistemic function of democratic institutions. Section 5 concludes.

## EXPLAINING THE EVOLUTION OF DESIGNED INSTITUTIONS

According to Hayek, our 'cultural heritage' (i.e., the universe of our commonly known learned rules and practices) is neither genetically programmed nor consciously designed by abstract reasoning,[4] but rather the product of 'a process of winnowing and sifting, directed by the differential advantages gained by groups from practices adopted for some unknown and perhaps purely accidental reasons' (Hayek 1979, p. 155; see also Hayek 1967, pp. 66–81). Following these rules allows the individuals (being, as they are, often unconscious about this fact) to establish and benefit from an extended order that in turn is capable of processing vast amounts of dispersed knowledge which would have gone unnoticed without it. Note that for Hayek, cultural evolution is to be categorically distinguished from biological evolution – any attempt to apply the latter's mechanisms 'mechanically' to the former is dismissed as 'scientistic' by him (Caldwell 2002). According to Hayek, cultural evolution differs from natural selection processes in exhibiting 'Lamarckian' features: rules and practices can be learned and transmitted to future generations – thus, cultural evolution accumulates knowledge in quite a different way to that of biological evolution.

Prima facie, however, designed institutions do not have a proper place within this theory of cultural evolution. For from a Hayekian perspective, practical (or cultural) knowledge is prior to theoretical knowledge ('reason'); attempts to consciously construct institutions will therefore necessarily result in epistemically inferior products. Hence, from a Hayekian viewpoint, they certainly look precarious. From a game-theoretic perspective, though, the role of designed institutions in structuring individual interactions appears in a different light. The spontaneously emerging institutions that are the object of the famous Ferguson quote cited above are then seen as solutions of coordination games. These institutions (often dubbed 'conventions' in the literature) are self-enforcing. Strategic interactions may, however, display a different structure of relative payoff combinations and result in a Prisoners' Dilemma (PD) situation with a conflict between individual and collective rationality. Then, some effort is needed in order to modify the payoffs and to transform the game into a coordination game. To be sure, this effort will sometimes be generated by the individuals themselves, i.e., cooperative behavior may emerge spontaneously. This happens if either (1) the game is infinitely repeated, for then even neoclassically rational players have the incentive to cooperate, or (2) if defective behavior is effectively punished. This costly punishment – the provision of which implies itself a PD problem – can be organized endogenously (i.e., a conditionally cooperative behavioral norm *cum* informal sanctioning mechanism has diffused within the relevant population of players, because its beneficial implications have been observed and learned over time) or exogenously, by an external enforcing agent (Witt 1989).

Given that real-world games are mostly only played over a finite number of rounds, the punishment option seems to be necessary. However, the first, endogenous way to provide for punishment may not always work. Consequently, during the course of human civilization, there have been many (often successful) attempts to organize the required transformation effort exogenously, i.e., to establish designed (enforcement) institutions. Apart from the fact that these externally imposed enforcement mechanisms most often *served* to promote the narrow self-interest of a powerful subset of the population (as Hayek describes it in, for example, Hayek 1973, ch. 6), they may, if properly constructed, contribute to overcome PD situations, i.e., they may have a sound economic *rationale*, too. As Hayek himself puts it, sometimes spontaneous institutions may simply evolve too slowly to provide the transformation needed (i.e., to solve a perceived dilemma); then, a discontinuous interference with the process of institutional evolution by way of institutional design may be necessary (see Witt 1994).

While most of Hayek's discussion of designed institutions has a strong normative and instrumental flavor (as will be seen in sections 3 and 4, below), there are clues concerning his conception of a positive theory of the evolution of designed institutions. Most strikingly, there are different mechanisms involved in the evolution of legislative rules, compared to the evolution of judge-made rules.[5]

## Legislative rules

Concerning Hayek's attempts to explain the positive evolution of legislative rules, two points have to be distinguished:

1. What is actually meant by 'legislative rules'?
2. How do legislative rules evolve over historical time? What determines the process of legislative rule-making?

First, Hayek identifies 'legislative rules' with what he calls 'theseis', i.e., public law rules (Hayek 1973, pp. 131–2; 1978, pp. 78–9). Public law (including constitutional law) in turn is identified as that subset of law which serves to (1) organize the structure of government and (2) to modify given and construct novel 'rules of just conduct'. The former category is rightly identified as having emerged much earlier in the course of legal history (Hayek 1973, ch. 6).

Generally, due to their original, viz. purely organizational, function, designed legislative rules are put into the same category as purposive rules that are established within firm organizations, i.e., in what Hayek idiosyncratically calls 'economy' (as contrasted to the 'catallaxy') *strictu sensu*. Hence, from this perspective, there is a self-evident tension between the rationale of legislative rules and the working properties of a catallactic order: in Hayek's view, legislative rules can per se only serve to co-ordinate activities within a closed, consciously arranged (government) organization. For originally they have been constructed to serve that function – hence, it is on a quasi-ontological level that they differ from informal 'rules of just conduct' in being specific and positive (instead of general and negative), aiming at the 'artificial' arrangement of particulars,[6] instead of constraining behavior in a general way. Hence, they are often referred to as 'commands' by Hayek.

It should be noted, however, that Hayek's notion of legislative rules or – synonymously – public law neglects the role that public law rules play in modern constitutional states. Though it is certainly true that their original organizational function remains valid for an important subset of public law rules, public law has also a qualitatively quite different economic role to play. This becomes most evident from a constitutional economics perspective (Vanberg 1999): Economic exchange requires a well-defined institutional framework in order to be carried out smoothly, i.e., without wasting too many resources in coping with transaction costs. In a wide sense, the constitutional 'rules of the game' define or demarcate the spheres within which the individuals can act freely according to their own self-interest. On a conceptual basis, markets cannot be defined independently of their institutional foundation.

Within complex social systems, however, the individually held expectations about adequate behavior, built on the basis of these pre-defined spheres, may often conflict. If the decentralized resolution of these conflicts (based, for example, on informal social norms, see Ellickson 1994) fails due to prohibitive transaction costs, an external agency is called for in order to re-define the individual action spheres – by re-specifying the individual property rights (Gunning 2000). Thereby, the 'legitimate content of market exchange' (Hayek 1960, p. 229) is specified anew. In other words, in this case the set of informal 'nomoi' proves incoherent and has to be selectively corrected by some *designed* institution. Hence, this designed institution has a *coordinative* role to play. Hayek, of course, concedes this (at least implicitly), for example when writing about the problem of externalities within urban agglomerations:

> There is a strong case for taking *whatever practical measures can be found* to cause the [price] mechanism to operate more efficiently by making owners take into consideration all the possible effects of their decisions. The framework of rules within which the decisions of the private owner are likely to agree with the public interest will therefore in this case have to be more detailed and more adjusted to particular circumstances than is necessary with other kinds of property. (Hayek 1960, p. 350, emphasis added)

While in this context, Hayek seems to have in mind the single *judge* as the competent agent to redefine and specify individual property rights, it is implausible to assume that complex externalities – as prevailing, for example, within urban agglomerations – can be accommodated by exclusively relying on the demarcation work of single judges. Concerning aspects like knowledge-processing capacity, democratic accountability, and administrative costs, it is not clear a priori that with regard to this task, judges have an overall comparative advantage relative to legislative bodies or administrative agencies. Rather, both kinds of governance mechanisms will display comparative advantages in some fields; hence, it is probably a reasonable working hypothesis to assume the superiority of some complementary use, i.e., some division of 'constitutional labor' (implying a division of knowledge), rather than a corner solution.[7]

From a constitutional economics perspective, the difference between the organizational and the coordinative role of designed legislative rules plays a key conceptual role. Vanberg (1999) proposes to distinguish between, on the one hand, those regulations that shift the dividing line between private and collective rights at the expense of the former (i.e., that decrease the 'domain within which market forces can work') and, on the other hand, those regulations that redefine, in a general way, the 'scope of permissible uses that private owners of assets may engage in' (ibid., p. 226; see also Gunning 2000). Since the private property rights that, from a constitutional economics viewpoint, constitute markets can never be truly unrestricted, the redefinition of their boundaries is no equivalent to the actual suspension of market forces – it is only at the limit, i.e. by interfering 'too much' that the redefinition amounts to a genuine suspension of private property.

While general, non-discriminatory regulations of the second kind do not aim at positively bringing about specific allocative end-states, they certainly are partly state-oriented (i.e., not exclusively procedural) by negatively aiming at the prevention of 'socially undesired' patterns of market results. From a Hayekian perspective, allowing for the option to recognize (necessarily imprecise) allocative or distributional *patterns* should not be an epistemological non-sequitur (Hayek 1967, pp. 22–42). What exactly counts as 'socially undesired' is, then, defined according to the contractarian general consensus criterion that has to be further justified, specified and made operational.

Thus, while Hayek implicitly concedes that even legislative rules can be compatible with (and sometimes even necessary for maintaining) the working properties of an extended order, as long as they are designed in a 'nomothetic' way (see also Hayek 1973, p. 127), he nonetheless classifies public law *in toto* as a set of 'commands' that only have an *organizational* role to play. This inconsistency obviously weakens the force of Hayek's proposed definition of designed legislative rules.

Concerning the second question ('How do designed legislative rules evolve over historical time? What determines the process of legislative rule-making?'), there are two aspects in Hayek's work which are worth considering. On the one hand, he seems to endorse the theoretical view that the process of legislative rule-making is largely driven by the activity of interest groups who attempt to channel the process into directions that favor their own narrow self-interest.[8] On the other hand, Hayek sketches a long-term historical trend toward an ever-wider crowding-out of private-law rules in favor of – epistemically inferior – public-law rules (cf., for instance, Hayek 1973, pp. 116–19). Apart from the well-known fact that he explicitly and repeatedly deplores this trend, he seems to see a mechanism at work here that promotes a kind of self-reinforcing increase in the public to private law ratio. Consequently, the catallactic order is incrementally transformed into a 'taxis'.[9] Moreover, from Hayek's writings about a 'model constitution' (Hayek 1979, see also Hayek 1990) one can conclude that he implicitly assumes that certain constitutional rules can indeed – as safeguards – influence this transformational process in a (from his viewpoint) desired direction. The same applies for the Hayekian concept of 'political competition', i.e., the competition of jurisdictions for relatively mobile production factors. While the possible effects of such a competitive order are clearly the object of positive research,[10] in the context of this chapter they would rather belong to the instrumental category of Hayek's theory, to be discussed below.

To sum up, Hayek does give only scant clues regarding his theoretical account of how designed legislative institutions evolve over time. The purely positive pillar of his political economy is incomplete. Note that the group selection argument that plays such a prominent role in his theory of the evolution of informal 'nomoi' appears to be hardly applicable in the context of legislative rules – quite apart from the question of whether it is still applicable to the evolution of informal institutions in modern societies. To be sure, it is plausible to assume that a subset of legislatively produced rules are inspired by the perceived success of designed rules that have been tried out in other societies. But it seems that any similarity to 'group selection' (with differential population growth due to more or less productive, i.e., adaptive rules) ends here. Within modern constitutional states that dispose of a fully developed multilayered set of law-making procedures, the evolution of designed legislative institutions is much more complex.

This, however, does not exclude the possibility that Hayek's ideas may inspire an evolutionary account of the development of legislative law. There are three aspects that appear to be in need of genuinely Hayekian concepts in order to be clarified:

## 1.   The role of political entrepreneurs

Given that the provision of productive institutions, i.e., institutions that provide for a 'better' adaptation of society to changed circumstances (in the sense of a better processing of productive dispersed knowledge) is a collective good, it may require the externally motivated effort of an agent who has the capability to introduce the required new institutions (see Wohlgemuth 2002b, pp. 235–6). Hayek seems to implicitly rely on such a figure when he proposes his own ideas for constitutional reform (Hayek 1979; 1990); conceptually, the entrepreneur idea is, however, rather weak, as long as the emergence of these Schumpeterian heroes (and their policy advisers) cannot be satisfactorily endogenized (Witt 1992).

## 2.   The role of mental models

Given Hayek's insights into the fundamental cognitive limitations of market participants and political agents,[11] the model of collective decision-making processes has to be revised. If there is only imperfect, fallible knowledge available concerning the effects of alternative rules on economic behavior and on the working properties of the extended order, then any proposed policy should be regarded as a conjectural hypothesis only. Moreover, not only are the problem solutions merely hypothetical, but the problem perception itself is subject to the same cognitive constraints (Slembeck 1997). Hence, what emerges as a key research issue is the question how these hypotheses are generated and learned in the first place. They are not 'given', as is commonly assumed in mainstream public choice approaches. Arguably, subjective, albeit partly shared mental models – as the 'internal representations that individual cognitive systems create to interpret the environment' (Denzau and North 1994) – play a key role in this context. They should be seen as comprising both a normative ('interest') and a positive ('theory') or instrumental component, specifying both what the individual aims at and the way she believes this aim can be realized (cf. Buchanan and Vanberg 1994). Note that Hayek seems to refer to these mental models as powerful restraining forces of political power, when elaborating on Hume's famous quip that 'it is … on *opinion* only that government is founded' (Hume 1777 [1987], p. 32, emphasis added), and that '[t]hough men be much governed by interest, yet even interest itself, and all human affairs, are entirely governed by opinion'.[12] Combined with this mental model aspect, it is evident that one central requirement for any political entrepreneur to be successful is to influence the perceived agenda of policy problems (e.g., by manipulating the way political issues are cognitively 'framed') and the perceived subset of all conceivable political problem solutions. Presumably, *mass media* play a key role, too, in these diffusion processes (Witt 1996). Finally, since at least the normative component of mental models is normally influenced to a large degree by the informal institutions (like, for example, normatively expected social norms) that prevail in a given social environment, research on politically relevant mental models also directs our attention to the question to whether there is a dynamic interplay between legislative ('formal') and informal institutions.[13]

### 3. The creative reactions of the individuals subject to policy interventions

While from the perspective of mainstream political economy, the market participants' reactions can be safely (i.e., at least probabilistically) anticipated by both the scientific observer (i.e., the economist-adviser) and all other agents, in light of Hayekian insights this is not an appropriate assumption. Rather, in an openly evolving social system, the agents' opportunities, perceived on the basis of idiosyncratic, mostly tacit knowledge, are not only largely unknown to the policy-making agency, but they also form a non-closed set. Put differently, agents can – and most often do – react in a creative way to policy interventions, thereby aiming at circumventing the – normally implied – restriction of their action parameters and the devaluation of their wealth (Wegner 1997; see also Backhaus 2001). This empirical observation has four key implications: First, a positive evolutionary theory of the evolution of legislative institutions should focus on the dynamic interplay between, on the one hand, the product of the policy-making process, and, on the other hand, the reactions of the market participants. Concerning this research issue, maybe fiscal sociology will prove a source of inspiration for economists in the future (Witt 2002). Second, with creativity on the part of the agents, policy interventions are prone to generate surprising results, i.e., they become riskier; policy-makers need more (and presumably harder to attain) knowledge about the social system they deal with than is assumed from a neoclassical point of view.[14] Third, creative reactions do also open up the possibility that policy interventions may (in light of the policy-makers' aim) be *more* successful than is commonly assumed from a Hayekian perspective. For if the direction of the agents' reactions can only imperfectly be anticipated, it is an unfounded ad hoc assumption to presume that policy interventions will *necessarily* fail (again, given whatever is aimed at by the intervening agency). Fourth and finally, the positive insight concerning the creative reactions to policy interventions makes it plausible to supplement the set of *normative* criteria by focusing on the question how far the agents' opportunity sets are effectively restrained by the policy intervention under review (Witt 1997).[15] If agents can no longer react in a creative way – i.e., if their opportunity set is too strongly restrained – Hayek's dismal cosmos-taxis transformation vision looms large indeed.

Hence, a study of Hayek's positive insights into the evolution of legislatively produced institutions does indeed only provide us with the contours of a theory that remains yet to be fully elaborated. Already at this point it becomes evident, though, that his original perspective, focusing, as it does, on the epistemic properties of spontaneous orders, can serve as a source of inspiration for all three strands – positive, instrumental, and normative – of a wider knowledge-oriented political economy.

### Judge-made rules

Die-hard Hayekians will find it surprising to see judge-made rules classified here as a subset of *designed* institutions. For Hayek describes the judicial law-making process (epitomized by the English common law-process), as it has emerged in the course of cultural evolution, as providing the institutional requirements for courts to develop judge-made law in an almost 'apolitical' way. From Hayek's perspective, the judge who applies legal rules to decide concrete cases 'has no choice in drawing the conclusions that follow from the existing body of rules and the particular facts of the case' (Hayek 1960, p. 153). Hence, judge-made law develops according to evolutionary mechanisms that differ markedly from those that shape the development of legislative law (Hayek 1973, ch. 5). First, it evolves more slowly than legislative law; moreover, it is subject to path-dependency effects (Hayek 1973, pp. 88–9). Second, according to Hayek, judges in the common-law tradition do not *create* (new) law when deciding new cases; they are rather able to *discover* the relevant 'rules of just conduct', as they have developed in the course of institutional evolution. For this reason, there is, for Hayek, actually no 'design' involved in the development of judge-made law. The judicial law-making process is thus seen as being complementary to the evolutionary process that brings about the informal 'nomoi'. These 'nomoi' are laid open and codified by the judge, who therefore acts as an 'unwitting tool' only (Hayek 1960, p. 153). The judge is capable of performing this task due to his highly specific legal intuition, acquired in the course of his socialization (Hayek 1973, pp. 117, 120). What's more, the common-law process exhibits an in-built constraint in limiting the content of adjudication according to the classical 'rule-of-law' requirements: Judge-made rules are then *per se* abstract, certain and negative. As such, they allow a maximum amount of reliable individual expectations to be formed (even if single expectations will necessarily be frustrated in any adjudication).

Here again, as in the case of his theory of legislative institutions, Hayek's approach suffers from an inadequate definition. First, rules cannot be 'abstract' or 'general' *and* 'certain' at the same time. Rather, there is a fundamental tension between those two rule-of-law conditions, which Hayek seems to ignore.

Second, the model of the judge that is implicit in Hayek's theory suffers from at least two shortcomings. If (1) the judge is able to 'discover', i.e., to correctly and objectively identify the *nomoi* that have emerged in the course of cultural evolution and to codify them in such a way that the resulting legal order is not only internally consistent, but also compatible with the institutional requirements of an extended order, then what we encounter in Hayek's writings is nothing less than a 'cognitive hero' who decides on grounds that are neither informationally nor motivationally biased. She seems to be free of any narrow self-interest (Okruch 1999, ch. D).[16] This applies even if Hayek (1973, pp. 117, 120) does not assume superior cognitive capacities on the level of 'reason' proper, but rather on the cultural level, in referring to the judge's allegedly superior socially learned 'intuition'. All this is nevertheless inconsistent with Hayek's fundamental assumption concerning the cognitive limitation of man, i.e., his fundamental subjectivism (Burczak 2002).

Furthermore, from a legal theory viewpoint, Hayek's model of the judge is unrealistic (Okruch 1999). Given the complexity of real-world regulation problems, legal rules almost always require creative specification in order to be applicable. In the course of this specification, they are almost always materially (if incrementally) 'enriched'. This gradual process of enrichment constitutes the very base of the development of judge-made law. Rather than subsuming the judge's activity under the category of 'discovery', it would be adequate to construct a model of the productive or *creative* judge. To be sure, this is to be distinguished from the idea, prevalent in the neoclassical law and economics literature, that the judge enjoys (or *should* enjoy) the full autonomy necessary to act as a 'social engineer'. In real-world cases, judges are creative within the bounds of legal precedent, principles and 'dogmatic theories'. More important, they take part in a highly structured and institutionalized discourse with other judges, legal scholars, politicians and the public about the adequate way to develop the law further. Viewing the judge's activity as genuinely creative allows one to conceptualize it as part of an overarching social learning process (on this see section 4).

Third and finally, the dynamic interplay between judge-made law and informal institutions also plays a key role in the evolution of the former (Mantzavinos 2001, ch. 5). While Hayek concedes this (e.g. in Hayek 1973, p. 100), he does not offer a coherent theoretical picture about how this interplay works. Given his thoughts about the economic function of the judge and the culturally evolving 'rule-of-law' doctrine, he seems to conceptualize informal institutions as the prime *material source* of judge-made law. Note however that it is unclear throughout all of his writings on the evolution of judge-made law if he takes a merely positive-theoretical perspective or a normative one. Thus, a fully satisfying interpretation of this part of Hayek's contribution to an evolutionary political economy is hard to get. As a result, there is paradoxically even less of a fully specified mechanism of endogenous, truly 'evolutionary' change in Hayek's theory of the judge-made law than in the neoclassical 'Efficiency theory of the common law', developed by Law & Economics scholars (Aranson 1986).

## HAYEK'S NORMATIVITY

Hayek's theory of cultural evolution – and in particular his conception of the evolution of designed institutions – is embedded in a social philosophical framework that specifies the epistemically adequate institutional underpinnings of the social order. This leads to a set of strong normative statements. According to Hayek, the extraordinary capacity of spontaneous orders to process decentralized knowledge and to exhibit a complexity unattainable for any intentionally organized 'taxis' is based on the individuals (consciously or unconsciously) following abstract, negative and certain 'rules of just conduct'. Due to their being a product of processes of spontaneous institutional evolution, they 'store' the knowledge necessary for epistemically rich macro orders to be sustained. Moreover, due to their negativity, they allow the individuals to autonomously pursue their own self-defined interests, i.e., to act according to their own (mostly tacit) idiosyncratic knowledge, which is thereby indirectly (viz., through the price mechanism) transmitted to the other market participants. If all individuals follow the 'rules of just conduct', all can form reliable expectations about the behavior of all others. The resulting web of coinciding expectations among anonymous market participants constitutes the extended order (Hayek 1973, p. 36).

From this point of view, the attempt to introduce 'thesis' rules potentially inhibits the market order's knowledge-processing capacity. According to Hayek, such attempts reflect the hubristic and anti-liberal[17] philosophy of 'constructivist rationalism'.

However, as has already been shown above, Hayek concedes that 'sometimes', spontaneously evolved institutions (or their designed counterpart: common or private-law rules) need to be 'corrected'. For processes of spontaneous institutional evolution can exhibit 'development traps', where from the viewpoint of the individuals concerned it would be advantageous to discontinuously modify certain elements of the institutional framework:

> 'The fact that all law arising out of the endeavour to articulate rules of conduct will of necessity possess some desirable properties not necessarily possessed by the commands of a legislator does *not* mean that in other respects such law may not develop in very undesirable directions, and that when this happens correction by deliberate legislation may not be the only practicable way out. For a variety of reasons the spontaneous process of growth may lead into an *impasse* from which it cannot extricate itself by its own forces or which it will at least not correct quick enough' (Hayek 1973, 88, italics added).

This modification, though, has to be organized in such a way as to avoid the pitfalls of 'constructivist rationalism'. It is in this context that Hayek proposes the 'rule of law' criterion (Hayek 1960, p. 222 (see also Caldwell, 2004, ch. 13)): If 'constructivist inputs' are universally applicable, i.e., if they are simultaneously negative, abstract and certain ('nomothetic'), then they will not negatively affect the catallaxy's epistemic capacities. This implies in particular that any attempt to positively attain pre-defined social *states* (for instance, in the name of some prespecified norm of 'social justice'[18]) are incompatible with the maintenance of a catallactic order.

This criterion, however, does not really help us in discriminating between 'adequate' and 'inadequate' constructivist interventions into market processes. For again, there is the incoherence within Hayek's catalogue of desired rule properties ('abstract' and 'certain'). In addition, Hayek's threefold catalogue of rule properties is purely formal. As has been argued before (Gray 1998), it actually does not provide effective protection against an anti-liberal transformation of the legislative order. Third (and more fundamentally), on closer inspection even in the contemporary Hayekian literature on the theory of economic policy the target of 'constructivist rationalism' (CR) is not well-defined. Finally, if it is plausibly seen as impossible to realize precisely pre-defined socio-economic states with certain desired properties, it is as implausible to argue that if the political principal (i.e., the individuals) wishes to *avoid* certain social states being realized, this would be a task impossible to fulfill without destroying the catallaxy's institutional underpinnings.

The first two objections are closely intertwined. If Hayek's 'rule of law' criterion could be developed in such a way that more or less general, *substantive* properties could be specified that indicate the compatibility of designed rules with the working properties of a spontaneous order, then the pure formalism with its inner contradictions ('abstract' versus 'certain') might be overcome. Concerning the third point, Hayek unfortunately is not very clear about what he exactly means by CR. In particular, he does not give clear guidance about (1) the appropriate roles of *tradition* or *culture* on the one hand and *reason* on the other hand in the purposive design of new rules, and (2) about the scope of harmful genuine CR ambition. This confusion further complicates the task of discriminating between adequate and inadequate rule design.

Let us take a brief look on the CR definitions that have been offered. According to one early definition of Hayek's, CR aims at reconstructing the social order *in toto*, on the basis of a prespecified comprehensive plan that is the product of abstract reasoning.[19] By invoking the primacy of practical or cultural (relative to theoretical) knowledge, Hayek emphatically rejects this concept. At other times, Hayek argues that CR aims at 'bettering' single social institutions on the basis of the theoretical knowledge available.[20] Not surprisingly, confusion also reigns among the Hayekians: Langlois and Sabooglu (2001, p. 239), for instance, define CR as the doctrine according to which 'human reason is capable of constructing a set of *ideal* institutions' (emphasis added). Then again, they say that by CR, Hayek very generally meant the attempt 'to arrive at a government based on reason' (ibid.). Obviously, the second approach does not necessarily imply the ambition expressed in the first quote. For it is certainly possible to develop and test propositions concerning the 'correction' of single institutions without ascribing an ideal status to the results of this process.[21] Modest and limited constructivism seems to be prima facie compatible with the working properties of an extended order.[22] That is however all that can be said at this moment. If we try to conceptualize a process of legislative trial-and-error (or 'piecemeal engineering', as Popper intrepidly called it), then at its current state, Hayekian political economy does not seem to offer practicable normative guidelines.

How could a further development proceed? To be compatible with the working properties of a spontaneous social order, i.e., to avoid the 'pretence of knowledge' trap, consciously designed institutions obviously have to meet three conditions:

- Their *status* should be a merely conjectural one. They should be designed and formulated in such a way that they can be revised in the light of new practical experiences and theoretical insights.
- Their *methodology* or mode of production has to avoid utopian assumptions concerning the availability of knowledge. In Hayek's view, it amounts to a scientistic fallacy to uncritically derive conclusions meant to apply for real-world settings from theoretical models (Schnellenbach 2002).
- Their *content* should be aligned with the institutional background of a given society. This refers to both the given set of informal institutions and the given web of legal rules. Though Hayek repeatedly criticizes the inborn behavioral instincts and attitudes of human beings (reflecting man's former life as a member of small hunter-gatherer bands) as being incompatible with the requirements of interaction within a complex extended order, he explicitly endorses Hume's concept of politically relevant 'opinions' (Hayek 1991). This contradiction may be resolved by constructing a procedure that, starting from the individuals' 'crude' social preferences, takes them as input into a social deliberation process where the preferences may be informed, discussed and possibly transformed in light of insights into the working properties of spontaneous social orders. These insights may, of course, be derived both from practical former experiences with constitutional rules and from theoretical reflection.

These conditions may be summed up in the methodological concept of 'immanent criticism', as proposed by Hayek (1976, pp. 24–5) himself and elaborated upon by Sugden (1993). This concept reflects the idea that the (at first sight contradictory) goals of (1) maintaining the knowledge-processing capacity of spontaneous orders and (2) 'bettering' the institutional framework of society in the face of new policy problems may be reconciled by the difficult attempt to gradually correct institutional 'development traps' without negatively affecting those elements of the interdependent web of institutions that maintain the mutual reliability of individual expectations. The trade-off between the valuable knowledge stored in grown cultural traditions and the possibility of processing and benefiting from new knowledge by way of institutional design has to be productively resolved. Evolutionary political economy can, however, only contribute to this complex task when the three Hayekian conditions sketched above are made much more operational.

Apart from this practical problem, a brief remark is in order concerning the relationship between a Hayekian political economy – conceptualized as described above – and constitutional economics with its strong contractarian orientation. Recently, some authors have argued that Hayek's approach to the problem of institutional design is in fact compatible with Constitutional Economics (Gray 1998; Sugden 1993; Vanberg 1994); see also Caldwell 2002, p. 293ff.). How is that possible, given that Hayek repeatedly targeted contractarianism when decrying the philosophy of 'constructivist rationalism'? Is the contradiction on the contractarians' or is it on Hayek's side?

In fact, both camps have to move in order for a conceptual integration to succeed. Hayek's normativity has been shown to lead not to an *a priori* objection to any institutional design, but rather to a catalogue of 'compatibility conditions'. The contractarians, in turn, have to dispense with a central element of their philosophical baggage, namely the Hobbesian concept of social order.

Hobbes clearly belongs to the (rightly targeted) 'creationist' camp within social philosophy according to which order can only be conceived as consciously planned by an agent whose relationship to society is hierarchical. From behind the famous veil of uncertainty, the *Leviathan* order is preferred to any anarchical state of nature. In his 'Of the Original Contract', Hume (1748 [1992]) puts forward a subtle argument against this concept. According to him, no social contract – specifying the rights and duties of the individuals, thereby constituting the non-anarchical social order – has normative binding force *per se*. It is rather some underlying informal *convention* (like, for example, the rule that 'pacta sunt servanda') that induces individuals to feel obliged to abide by the rules stipulated in the contract. Thus, informal conventions are not only historically prior to designed constitutions, but they are also legitimatorily superior.

Analogously, if the social contract is merely *hypothetical* (as is realistically most often assumed in modern Constitutional Economics), then in order to be normatively binding, *real* individuals will have to be effectively *convinced* by its contents. This is the easier the stronger aligned are the proposed constitutional rules with the informal institutions prevalent in a given society. Thus, effective constitutional reform proceeds 'from within' a given institutional background, instead of aiming at a total reconstruction of the social order.

This material orientation toward the culturally contingent institutional peculiarities of a given society also implies a more modest approach on a methodological level: Constitutional Economics' statements about the capacity of alternative rules of the game to command general assent cannot be regarded as hard logical deductions from a universalizable 'veil of uncertainty' model. They are rather to be understood as conjectural statements that are valid only for a well-specified society in historical time. More precisely, they are to be seen as statements of the following mode: 'Given what we know about (1) the preferences of the individuals [i.e., our normative knowledge] and (2) how the social order in fact works [i.e., our positive/instrumental knowledge], we hypothesize that policy X should be capable of commanding general assent, i.e., should be legitimate in this sense.'

This material orientation toward the given institutional structure of a society can be organized according to the 'reflective equilibrium' model proposed by the political philosopher John Rawls (Rawls 1971 [1995]; O'Neill 1998).[23] He specifies a model of 'fair' procedures that allow the endogenization of the concrete shape of the contractarian 'veil of uncertainty' model which he labels 'veil of ignorance' and which is traditionally specified in an *aprioristic* way in the contractarian literature. The individual social preferences are channelled into a public deliberation process, in the course of which their universalizable and well-informed parts are identified and taken as a guideline to formulate the 'veil of ignorance' construct. Consequently, Constitutional Economics undergoes a paradigm shift. Instead of the radically subjectivist route taken by, for example, Buchanan (1975), a Humean approach would attempt to specify the *material substance of the constitutional consensus of a society* at any point in time. Arguably, this conceptual strategy will permit the integration of contractarianism with Hayekian ideas.[24]

## ON DEMOCRACY

Besides his positive and normative theories, Hayek's work contributes a third aspect to an evolutionary political economy, namely his concept of democracy as a 'discovery mechanism'.

While in the relevant literature, Hayek is most often cited as a staunch critic of democratic institutions (for their potential to allow arbitrarily emerged majorities to exploit the minority, motivated by Rousseau's famous *volonté générale* dictum), he also offers a constructive approach to view these institutions in a genuinely 'evolutionary' light, i.e., from the perspective of the precarious epistemic basis of political problem solutions (see in particular Hayek 1960, ch. 7). In a pointed contrast to the dominant neoclassical view on collective decision-making procedures, shaped by Arrow and the *Social Choice* school, Hayek proposes to model them as adaptive, if necessarily imperfect, solutions to the problem of the fallible knowledge on policy issues and the quality of alternative political problem solutions. For by means of democratic decision-making procedures, a forum can be institutionalized that allows the entry to a collective deliberation process, implying interactive learning, in the course of which new knowledge on policy issues may be generated.

This approach differs from Arrow's in taking a 'transformation' rather than an 'aggregation' view on individual (political) preferences. Instead of aggregating given and constant individual preference orderings, it is now (at least implicitly) assumed that the mental models underlying the formation of these preferences or their underlying 'opinions' are imperfect in containing fallible – and probably often false – theoretical assumptions on, for example, economic means–ends relationships, the economic effects of alternative institutions, etc. Some political *learning* mechanism is thus called for.[25] The given imperfect knowledge may be enriched by channelling the preferences that are based on it into a public discourse, where competing views on the same policy issue are offered and confronted with one another. Put differently, '[t]he central belief from which all liberal postulates may be said to spring is that more successful solutions of the problems of society are to be expected if we do not rely on the application of anyone's given knowledge, but encourage the interpersonal process of the exchange of opinion from which better knowledge can be expected to emerge' (Hayek 1978, p. 148).

What's more, the Hayekian approach (on which see also Wohlgemuth 2002a, 2002b; Peacock 2004) avoids the collectivist concept of a 'social preference' which Arrow takes as the well-defined product of his mechanical aggregation process.

Note, though, that if we regard democracy 'above all, [as] a process of forming opinion', i.e., if we evaluate it 'in its dynamic, rather than its static aspects' (Hayek 1960, p. 109), then it is much more difficult to develop operational criteria that indicate the degree to which given democratic institutions (as a subset of the many conceivable ones) adequately perform their function. Candidates for criteria include, for instance, the question how well democratic institutions structure the informed discourse on the positive or normative components of individual preferences; how well they contribute to overcoming the PD problem implied in individually investing in 'constitutional knowledge' (Buchanan and Vanberg 1991) or providing constitutional expertise; how well 'biases' in the individual perception of, for example, risk are corrected (Sunstein 2000); if divergent opinions are channelled into the discourse in such a way that they are effectively contestable, etc. Quite obviously, much theoretical work remains to be done here, in order to complement the positive and normative pillar of an evolutionary theory of designed institutions by an instrumental one.

## CONCLUDING REMARKS

To sum up, Hayek has left us with a multitude of theoretical ideas that, if not internally inconsistent, do not form an overarching conception of the evolution of designed institutions, i.e., an evolutionary political economy.

As Hayek (1973, pp. 45–6) observed, '[t]he spontaneous character of the [social] order must ... be distinguished from the spontaneous origin of the rules on which it rests'. The latter can partly be the object of purposeful design without necessarily affecting the former's spontaneous character. Consequently, *reason* plays a role in institutional evolution, and this role has to be thoroughly investigated. A theory of designed institutions is thus called for, if we wish to (1) fully understand and (2) maybe even purposefully influence the driving forces of cultural evolution.

If we assume that a complete theory of the evolution of designed institutions comprises a positive, an instrumental, and a normative part, then Hayek's contribution and the conceivable further developments may be summed up as follows.

### The positive view

With regard to the *positive* view on the evolution of designed institutions, Hayek's approach suffers from definitions of legislative and judge-made law that are somewhat unconvincing. His highly original focus on the precarious epistemic dimension of policy problems and problem solutions proves, however, a fruitful source of inspiration for a positive account of the evolution of designed law. Relevant research questions include, *inter alia*, the mechanisms of individual (and presumably interdependent) belief formation; the diffusion of subjective beliefs (both theoretical and normative) regarding the substance of policy issues, given the cognitive limitations of all agents concerned; the role of political entrepreneurs in influencing these diffusion processes; the development of law as a product of the dynamic interplay between policy interventions and creative attempts on the part of the individuals to circumvent those interventions; and the role of mass media in this context. Hayek's own approach is relatively silent on these positive issues, because he generally neglected the problem of the genesis and diffusion of knowledge in *non-market* settings, like the political or judicial arena (Schnellenbach 2002).

### The normative view

With regard to the *normative* view, Hayek's most important legacy seems to be his overall focus on the epistemic (knowledge-processing) 'welfare contribution' of spontaneous social orders. While this focus is not necessarily incompatible with a constitutional economics approach on the problems of policy and legal reform, two main obstacles hamper the integration so far: first, Hayek's 'rule of law' condition that is meant to serve to distinguish adequate ('nomothetic') from inadequate designed institutions appears to be hardly operational. Second, on the part of constitutional economics itself, the traditional Hobbesian paradigm does not conform well with the Hume–Smith–Menger–Hayek view on the characteristics of spontaneous social evolution. Within constitutional economics, then, a conventionalist 'Humean' paradigm shift would seem to be called for.

## The instrumental view

Finally, on the subject of the *instrumental* view, what appears to be most interesting is Hayek's concept of democracy. While on the one hand, he gives warnings of Rousseau's idea of the absolute status of the *volonté générale*, on the other hand, he regards democratic institutions as intelligent adaptations to the fundamental cognitive limitations of the *citoyen*. For they allow individuals to participate in an interactive deliberation and learning process that ideally (i.e., if well-organized) brings about well-informed and universalizable opinions on policy issues. Elaborating upon this idea requires one to overcome the narrow concept of 'normative individualism' prevalent in mainstream normative economics: to assume individual autonomy necessarily implies assuming the individual capacity to *further develop* one's (political) preferences in light of new practical experiences and new theoretical insights.

Hence, Hayek's fundamental contribution to an evolutionary political economy appears to be his integration of insights into the evolutionary nature of the social order with political economy proper. Political and legal institutions should be designed in such a way that the working properties of the extended order are not negatively affected. Elaborating on this idea in order to establish a knowledge-oriented political economy that is both conceptually well-founded and operational in providing reasonable solutions to real-world policy problems will require far-ranging efforts by evolutionary theorists and constitutional economists alike.

## NOTES

1. In this sense 'institutional', can be understood as behavioral regularities that co-ordinate the interactive behavior of individuals, and which are both commonly known and mutually (positively and/or normatively) expected to be followed. The set of informal (or spontaneous) and formal (or designed) institutions defines the 'rules of the game' of a society.
2. At least in continental civil-law systems, they are mostly also explicitly codified (and enforced according to the specific way they are codified); this is however less valid in the common law world that has inspired Hayek's views on the evolution of the *judge-made* part of designed institutions.
3. See Witt (2003) for a similar methodological classification.
4. In other words, it occupies a place between 'instinct' and 'reason', cf. Hayek (1988, ch. 1).
5. On this positive-theoretical aspect of a theory of designed institutions, cf. also the first attempts by Witt (1992), Schnellenbach (2002), and Voigt (1999).
6. Or, to quote Hayek (1973, p. 142), to 'secure particular results for particular groups'.
7. Note that there are some scattered remarks, as in Hayek (1944, p. 37), concerning the productive co-ordinate role of legislative rules when it comes to, for example, restricting 'allowed methods of production' in a non-specific way (ibid.).
8. Cf., for example, Hayek (1973, p. 89), where he also alludes to the possibility that judges, if systematically recruited from a particular social group, might have furthered that social group's particular interests by somehow biasing adjudicatory practice.

9. Cf., for example, Hayek (1973, pp. 141–3; 1994, pp. 116–19, 187ff.); cf. Buchanan's (1975) analogous remarks concerning the 'constitutional disorder' he perceives to reign in the United States.

10. See, for example, Bünstorf (2002) for a skeptical view about the – often claimed – analogy between the implications of economic compared to political competition.

11. It is not clear if, for Hayek, this applies for judges, too. See the following subsection.

12. As cited by Hayek (1973, 168, note 39). See also Hayek (1960, pp. 107–10) and his definition of 'opinion' as opposed to 'will' in Hayek (1976, pp. 12–14, emphasis in the original): '[W]e shall call *opinion* the view about the desirability or undesirability of different forms of action...which leads to the approval or disapproval of the conduct of particular persons according as they do or do not conform to that view' (ibid., p. 13). On the problematics of Hayek's 'opinion' concept see Peacock (2004).

13. See, for example, Ellickson's (1994) programmatic objections against 'legal centralism'.

14. Note that in order to intervene successfully, the policy-maker would need reliable information on the agents' opportunities. Many of them, though, emerge only in the course of the interactions that are triggered by the policy intervention itself, i.e., they develop endogenously.

15. On normative issues, see section 3, below.

16. Though Hayek concedes the possibility of judicial self-interest (cf. note 8, above), this is not systematically integrated into his own theory of the evolution of judge-made law.

17. See Hayek (1967: 94).

18. For Hayek, it is only individual behavior that can be judged as 'just' – this is the case if the individual conforms to the given 'rules of just conduct'. Hence, he conceptualizes 'justice' as (1) a procedural value on (2) the level of the individual only.

19. See, for example, his Descartes quote in Hayek (1949, p. 9).

20. On the different CR conceptions, cf. Hayek (1949), (1967, pp. 82–95), (1973, pp. 10, 24–26), and (1991).

21. This appears to be neglected, for example, by Hayek (1967, p. 85, emphasis added), where he objects to the approach ascribed to 'CR', that institutions 'are to be approved and respected only to the extent that we can show that the particular effects they will produce in any given situation are preferable to the effects another arrangement would produce; that we have it in our power so to shape our institutions that *of all possible sets of results* that which we prefer *to all others* will be realized'.

22. See also Hayek (1978, p. 19, italics added): 'The social scientist ... must claim the right critically to examine, and even to judge, every single value of our society. The consequence of what I have said is merely that we can never *at one and the same time question all its value*'. See also (ibid., p. 167): 'There is...certainly room for improvement, but we cannot redesign but only further evolve what we do not fully comprehend.'

23. On Rawls' 'reflective equilibrium' approach see also Gray (1998, ch. 6). The ethical background is discussed in Daniels (1979). What is specifically referred to in the chapter is Rawls's *wide* (as opposed to narrow) reflective equilibrium concept (see also Daniels 1979).

24. Note, though, that Hayek himself misreads Rawls' 'justice as fairness' approach by reducing it to its purely procedural aspects, as in Hayek (1976, pp. xiii, 100, 166, 179). Rawls's reflective equilibrium concept encompasses a procedural as well as a substantive, if not detailed, check of market outcomes, see Schubert (2003).

25. On the need of which see also Buchanan and Vanberg (1991).

# REFERENCES

Aranson, P.H. (1986), 'Economic efficiency and the common law: a critical survey', in J.-M. von der Schulenburg and G. Skogh (eds), *Law and Economics and the Economics of Legal Regulation*, Dordrecht: Kluwer, pp. 51–84.

Backhaus, J. (2001), 'Fiscal sociology: what for?', mimeo, University of Erfurt, reprinted in *American Journal of Economics and Sociology*, **61**, 2002, 55–77.

Buchanan, J.M. (1975), *Limits of Liberty: Between Anarchy and Leviathan*, Chicago: University of Chicago Press.

Buchanan, J.M. and V.J. Vanberg (1991), 'Constitutional choice, rational ignorance and the limits of reason', *Jahrbuch für Neue Politische Ökonomie*, **10**, 61–78.

Buchanan, J.M. and V.J. Vanberg (1994), 'Interests and theories in constitutional choice', in V. Vanberg (ed.), *Rules and Choice in Economics*, London: Routledge, pp. 167–77.

Bünstorf, G. (2002), 'Über den Wettbewerb als allgemeines Aufdeckungs-, Ordnungs- und Erkundungsverfahren', *ORDO*, **53**, 189–205.

Burczak, T.A. (2002), 'The contradictions between Hayek's subjectivism and his liberal theory', in J. Birner, P. Garrouste and T. Aimar (eds), *F.A. Hayek as a Political Theorist*, London: Routledge, pp. 183–201.

Caldwell, B.J. (2002), 'Hayek and cultural evolution', in U. Mäki (ed.), *Fact and Fiction in Economics: Models, Realism, and Social Construction*, Cambridge: Cambridge University Press, pp. 285–303.

Caldwell, B.J. (2004), *Hayek's Challenge*, Chicago: University of Chicago Press.

Daniels, N. (1979), 'Wide reflective equilibrium and theory acceptance in ethics', *Journal of Philosophy*, **76**, 256–82.

Denzau, A.T. and D.C. North (1994), 'Shared mental models', *Kyklos*, **47**, 3–31.

Ellickson, R.C. (1994), 'The aim of order without law', *Journal of Institutional and Theoretical Economics*, **150**, 97–100.

Gray, J.N. (1998), *Hayek on Liberty*, 3rd edn, London: Routledge.

Gunning, J.P. (2000), 'The property system in Austrian economics: Ronald Coase's contribution', *Review of Austrian Economics*, **13**, 209–20.

Hayek, Friedrich A. von (1948), *Individualism and Economic Order*, Chicago: University of Chicago Press.

Hayek, Friedrich A. von (1949), 'Individualism: True and False', in *Individualism and Economic Order*, London: Routledge, pp. 1–32.

Hayek, Friedrich A. von (1960), *The Constitution of Liberty*, London: Routledge.

Hayek, Friedrich A. von (1967), *Studies in Philosophy, Politics and Economics*, Chicago: University of Chicago Press.

Hayek, Friedrich A. von (1973), *Law, Legislation and Liberty*, vol I: *Rules and Order*, London: Routledge & Kegan Paul.

Hayek, Friedrich A. von (1976), *Law, Legislation and Liberty*, vol II: *The Mirage of Social Justice*, Chicago: University of Chicago Press.

Hayek, Friedrich A. von (1978), *New Studies in Philosophy, Politics, Economics and the History of Ideas*, London: Routledge & Kegan Paul.

Hayek, Friedrich A. von (1979), *Law, Legislation and Liberty*, vol III: *The Political Order of a Free People*, Chicago: University of Chicago Press.

Hayek, Friedrich A. von (1988), 'The fatal conceit', in W.W. Bartley (ed.), *The Collected Works of F.A. Hayek*, vol 3, Chicago: University of Chicago Press.

Hayek, Friedrich A. von (1990), *The Denationalisation of Money: The Argument Refined*, London: Institute of Economic Affairs.

Hayek, Friedrich A. von (1991), 'The legal and political philosophy of David Hume (1711–1776)', in W.W. Bartley and S. Kresge (eds),*The Collected Works of F.A. Hayek*, vol III, Chicago: University of Chicago Press, pp. 101–18.

Hayek, Friedrich A. von (1994), *Freiburger Studien*, 2nd edn, Tübingen: Mohr.

Hume, D. (1748), 'Of the original contract', in T. Hill Green and T.H. Grose (eds),

1992, *David Hume. The Philosophical Works*, vol 3, Aalen, Germany: Scientia, pp. 443–60.

Hume, D. (1777), 'First principles of government', in *Essays, Moral, Political and Literary*, ed. by E.F. Miller, 1987, Indianapolis: Liberty Press, pp. 32–41.

Langlois, R.N. and M.M. Sabooglu (2001), 'Knowledge and meliorism in the evolutionary theory of F.A. Hayek', in K. Dopfer (ed.), *Evolutionary Economics: Program and Scope*, Boston: Kluwer, pp. 231–51.

Mantzavinos, C. (2001), *Individuals, Institutions, and Markets*, Cambridge: Cambridge University Press.

Okruch, S. (1999), *Innovation und Diffusion von Normen*, Berlin: Duncker & Humblot.

O'Neill, O. (1998), 'The method of a theory of justice', in O. Höffe (ed.), *John Rawls. Eine Theorie der Gerechtigkeit*, Berlin: Akademie-Verlag, pp. 27–43.

Peacock, M.S. (2004), 'On political competition: democracy, opinion and responsibility', *Constitutional Political Economy*, **15**, 187–204.

Rawls, J. (1971), *A Theory of Justice*, 1995, Cambridge, MA: Belknap Press.

Schnellenbach, J. (2002), 'New political economy, scientism and knowledge', *American Journal of Economics and Sociology*, **61**, 193–214.

Schubert, C. (2003), 'A contractarian view on cultural evolution', *Papers on Economics & Evolution*, # 0311, Max Planck Institute for Research Into Economic Systems, Jena.

Slembeck, T. (1997), 'The formation of economic policy: a cognitive-evolutionary approach to policy-making', *Constitutional Political Economy*, **8**, 225–54.

Sugden, R. (1993), 'Normative judgments and spontaneous order: the contractarian element in Hayek's thought', *Constitutional Political Economy*, **4**, 393–424.

Sunstein, C.R. (2000), 'Cognition and cost–benefit analysis', *Journal of Legal Studies*, **29**, 1059–103.

Vanberg, V.J. (ed.) (1994), 'Individual choice and institutional constraints', in *Rules and Choice in Economics*, London: Routledge, pp. 208–34.

Vanberg, V.J. (1999), 'Markets and regulation: on the contrast between free-market liberalism and constitutional liberalism', *Constitutional Political Economy*, **10**, 219–43.

Voigt, S. (1999), 'Positive constitutional economics: A Survey', *Public Choice*, **90**, 11–53.

Wegner, G. (1997), 'Economic policy from an evolutionary perspective – a new approach', *Journal of Institutional and Theoretical Economics*, **153**, 485–509.

Witt, U. (1989), 'The evolution of economic institutions as a propagation process', *Public Choice*, **62**, 155–72.

Witt, U. (1992), 'The endogenous public choice theorist', *Public Choice*, **73**, 117–29.

Witt, U. (1994), 'The theory of societal evolution: Hayek's unfinished legacy', in J. Birner and R. Van Zijp (eds), *Hayek, Co-ordination and Evolution: His Legacy in Philosophy, Politics, Economics and the History of Ideas*, London: Routledge, pp. 178–89.

Witt, U. (1996), 'The political economy of mass media societies', *Papers on Economics & Evolution*, # 9601, MPIEW, Jena.

Witt, U. (1997), 'Markteingriffe – eine prozeßorientierte Betrachtung', in H. Schmid and T. Slembeck (eds), *Finanz- und Wirtschaftspolitik in Theorie und Praxis – FS A.Meier*, Bern: Haupt, pp. 245–67.

Witt, U. (2002), 'Evolutorische Finanzwissenschaft – worum geht es?', in M. Lehmann-Waffenschmidt (ed.), *Perspektiven des Wandels*, Marburg: Metropolis, pp. 457–63.

Witt, U. (2003), 'Economic policy making in evolutionary perspective', *Journal of Evolutionary Economics*, **13**, 77–94.
Wohlgemuth, M. (2002a), 'Evolutionary approaches to politics', *Kyklos*, **55**, 223–46.
Wohlgemuth. M. (2002b), 'Democracy and opinion falsification: towards a new Austrian political economy', *Constitutional Political Economy*, **13**, 223–46.

# 5. Hayek on entrepreneurship: competition, market process and cultural evolution

**Alexander Ebner**

## INTRODUCTION

Friedrich August von Hayek's theory of cultural evolution is usually regarded as a crucial contribution to an analysis of the institutional dynamism of market economies. It highlights the impact of rules and conventions in maintaining the extended order of modern civilisation. The role of entrepreneurship in that line of reasoning, however, seems to have been largely neglected. Indeed, it is a well-established position in discussions on the theoretical foundations of modern Austrian economics, that entrepreneurship has been most promisingly discussed in Ludwig von Mises' theory of human action, whereas Hayek is said to have focused more intensely on the evolutionary mechanism of the competitive coordination of dispersed knowledge. Indeed, it is usually argued that Hayek dismissed the matter of entrepreneurship, for he neglected theorising on individual behaviour in favour of the analysis of rules and institutions.

Quite in contrast to that view, the present chapter argues that Hayek's theory of cultural evolution is based on a conceptualisation of entrepreneurial activities which is decisive for the related concept of institutional change. The evolutionary role of entrepreneurship in the market process pinpoints the matter of search, experimentation and discovery. Despite its rather implicit character in Hayek's theorising, entrepreneurship provides Hayek's theory of cultural evolution with constitutive arguments on the interplay of individuals, groups and institutions in the evolutionary process of economic development. The underlying line of reasoning ranges from entrepreneurial behaviour in competition to knowledge dispersion in the market process, informing the theory of cultural evolution as a comprehensive approach to institutional change in economic development.

In dealing with that subject, the chapter proceeds as follows. First, the Austrian framework of theorising on entrepreneurship is brought to the fore, exploring the diverse conceptual strands of economic analysis that have shaped the Austrian perspective. In particular, the contributions of Menger, Wieser and Mises are emphasised. Second, Hayek's theory of the market process is examined with regard to the role of entrepreneurship in the experimentation and discovery procedures of knowledge coordination in market competition. It is pointed out that entrepreneurship promotes gradual evolutionary change within the economic system. Third, the related aspects of entrepreneurship are traced in Hayek's theory of cultural evolution, highlighting the matter of rules, traditions and knowledge. Indeed, in Hayekian terms, it is the developmental impact of pioneering entrepreneurs that facilitates those institutional and structural changes which characterise the growth of modern civilisation. In conclusion, Hayek's approach to entrepreneurship is assessed as an indispensable contribution to modern Austrian positions in economic analysis.

## AUSTRIAN THEMES IN THE THEORY OF ENTREPRENEURSHIP

Traditional contributions to neoclassical marginalism denote an analytical framework, in which scarce resources are allocated to meet given ends. Neglecting the role of entrepreneurship, equilibration is assumed to result from a seemingly automatic adjustment mechanism (Hébert and Link 1982, 52n). In particular, the essentials of the 'marginalist revolution' of neoclassical economics have been summarised by the concept of opportunity costs, rational behaviour and individual choice, as well as by problems of information procession that lead to the question of the stability of equilibrium (Spengler 1973, 211n). Walrasian theory represents the most abstract variant in that theoretical endeavour. In its static exchange model, the entrepreneur comes into play as a buyer of services which are used as inputs in production, operating with fixed technical coefficients (Jaffé 1967, 6n). Due to the zero-profit situation in equilibrium, the opportunity for entrepreneurial profit arises basically from arbitrage between competitive market prices and average costs. Thus, Walrasian entrepreneurship is essentially an equilibrating force (Walker 1986, 396n).

The Austrian School in the Mengerian tradition represents a variation of marginalism that promotes the case for entrepreneurship most explicitly in the context of uncertainty, knowledge and time (Martin 1979, 272n).[1] Menger's approach to entrepreneurship is part of his theory of production, in which the intertemporal coordination of the factors of production is of paramount analytical importance, with the entrepreneurial position depending on the knowledge-based direction of resources on markets and in the production process (Hébert and Link 1982, 59n). Menger's argumentation rests on a typology of goods that reflects the time structure of production and its rationale, namely the satisfaction of consumptive needs. It indicates that production is time-consuming, as its outcome remains uncertain (Menger 1871/1923, 27n).

These arguments shape the Mengerian concept of entrepreneurial activities as he argues that the economic process of transforming higher-order goods into lower-order goods needs to be arranged and guided by an economising subject, as it proceeds with economic calculations while providing the required set of higher-order goods, including technological performance (Menger [1871] 1923, p. 153).

The latter would include information on the economic situation, calculation required for arranging production; an act of will by which higher order goods are supplied to production, as well as supervision of actual production, but definitely not risk-taking. Entrepreneurial activities could be exercised by an individual in small enterprises, while they are often split among employees in large enterprises (Menger [1871] 1923, p. 154). Hence, Menger brought together entrepreneurship and production in a common framework, stressing the satisfaction of consumer needs as a rationale of entrepreneurship.

In the succeeding generation of Austrian economists, Böhm-Bawerk's theory of production added nothing specific to that scheme of entrepreneurship, supposedly due to his analytical focus on time preference in the intertemporal coordination of production, Instead, it was Friedrich von Wieser, who stood out in the Austrian School with his theses on entrepreneurial leadership that would especially influence Schumpeter's theorising, in addition to the introduction of subjectivist principals of value theory such as the concept of imputation, which allows for determining factor prices by output prices, as well as the related notion of opportunity costs (Streissler 1981, 66n).[2] According to Wieser, the impulse for development corresponds with the impact of novelty and leadership. While the leadership function proves to be the decisive aspect of entrepreneurship, it is accompanied by the role of the entrepreneur as a risk-taker. Both leadership capabilities and property of capital are addressed as indispensable conditions for achieving an entrepreneurial position (Wieser 1914, p. 353n). Consequently, Wieser maintains that the historical emergence of capitalist enterprise is related with 'pioneers' who 'open up new ways' by making use of technological knowledge and organisational leadership, characterised by the 'courage of the innovator' (Wieser 1914, p. 375n). Large enterprises evolve as a result of entrepreneurial leadership, quite in keeping with the formation of dynastic empires (Wieser 1914, 406n).

Wieser even maintains that the emergence of large bureaucratic enterprises stimulates an institutional transformation of entrepreneurship, for personal talent is replaced by the disposal of capital, while technological problems and their solutions could be treated as data, to be solved by professional engineers and managers (Wieser 1892, p. 110). Wieser thus puts forward a transformation to a bureaucratic-administrative type of governance, in which economic leadership and enterprise are detached. The emerging mass character of economic life is illustrated by invoking the image of anonymous shareholders and employees in corporate business organisations (Wieser 1914, 354n). Yet Wieser points out that entrepreneurial leadership retains its function of also establishing organisational guidance in a socialist society (Wieser 1892, p. 122). This developmental vision underlines major concerns that are shared by Schumpeter's theory of economic development.

Schumpeter deals with innovation as the internal force of discontinuous evolutionary change, carried out by means of entrepreneurial leadership. Indeed, Schumpeterian entrepreneurship should reflect the impact of leadership, based on the interplay of imagination and creation, identified as a most relevant endogenous source of socio-cultural change in general, and of economic development in particular (Schumpeter 1912, 124n). The role of entrepreneurial leadership is derived from the innovative disruption of the routines of the circular flow, as novelty is forced upon the majority of economic agents (Schumpeter 1912, 185n). The clustering of innovations is resulting from these effects of entrepreneurial leadership, for pioneering innovations enlarge opportunities for further ventures (Schumpeter 1939, 100n). With ongoing processes of bureaucratisation and rationalisation, however, the obsolescence of personal entrepreneurship heralds socialist transformation, accompanied by government interventions and the establishment of innovation as an organisational routine (Schumpeter 1942, 131n).

This perspective on the dynamism of capitalism reflects a discourse on the advent of socialism and its Marxist prophets that had been prevalent in Austrian marginalism, as exemplified by Böhm-Bawerk's criticism of the labour theory of value. Wieser also confronts Marxian ideas, especially regarding the theoretical aspects of economic organisation in a collectivist setting (Streissler 1986, p. 100). Indeed, Austrian contributions to the socialist calculation debate, as introduced by Mises, were directed at the same set of problems, namely a critique of socialist organisation. Yet in contrast to subsequent Schumpeter's argumentation, which was influenced by Walrasian theory, Mises always kept the Austrian position of an unfeasibility of socialism. Hayek then emerged as an eminent representative of that Austrian criticism of policy interventionism and the ideal of central planning.

Indeed, with a focus on these aspects, the modern Austrian perspective in economic theory was established by Mises and Hayek following major efforts in monetary business cycle theory and capital theory since the late 1930s (Kirzner 1999, 19n). The commonly shared theoretical position of modern Austrian economics highlights key categories of time and ignorance, pointing to novelty and uncertainty in the irreversible historical flow of events as well as to the subjective character of knowledge. Austrian economics then deals with an unforeseeable process of coordination and discovery, shaped by institutional rules, while unintended consequences of individual action are perceived as constitutive factors of the economic process in terms of a spontaneous order (O'Driscoll and Rizzo 1985, 5n).

Mises' approach of 'praxeology' pinpoints a theory of human action that formulates universally valid principles underlying human behaviour which are needed as a priori devices for categorising and explaining the objects of inquiry (Mises 1949, p. 32). Lionel Robbins' landmark definition characterises economics as a science that studies human behaviour as a relationship between a given hierarchy of ends and scarce means which have alternative uses. For Mises, however, a theory of choices regarding the allocation of scarce resources according to alternative ends–means frameworks should constitute the analytical focus. His aprioristic approach is concerned with the logic of choice and action (Koslowski 1990, p. 6). Hence Mises suggests on the subject matter of economics: 'The sole task of economics is analysis of the actions of men, is the analysis of processes' (Mises 1949, p. 354).

The notion of entrepreneurship represents a major concern in that theoretical scheme. A point of departure is provided by the notion of the evenly rotating economy, in which no specific functions for entrepreneurs are exercised, while economic agents behave like mechanical devices, with no choices to make and no purpose to proceed with (Mises 1949, p. 249). Economic change sets in as soon as choices need to be made. According to Mises, entrepreneurship belongs to the core features of economic processes which are time-consuming and uncertain. Mises then presents a concept of entrepreneurship that is attributable to all economic agents who participate in the equilibration of market constellations (Mises 1949, 253n). In particular, entrepreneurship should imply activity in the face of uncertainty: 'Entrepreneur means acting man in regard to the changes occurring in the data of the market' (Mises 1949, p. 255). Indeed, Misesian entrepreneurship needs to be assessed in the framework of this concept of the '*homo agens*' that senses rational behaviour as a universally valid pattern, based on a methodology of apriorism.

While the latter position has become subject to considerable controversy in modern Austrian economics, its major proponents still tend to underline their intellectual indebtedness to Mises' theorising. Further explorations into the Austrian approach to entrepreneurship follow that line of reasoning, well represented by Kirzner's market process theory with its concept of entrepreneurial alertness that underlines an understanding of human action as active and creative (Kirzner 1973, p. 35). Kirznerian entrepreneurship deals with gradual patterns of economic change by means of individual alertness in the discovery procedures of the market process. Yet these aspects are also part of Hayek's research agenda, which goes beyond Mises' efforts in accounting for the evolutionary qualities of knowledge and institutions. Still, in the discussion on the intellectual orientation of modern Austrian economics it is usually argued that Hayek has neglected the theoretical complexity of entrepreneurship, whereas Mises has underestimated the theoretical impact of knowledge coordination (Kirzner 1999, p. 22n). This is in agreement with the proposition that Hayek's methodological individualism differs both from neoclassical standard theory and Mises' apriorism in denying the 'given' status of individual rationality as a basis of human action, while focusing on supra-individual patterns on the level of markets and institutions (Caldwell 2001, 550n).[3]

However, the following section proceeds with the argument that the notion of entrepreneurship is not only constitutive for the Hayekian approach to the competitive dynamism of the market process, but also for the related theory of cultural evolution. The Hayekian entrepreneur resembles an agent of change, whose activities are relevant both in the market process and in the even more encompassing cultural sphere of rules and traditions that reflect the increasing complexity of the extended order of modern society. With regard to the matter of individual behaviour and institutional change as an area of theoretical clarification in the Hayekian framework, it is argued that the reconsideration of the notion of entrepreneurship contributes to an adequate understanding of the relationship between individuals and institutions in Hayekian thought. The following section thus explores the role of entrepreneurship in Hayek's theory of the market process.

## HAYEK ON THE ROLE OF ENTREPRENEURSHIP IN THE MARKET PROCESS

The distinction between made order and spontaneous order outlines the conceptual foundations of Hayek's theory of the market process. The made order represents an artificial construction that needs to be understood as a deliberately designed type of order in terms of an organisation, while the spontaneous order is perceived as a self-generating and self-organising type of grown order – a product of human action but not of human design (Hayek 1973, p. 37). In this framework, the market process is characterised as an economic manifestation of the general principles of the spontaneous order. In particular, Hayek's theory of the market process takes as its analytical point of departure, explorations of the decentralised coordination of individual economic plans by proceeding with research in business cycle analysis. These initial efforts in business cycle theory highlight exogenously generated disturbances of the economic process, as banks would erroneously reduce monetary rates of interest below the corresponding natural rates, fuelling investment decisions which are not in accordance with prevailing time preferences, and thus contribute to disequilibrium. Subjective knowledge and market coordination then constitute basic analytical challenges. In particular, Hayek argues that the division of knowledge, fashioned in analogy with the division of labour, brings about the problem of coordinating fragmented knowledge no central authority can posses on its own (Hayek 1937, p. 49).

While emphasising the subjective character of knowledge in economic coordination, Hayek's use of the category of knowledge should involve both scientific knowledge as a universal type and the subjective knowledge of particular circumstances, conditioned by time and space, which is not to be quantified and measured statistically. The subjective acquisition of knowledge in learning processes then shifts established traditions and routines; an argument that underlines once more the subjective sources of institutional change in the Hayekian scheme of analysis (Garrouste 1994, p. 279). Accordingly, the matter of coordination transcends the static limitations of Lionel Robbins' famous formulation on allocation as the constitutive economic problem: 'The economic problem of society ... is a problem of the utilization of knowledge not given to anyone in its totality' (Hayek 1945, 519n).

Hayek characterises the price system of the market order as the most efficient mechanism for the decentralised communication of information in complex economic systems, characterised by a dispersion of subjective knowledge among the economic agents. The subjectivist underpinnings of that position also inform the Hayekian critique of Walrasian equilibrium theory with its characterisation of market prices as carriers of objective knowledge. Related attempts at modelling a socialist system of administrative planning by using Walrasian arguments are thus dismissed. This is quite in agreement with the Austrian concept of the entrepreneur as a figure who performs equilibrating feedback functions which are similar to the Walrasian auctioneer, although the former dispenses from the centralist coordination structure of the Walrasian approach by contributing to the decentral coordination of the plans of economic agents in the market process (Schmidtchen 1990, p. 141). Affirming the evolutionary character of market processes, Hayek points to the persistence of change as a crucial feature of market economies:

> (E)conomic problems arise always and only in consequence of change. So long as things continue as before, or at least as they were expected to, there arise no new problems requiring a decision, no need to form a new plan. The belief that changes, or at least day-to-day adjustments, have become less important in modern times implies the contention that economic problems also have become less important. (Hayek 1945: 523)

Entrepreneurship denotes the search, discovery and adjustment procedures of economic agents who are active in promoting those changes which characterise the market process. In particular, entrepreneurship in Hayekian terms mirrors the relationship between competition and knowledge, rooted in the condition that every economic agent commands a specific advantage in his subjective knowledge. This is exemplified by the entrepreneurial figure of an arbitrageur who gains from local price differentials (Hayek 1945, p. 521n). The orientation of entrepreneurship is shaped by the signalling function of relative prices: 'Price relations alone tell the entrepreneur where return sufficiently exceeds costs to make it profitable to devote limited capital to a particular undertaking. Such signs direct him to an invisible goal, the satisfaction of the distant un-known consumer of the final product' (Hayek 1988, p. 100). While following these price signals in the market process, entrepreneurs are guided by the profit motive as a general type of motivation that abstracts from personal specificity in proceeding with economic interactions, thus allowing for discovery and innovation as developmental functions: 'The entrepreneur *must* in his activities probe beyond known uses and ends if he is to provide means for producing yet other means which in turn serve still others, and so on – that is, if he is to serve a *multiplicity* of ultimate ends' (Hayek 1988, p. 104, emphasis in original).

The ethos of that kind of rule-based open society with its extended division of labour and system of market exchange highlights the virtues of entrepre-neurial activity with reference to the values of Calvinism, among others: 'In its purest form this ethos regards it as the prime duty to pursue a self-chosen end as effectively as possible without paying attention to the role it plays in the complex network of human activities' (Hayek 1976, p. 145). This ethic does not necessarily include an egoist striving for material gain, as outlined by Adam Smith, for the decisive point is the satisfaction of anonymous needs in the context of the market process, allowing for complex economic activi-ties beyond the confines of separate groups, while the earned entrepreneurial profits may be used for non-economic ends which may reflect community-based ideals (Hayek 1976, p. 145). However, this relativity of motives coincides with the appreciation of the economic self-interest of economic agents: 'Com-petition as a discovery procedure must rely on the self-interest of the producers, that is it must allow them to use their knowledge for their purposes, because nobody else possesses the information on which they must base their deci-sion' (Hayek 1979, p. 70).

Apart from motivational aspects, the specific gain from entrepreneurial activities in the market process is legitimised through the indispensable de-velopmental impact of competitive discovery:

> Yet there can be no doubt that the discovery of a better use of things or of one's own capacities is one of the greatest contributions that an individual can make in

our society to the welfare of his fellows and that it is by providing the maximum opportunity for this that a free society can become so much prosperous than others. The successful use of this entrepreneurial capacity (and, in discovering the best use of our abilities, we are all entrepreneurs) is the most highly rewarded activity in a free society, while whoever leaves to others the task of finding some useful means of employing his capacities must be content with a smaller reward. (Hayek 1960, p. 81)

This type of entrepreneurship is presented as an institutional characteristic of market systems, involving 'creative powers of a free civilization' that parallel 'spontaneous forces of growth' in terms of the decentral coordination of economic activities (Hayek 1960, p. 38). However, the decisive role of entrepreneurship in the market process remains usually unnoticed in terms of increasing productivity and rising standards of living; a situation that fuels atavistic judgements on the unjust character of entrepreneurial activities and related earnings (Hayek 1988, p. 92n).

At this point, Hayek is quite in agreement with Mises in pointing to egalitarian demands for social justice as well as to the related idea of socialism as an outcome of group-oriented atavism and its collective instincts, which need to be overcome by the individualism of the market order, whereas Wieser and Schumpeter as Austrian counterparts actually view entrepreneurship as driven by motives of atavism, relating it with socio-economic functions of leadership (Ebner 2003, p. 117n). Still, some common ground with the latter is provided by Hayek's suggestion that economic change reflects the innovation efforts of a pioneering minority of producers and consumers, who shape the pattern of diffusion and learning: 'All new tastes and desires are necessarily at first tastes and desires of a few, and if their satisfaction were dependent on approval by a majority, much of what the majority might learn to like after they have been exposed to it might never become available' (Hayek 1979, p. 49).

However, due to the character of subjective knowledge, involving non-codified tacit knowledge as well as local knowledge that reflects the impact of particular settings and circumstances, entrepreneurial activities prove to be unpredictable:

> Much of the knowledge of the individuals which can be so useful in bringing about particular adaptations is not ready knowledge which they could possibly list and file in advance for the use of a central planning authority when the occasion arose; ... what they possess is a capacity of finding out what is required by a given situation, often in acquaintance with particular circumstances which beforehand they have no idea might become useful. (Hayek 1976, p. 187)

Accordingly, the Hayekian notion of knowledge-based entrepreneurial discovery underlines the substantial uncertainty of economic development, paralleling the progress of knowledge in science, with all of its systematic as well as spontaneous characteristics:

> (M)ost scientists realize that we cannot plan the advance of knowledge, that in the voyage into the unknown – which is what research is – we are in great measure dependent on the vagaries of individual genius and of circumstance, and that scientific advance, like a new idea that will spring up in a single mind, will be the result of a combination of conceptions, habits, and circumstances brought to one person by society, the result as much of lucky accidents as of systematic efforts. (Hayek 1960, p. 33)

Indeed, the matter of determinism in economic processes fuels Hayek's criticism of arguments on the developmental inevitability of industrial concentration, as promoted by Schumpeter among others, interpreting the emergence of large enterprises as carriers of large-scale technologies in terms of an organisational shift towards central coordination. At this point, Hayek claims that decentral adjustment would remain crucial in economic change, not losing in importance at all due to an increase of technological knowledge and a related extension of time intervals in investment decisions (Hayek 1945, p. 523).

In accordance with that position, the persistence of the competitive patterns of the market process implies that continuous learning is necessary for all economic agents, while competition drives the diffusion of rationality all over the economic system: 'And it is therefore in general not rationality which is required to make competition work, but competition, or traditions which allow competition, which will produce rational behaviour' (Hayek 1979, p. 76). In Hayekian thought, competition, entrepreneurship and innovation go hand in hand, based on the rationalising impact of pioneers on established patterns of economic behaviour and organisation. Indeed, economic competition and institutional change tend to run parallel, as long as the general rules that constitute market competition prevent the majority of economic agents from obstructing the introduction of innovations by the use of force and coercion against the pioneering minority, which is itself held to stick to the rules of competition:

> Competition is, after all, always a process in which a small number makes it necessary for larger numbers to do what they do not like, be it to work harder, to change habits, or to devote a degree of attention, continuous application, or regularity to their work which without competition would not be needed. (Hayek 1979, p. 77)

However, complementing entrepreneurial discovery and innovation as driving forces of the market process, related procedures of imitation are identified as crucial economic activities that stabilise and maintain the order of the market: 'It was the thousands of individuals who practised the new routine more than the occasional successful innovators whom they would imitate that maintained the market order' (Hayek 1979, p. 165). This is in agreement with Hayek's emphasis on the gradual character of technological and institutional change, highlighting the embeddedness of innovation and imitation in established rules and traditions, as 'all progress must be based on tradition' (Hayek 1979, p. 167). At this point it may be argued that Hayek seemingly neglects the matter of novelty in economic change and related evolutionary processes, upholding a focus on gradual variations within an established setting. Therefore, Hayek's concern with innovation as an entrepreneurial outcome has been largely underrated in corresponding assessments of his theory of the market process. Moreover, even the more encompassing theory of cultural evolution, which applies the notion of spontaneous order to the evolution of rules and institutions in the historical development of civilisations, has been primarily perceived in terms of Hayekian ideas on imitation and adaptation. Confronting that position, the following section presents an account of the role of entrepreneurship as the driving force of institutional change in Hayek's theory of cultural evolution.

## ENTREPRENEURSHIP IN THE HAYEKIAN THEORY OF CULTURAL EVOLUTION

The notion of market competition as a discovery procedure points to the theory of cultural evolution which is also concerned with the matter of knowledge and learning, that is, the process of competitive selection among rules and other institutions that define frameworks for social interaction. According to Hayek, the trial and error procedures of the market process, that are also dealing with rules as problem-solving devices, are to be viewed as an element of the innovation and selection of rules and institutions in cultural evolution, shaping the market order and allowing for the combination of individual liberty and societal complexity in the progress of civilisation (Vanberg 1994, 100n). Crucially, Hayek thus suggests that the rules and institutions of society are shaped by customs and habits, which are not the result of efforts in purposeful design.

These rules that constitute the character of the market order by governing individual behaviour are either almost invariant genetically inherited rules or historically variable learned, culturally transmitted rules which are subject to institutional competition in cultural evolution (Vanberg 1994, 78n). Accordingly, rules which guide human behaviour in terms of underlying traditions result from an evolutionary selection procedure that contradicts the constructivist position on cultural evolution as driven by human reason: 'Man is as much a rule-following animal as a purpose-seeking one' (Hayek 1973, p. 11). In that context, Hayek underlines that competition constitutes the basic feature of both biological and cultural evolution; highlighting competition as the decisive evolutionary force (Hayek 1988, p. 26).

Even in his earliest elaborations on that subject, Hayek applies his arguments to a historical process like industrialisation, which is attributed to market competition as a discovery procedure regarding material and human resources. This role of competition also seems to be most important in cases of underdevelopment, for the particular discovery procedures in developing economies are settled in an early stage, leaving habitually oriented economic agents without experience from past competition as a device for future decisions (Hayek 1978b, p. 188). Already in the *Road to Serfdom*, Hayek analyses the institutional dynamism of economic development in terms of the spontaneous order:

> During the whole of this modern period of European history the general direction of social development was one of freeing the individual from the ties which had bound him to the customary or prescribed ways in the pursuit of his ordinary activities. The conscious realization that the spontaneous and uncontrollable efforts of individuals were capable of producing a complex order of economic activities could come only after this development had made some progress. (Hayek 1944, 18n)

In particular, Hayek proposes that the evolution of knowledge since the Renaissance contributed decisively to that development process, based on individual economic initiative, which led to the establishment of modern capitalism, defined as 'a competitive system based on free disposal over private property' (Hayek 1944, p. 77). Individualism reinforced the progress of scientific knowledge in the discovery procedure of market competition, thus contributing to the comparative success of capitalist economies:

> Perhaps the greatest result of the unchaining of individual energies was the marvellous growth of science which followed the march of individual liberty from Italy to England and beyond. ... Only since industrial freedom opened the path to the free use of knowledge, only since everything could be tried – if somebody could be found to back it at his own risk – and, it should be added, as often as not from outside the authorities officially intrusted with the cultivation of learning, has science made the great strides which in the last hundred and fifty years have changed the face of the world. (Hayek 1944, p. 19)

Cultural evolution is thus linked to the growth and diversification of knowledge; a topic that is explored furthermore in the *Constitution of Liberty*. There, Hayek argues that the growth of knowledge implies a decrease of individual shares in the total complex of the division of knowledge, thus contributing to a relative deepening of subjective ignorance, while advancing the requirement for a coordination of decentralised knowledge. These coordination efforts should involve specific institutional forms of knowledge, like habits, rules and even technological aspects; all of them subject to an inherent variety of forms that shapes individual behaviour:

> The growth of knowledge and the growth of civilization are the same only if we interpret knowledge to include all the human adaptations to environment in which past experience has been incorporated. ... Our habits and skills, our emotional attitudes, our tools, and our institutions – all are in this sense adaptations to past experience which have grown up by selective elimination of less suitable conduct. They are as much an indispensable foundation of successful action as is our conscious knowledge. Not all these non-rational factors underlying our action are always conducive to success. Some may be retained long after they have outlived their usefulness and even when they have become more an obstacle than a help. Nevertheless, we could not do without them: even the successful employment of our intellect rests on their constant use. (Hayek 1960, p. 26)

Innovations in institutional and technological terms should be perceived as adaptations to changing data:

> The undesigned novelties that constantly emerge in the process of adaptation will consist, first, of new arrangements or patterns in which the efforts of different individuals are coordinated and of new constellations in the use of resources, which will be in their nature as temporary as the particular conditions that have evoked them. There will be, second, modifications of tools and institutions adapted to the new circumstances. (Hayek 1960, p. 32n)

Hence, cultural evolution according to Hayek is based on a trial-and-error process which combines intentional and unintentional experiments in proceeding with institutional and technological innovations as an adaptation to changing socio-economic conditions (Vanberg 1992, p. 109).

Hayek's evolutionary theory of institutional change then follows a scheme of variety, transmission and selection. Underlining the aspect of efficacy in cultural evolution, Hayek suggests: 'It is in the pursuit of man's aims of the moment that all the devices of civilization have to prove themselves; the ineffective will be discarded and the effective retained' (Hayek 1960, p. 36). The introduction and dissemination of novelty is promoted by an institutional framework which allows for variety in the competitive discovery procedures that drive economic development (Hayek 1960, p. 37). The institutional structuration of particular groups serves as the basis of knowledge transmission, while selection also intervenes on the group level, in accordance with capabilities for learning and innovation (Hayek 1960, p. 36).

This hint at the group level of evolutionary selection is explored in more detail in the volumes on *Law, Legislation and Liberty*. Hayek suggests that

the evolution of rules coincides with the cultural evolution of groups, societies and whole civilisations, as groups that adopt those rules within their
particular order which are most conducive to growth and development in a
certain setting tend to be more successful in terms of material reproduction.
Decisive is not only the coherent order that is achieved within the networks
of personal relationships inside the particular groups, but also the opportunities that are offered for outward-oriented contacts which contain impersonal
relationships (Hayek 1973, p. 99). Indeed, the market system in the extended
order of the Hayekian 'Great Society' presupposes institutional conditions
for complex exchange relations among anonymous participants in the division of labour. Therefore, entrepreneurship in cultural evolution denotes a
behavioural pattern of extending the domain of individual interaction and
exchange driven by 'rule-breakers' who would become 'path-breakers': 'Most
of these steps in the evolution of culture were made possible by some individuals breaking some traditional rules and practising new forms of conduct
– not because they understood them to be better, but because the groups
which acted on them prospered more than others and grew' (Hayek 1979,
p. 161). This line of reasoning is also addressed in Hayek's *Fatal Conceit*,
suggesting that entrepreneurship is an indispensable factor in the evolution of
the extended order of the market, based on the division of labour and far-
reaching exchange relations beyond the confines of established communities:

> In any case, some individuals did tear away, or were released, from the hold and
> obligations of the small community, and began not only to settle to other commu-
> nities, but also to lay the foundations for a network of connections with members
> of still other communities – a network that ultimately, in countless relays and
> ramifications, has covered the whole earth. Such individuals were enabled to
> contribute their shares, albeit unknowingly and unintentionally, towards the build-
> ing of a more complex and extensive order – an order far beyond their own or their
> contemporaries' purview. (Hayek 1988, p. 42)

In discussing this process, Hayek focuses on the correspondence between the
transfer of goods and the transfer of knowledge, with trade based on the
distinctive individual knowledge of the competing trading agents, then continuously promoting initiatives in discovering new opportunities. Innovations
would turn to customs in the context of institutional conditions and distinct
advantages that allow for an expansion of the innovative groups (Hayek
1988, p. 43).

These arguments also inform Hayek's policy conclusions concerning the
rejection of development planning and extensive public regulation, because
modes of technological advance and the emergence of related social structures are not to be foreseen and controlled (Hayek 1978b, p. 188). Hayek
claims that development planning would imply attempts to regulate and

shape economic processes in a scientifically founded manner, related with a predictive anticipation of future developments that was typical for constructivism, denoting a belief in the design and engineering of the institutional and social order of a society at large (Hayek 1978a, p. 3n). In contrast to these types of development planning schemes, the relationship between competition and entrepreneurship should be held responsible for the dynamism of economic development, based on the institutional order of a particular economy under consideration.

Also in the context of that discussion of development policy, the perception of a pioneering minority that confronts a traditional majority resembles the Wieser–Schumpeter line of reasoning on the leadership qualities of pioneering individuals:

> This is that required changes in habits and customs will be brought about only if the few willing and able to experiment with new methods can make it necessary for the many to follow them, and at the same time to show them the way. The required discovery process will be impeded or prevented, if the many are able to keep the few to the traditional ways. (Hayek 1978b, p. 189)

Therefore, the implementation of an institutional order that is conducive to entrepreneurship, based on private property, would provide the most promising device for the formulation of development polices:

> The much lamented absence of a spirit of enterprise in many of the new countries is not an unalterable characteristic of the individual inhabitants, but the consequence of restraints which existing customs and institutions place upon them. This is why it would be fatal in such societies for the collective will to be allowed to direct the efforts of individuals, instead of governmental power being confined to protecting individuals against the pressures of society. (Hayek 1978b, p. 189n)

Again, it is evident that a reconsideration of the notion of entrepreneurship is of major importance for understanding the dynamism of economic development and the underlying processes of cultural evolution. Still, it remains noteworthy that Hayek pinpoints the role of institutions in articulating the entrepreneurial potential of the market process, whereas the behavioural dimension of entrepreneurship is not addressed as a decisive topic to be explored.

In assessing Hayek's theory of cultural evolution, then, it has been pointed out that in reality it is comprised of two subprocesses, namely the process of variation that generates novel variants of behaviour that are to be transmitted, and the process of selection which results in the selective establishment of specific regularities out of the pool of available variants of behaviour. Individualist arguments in Hayek's theorising then point to the role of specific individuals, who act as innovators, for they deviate from established traditions by experimenting with new practices that may turn into regularities during competitive selection as they are adopted within groups and then spread all over the socio-economic system. However, as argued by Vanberg, this perspective suffers from a lack of well-defined individualist arguments, for it remains unclear whether it is behaviour advantageous to individuals or groups which prevails in the competitive process of cultural evolution (Vanberg 1994, p. 82n). Moreover, apart from these aspects, Hayek's approach has been criticised on the grounds that it lacks an adequate elaboration of evolutionary theory. In particular, Hodgson has asserted that Hayek fails to specify the process that leads to the adoption and routine operation of advantageous rules within a group; a lack of analytical rigour which is especially relevant with regard to the matter of organisations (Hodgson 1993, p. 171n). Accordingly, it seems that Hayek underestimates the extent to which evolutionary processes tend to require an institutional variety that allows for a plurality of market structures and other institutional forms of socio-economic interaction (Hodgson 1993, p. 176n).

In conclusion, these critical assessments do in fact, highlight the specific role of the notion of entrepreneurship in Hayek's theorising. After all, Hayek does not present a distinct theory of entrepreneurship with an elaborate apparatus of behavioural arguments. Instead, both his theory of the market process and the theory of cultural evolution focus on the coordinative impact of rules, which derive their functional importance from the subjectivity of knowledge as well as from the related complexity of evolving socio-economic systems. All of this is outlined in a mode of reasoning that approaches entrepreneurship in terms of a potential which does not require further analytical efforts. Indeed, the theoretical problems of Hayek's theory of cultural evolution, as outlined above, may be related with that lack of analytical rigour in sorting out the behavioural foundations of entrepreneurship.

Still, entrepreneurship plays a major role in Hayek's approach, highlighting search, experimentation and discovery as crucial factors in the stimulation of economic change – which is identified as the constitutive problem of economic theory. Accordingly, entrepreneurship is viewed as the decisive force in the growth of civilisation, interpreted as a historical process that coincides with cultural evolution. The 'rule-breaking' and 'path-breaking' qualities of Hayekian entrepreneurship then combine segments of theorising that resemble Mises' theory of human action as well as the approaches of Wieser and Schumpeter to entrepreneurial leadership, although Hayek does not elaborate on a detailed exploration of behavioural aspects in the carrying out of the entrepreneurial function. In this context, it is also noteworthy that Hayek, rather than discussing the introduction of novelty, emphasises the matter of imitation and dissemination, with entrepreneurship perceived as pioneering initiative in a comprehensive evolutionary process of gradual change. Based on these considerations, Hayek's theorising may serve as a point of departure for future research on the role of entrepreneurship in economic change, providing further insights for an analysis of the institutional foundations of cultural evolution.

## CONCLUSION

The present chapter has argued that Hayek's theory of cultural evolution is based on a conceptualisation of entrepreneurial activities which is constitutive for the underlying concept of institutional change, reflecting a specific constellation of search, discovery and innovation. All of these particular activities resemble the entrepreneurial function in the competitive procedures of the market process. Therefore it has been suggested that the matter of entrepreneurship provides Hayek's theory of cultural evolution with constitutive arguments on the interplay of individuals, groups and institutions in the evolutionary process of economic development. These aspects have been examined by taking the point of departure in the Austrian framework of theorising on entrepreneurship. In particular, the contributions of Wieser and Mises proved to be influential with regard to Hayek's account of the entrepreneurial function in cultural evolution, pointing to the pioneering positions and knowledge qualities of entrepreneurship. In Hayek's theory of the market process, these arguments shape the characterisation of entrepreneurship in the search and discovery procedures that drive competition. Dealing with related aspects of entrepreneurship in the promotion of evolutionary change, Hayek's theory of cultural evolution then highlights rules, traditions and knowledge as parameters of entrepreneurial activities, for entrepreneurs are said to facilitate those institutional and structural changes which characterise the growth of modern civilisation. After all, it is this emphasis on the interaction of long-run rules and individual initiative in the context of a gradually extending order that characterises Hayek's approach to entrepreneurship as an unjustly neglected major contribution to modern Austrian theory. In this sense, despite analytical limitations regarding a stringent elaboration on behavioural aspects, Hayek's approach to entrepreneurship provides indispensable arguments for theorising on the market process and cultural evolution. Thus it represents a major effort in exploring the entrepreneurial dynamism of economic development.

## NOTES

1. Compared with the related theories of Walras and Jevons, it has been proposed that the Mengerian position resembled a kind of institutional economics (Jaffé 1976, p. 520).

2. Lasting Wieserian contributions to economic theory include the concept of optimal resource allocation according to marginal productivity of the factors of production and the role of prices as carriers of information (Streissler 1986, p. 85).
3. It even has been proposed that Hayek's emphasis on the role of subjective knowledge in the market coordination of individual plans is at odds with Mises' emphasis on economic calculation through market prices as a means of purposeful economic behaviour (Salerno 1993, p. 130).

# REFERENCES

Caldwell, B. (2001), 'Hodgson on Hayek: a critique', *Cambridge Journal of Economics*, **25** (4), 539–53.

Ebner, A. (2003), 'The institutional analysis of entrepreneurship: historist aspects of Schumpeter's development theory', in J.G. Backhaus (ed.) *Joseph Alois Schumpeter: Entrepreneurship, Style and Vision*, Boston, MA: Kluwer, pp. 117–39.

Garrouste, P. (1994), 'Menger and Hayek on institutions: continuity and discontinuity', *Journal of the History of Economic Thought*, **16** (2), 270–91.

Hayek, Friedrich A. von (1937), 'Economics and knowledge', *Economica*, **4** new series, 33–54.

Hayek, Friedrich A. von (1944), *The Road to Serfdom*, Chicago: University of Chicago Press.

Hayek, Friedrich A. von (1945), 'The use of knowledge in society', *American Economic Review*, **35** (4), 519–30.

Hayek, Friedrich A. von (1960), *The Constitution of Liberty*, Chicago: University of Chicago Press.

Hayek, Friedrich A. von (1973), *Law, Legislation and Liberty, Vol.1: Rules and Order*, Chicago: University of Chicago Press.

Hayek, Friedrich A. von (1976), *Law, Legislation and Liberty, Vol.2: The Mirage of Social Justice*, Chicago: University of Chicago Press.

Hayek, Friedrich A. von (1978a), 'The errors of constructivism', in Friedrich A. von Hayek, *New Studies in Philosophy, Politics, Economics and the History of Ideas*, London: Routledge, pp. 3–22.

Hayek, Friedrich A. von (1978b), 'Competition as a discovery procedure', in Friedrich A. von Hayek, *New Studies in Philosophy, Politics, Economics and the History of Ideas*, London: Routledge, pp. 179–90.

Hayek, Friedrich A. von (1979), *Law, Legislation and Liberty, Vol.3: The Political Order of a Free People*, Chicago: University of Chicago Press.

Hayek, Friedrich A. von (1988), *The Fatal Conceit: The Errors of Socialism*, London: Routledge.

Hébert, R. and A.N. Link (1982), *The Entrepreneur: Mainstream Views and Radical Critiques*, New York: Praeger.

Hodgson, G.M. (1993), *Economics and Evolution: Bringing Life back into Economics*, Cambridge: Polity Press.

Jaffé, W. (1967), 'Walras' theory of tatônnement: a critique of recent interpretations', *Journal of Political Economy*, **75** (1), pp. 1–19.

Jaffé, W. (1976), 'Menger, Jevons and Walras de-homogenised', *Economic Inquiry*, **XIV**, December, 511–24.

Kirzner, I.M. (1973), *Competition and Entrepreneurship*, Chicago: University of Chicago Press.

Kirzner, I.M. (1999), 'Paradox upon paradox: economic order and entrepreneurial activity', in *Lectiones Jenenses Vol.19*, Jena: Max-Planck-Institute for Research into Economic Systems.

Koslowski, P. (1990), 'The categorical and ontological presuppositions of Austrian and neoclassical economics', in A. Bosch, P. Koslowski and R.V. (eds), *General Equilibrium or Market Process: Neoclassical and Austrian Theories of Economics*, Tübingen: Mohr, pp. 1–20.

Martin, D.T. (1979), 'Alternative views of Mengerian entrepreneurship', *History of Political Economy*, **1** (2), 271–85.

Menger, C. [1871] (1923), *Grundsätze der Volkswirtschaftslehre*, 2nd edn, ed. by K. Menger, Vienna: Hölder.

Mises, L. v. (1949), *Human Action: A Treatise on Economics*, London: Hodge.

O'Driscoll Jr., G.P. and M.J. Rizzo (1985), *The Economics of Time and Ignorance*, Oxford: Blackwell.

Salerno, J. (1993), 'Mises and Hayek dehomogenized', *Review of Austrian Economics*, **6** (2), 113–46.

Schmidtchen, D. (1990), 'Neoclassical and Austrian theory of economic policy: differences in constitutional policies', in A. Bosch et al. (eds), *General Equilibrium or Market Process: Neoclassical and Austrian Theories of Economics*, Tübingen: Mohr, pp. 123–44.

Schumpeter, J.A. (1912), *Theorie der wirtschaftlichen Entwicklung*, Berlin: Duncker und Humblot.

Schumpeter, J.A. (1939), *Business Cycles: A Theoretical, Historical and Statistical Analysis of the Capitalist Process*, 2 vols, New York: McGraw-Hill.

Schumpeter, J.A. (1942), *Capitalism, Socialism and Democracy*, London: Allen and Unwin.

Spengler, J.J. (1973), 'The marginal revolution and concern with economic growth', in R.D.C. Black, A.W. Coats and C.D.W. Goodwin (eds), *The Marginal Revolution in Economics: Interpretation and Evaluation*, Durham, NC: Duke University Press, pp. 203–32.

Streissler, E.W. (1981), 'Schumpeter's Vienna and the role of credit in innovation', in H. Frisch (ed.), *Schumpeterian Economics*, New York: Praeger, pp. 60–83.

Streissler, E.W. (1986), 'Arma virumque cano: Friedrich von Wieser, the bard as economist', in N. Leser (ed.), *Die Wiener Schule der Nationalökonomie*, Vienna: Böhlau, pp. 83–106.

Vanberg, V. (1992), 'Innovation, cultural evolution, and economic growth', in U. Witt (ed.), *Explaining Process and Change: Approaches to Evolutionary Economics*, Ann Arbor: University of Michigan Press, pp. 105–21.

Vanberg, V. (1994), *Rules and Choice in Economics*, London and New York: Routledge.

Walker, D.A. (1986), 'Walras's theory of the entrepreneur', *De Economist*, **134** (1), pp. 1–24.

Wieser, F. von (1892), 'Großbetrieb und Produktionsgenossenschaft', *Zeitschrift für Volkswirtschaft, Sozialpolitik und Verwaltung*, vol. 1, reprinted in F. von Wieser (1929) *Gesammelte Abhandlungen*, ed. by Friedrich A. von Hayek, Tübingen: Mohr, pp. 278–333.

Wieser, F. von (1914), 'Theorie der gesellschaftlichen Wirtschaft', in K.Bücher, J. Schumpeter and F. von Wieser (1914) *Grundriss der Sozialökonomik*, vol.1, Grundlagen der Wirtschaft: Wirtschaft und Wirtschaftswissenschaft, Tübingen: Mohr, pp. 125–444.

# 6. Hayek's 'free money movement' and the evolution of monetary order in historical perspective

## Martin T. Bohl and Jens Hölscher

## INTRODUCTION

The role of money in society and for economic order has been a longstanding subject of academic dispute. Hayek's work (1976, 1990) stands out in this field as being the most provocative and at some stage politically influential contribution, which culminated in the call for a 'Free Money Movement' in order to abolish the state privilege of issuing banknotes. Hayek saw this as not less important than 'a crucial reform that may decide the fate of civilisation' (Hayek 1976, p. 110). His approach is closely related to the general idea of spontaneous evolution of civilisation, which needs protection from the state. Before Hayek's study and its reception are inspected in detail within the next section, the aims and objectives of this study will be laid out.

The motivation of this study stems from the high times of the debate of establishing the Eurozone. In the 1980s and 1990s the Thatcher government in the UK was deeply impressed by Hayek's proposal of currency competition and the plan of a 'parallel currency' system rather than a single European currency was setting part of the agenda of economic policy. As this idea has vanished at least for the time being, the authors of this study wonder whether or not it might be time to say goodbye to the whole concept of 'free banking', as it was advocated by Hayek. In order to find an answer to this question this study operates on two levels: section 2 will review Hayek's position on money from an evolutionary point of view, which will focus on money as a cultural institution of society. Although this approach seems to be slightly offbeat we will show that Hayek's contribution still attracts some interest in contemporary monetary economic theory.

The third and fourth sections will try to present some empirical evidence of 'free banking' and monetary stability. We believe ourselves to be better informed than Hayek, who thought, that 'indeed, our experience [with 'free banking'] is so limited that we have to fall back upon the usual procedure ...

of a sort of mental model' (Hayek 1976, p. 38). In fact there is some historical experience with 'free banking', which will be reviewed against its institutional background. The second step of the empirical analysis will use latest advances in econometric techniques, which were not available in Hayek's days. We believe that Hayek would have been happy, if he had seen the results, as we are indeed able to present some evidence in support of a positive relationship between money supply by private bankers and monetary stability. The conclusion discusses whether and how far the findings can be generalised. This will be undertaken against the analytical discussion in order to detect potential implications for economic policy.

## HAYEK'S PAMPHLET IN DISCUSSION

We call Hayek's work *Denationalisation of Money* (1976) a pamphlet, because it does not meet standards of ordinary academic papers, as it is implicitly acknowledged in the introduction by Hayek himself. The work is written 'in my despair about the hopelessness of finding a politically feasible solution to what is technically the simplest possible problem, namely to stop inflation' (ibid, p. 13). The pamphlet is divided into 25 chapters ranging from the practical proposal of 'free banking' over discussions of the persistent abuse of the government's prerogative of issuing money to the call for a 'Free Money Movement'. However, apart from the abuse of power, Hayek does not offer a theory of why the state monopoly on money supply emerged in the first place.

We believe Hayek would have agreed with an evolutionary approach of the development of the state monopoly of money supply, although he would of course not have accepted this explanation as any kind of justification. Usually a state monopoly would be justified on the grounds that the products have the attributes of a public good. Be the theory of public goods as bad as we know since Coase, it would be particularly tricky to claim non-rivalry of money, be it in consumption or production.[1] Glaser (1997) proposes to understand the emergence of the state monopoly of money supply as a weapon of the state against internal and external threats. However, Glaser's defence-sovereignty approach has little to say about monetary stability and the state monopoly of money supply. He offers a theory of the state, in which state monopoly over money supply has a reason, but in Hayek's terms – although this theory appears to be the best available – this would be like holding the tiger by its tail.

The intellectual discussion focuses first of all on whether or not Gresham's law applies in the sense that private competition of money supply would lead to monetary instability rather than stop inflation. This aspect is already discussed in Hayek's pamphlet, where he convincingly argues that this only applies to monetary regimes, where exchange rates between different monies are enforced by law – circumstances which could be taken for granted in Elizabethan times but not today. This aspect should be emphasised, as it puts Hayek into a very different position compared to other proponents labelled as 'free banking' campaigners such as Gesell (1916) or his disciples, who aimed for free money in the sense that it would be ubiquitous in terms of liquidity.

Buiter and Panigirtzoglou (2003) follow this tradition exactly in that they are proposing a 'carry tax' for money, i.e. negative interest rates as an option to escape from the liquidity trap. Here Gesell (probably to Hayek's dismay) is revived. Neldner (2003) tries to show in an empirical study, which does not even refer to Hayek, that the result of 'free banking' was indeed excessive money supply by private banks in the years of 1826–1907, i. e. that Gresham's law did apply and led to inflation. We leave the discussion of the applied methodology to a later stage, but would like to contrast the results with the ones of a concurrent study.

Gorton (1999) shows that 'free banking' was efficient in the sense that market participants were able to price 'free' bank notes in the pre-civil war period of the United States. The notes were priced properly according to risks and transaction costs. The underlying implication would be that market discipline was strong enough to prevent wildcat banking of excessive money supply. We will compare these findings with our own results at a later stage.

The second intellectual challenge refers to the possibility that currency competition might lead to deflation. Hayek reflects on this possibility himself (Hayek 1976, p. 76) and not having the benefit of living in an era of a Japanese liquidity trap he has no further arguments than the faith in the 'effective conduct of capitalist enterprise' (p. 77).


## INSTITUTIONAL BACKGROUND

During the eighteenth century America experienced an important monetary regime change (see Grubb (2002) for further details). It actually began in 1696 when Massachusetts issued small-denomination paper money to its soldiers participating in King William's War. These bills began to circulate as a medium of exchange within the colony. Soon other colonies also adopted this innovation: South Carolina in 1703, New York and New Jersey in 1709, Rhode Island in 1710, North Carolina in 1712, Pennsylvania in 1723, Maryland in 1723, Georgia in 1735 and Virginia in 1755. These colonies issued bills not only to meet wartime expenses but also to meet normal peacetime expenses. Each colony's bills were denominated in pound units for example, New York pound, Virginia pound, earned zero nominal interest and circulated at market-determined rates of exchange. Prices within each colony were quoted in their respective paper currencies.

During the revolution the US government, both individual states and the Continental Congress, continued to issue their own paper money. Beginning in 1775 the Continental Congress issued the Continental dollar that depreciated to zero by April 1781 and thereafter ceased to circulate. Each of the 13 states also issued their own paper currencies that, while also depreciating, held their value to a greater extent than did the Continental dollar.

After the collapse of the Continental dollar, the Bank of North America was established in 1782 to restore the confederation's finances. The bank was intended to be the federal government's bank with branches throughout the states. In 1787 the Constitutional Convention drafted the new US constitution and created a currency union within the USA. After 1787 states could no longer issue new bills. Outstanding state bills could continue to circulate until they were redeemed and destroyed by their respective states. After a transition phase, in 1791 the First Bank of the USA was chartered by Congress. This issued dollar-denominated bank notes as the chief circulating medium of exchange.

In summary, the year 1791 splits the monetary history of North America into two periods. Prior to 1791 the monetary system consisted of individual state-issued pound-denominated paper money and after 1791 the US dollar as a common unit of account existed with in the USA. It is this institutional characteristic we exploit to investigate the hypothesis that the transition from a multi-currency monetary system to a monetary union is associated with an increase in inflation.

## DATA, TIME SERIES MODEL AND EMPIRICAL RESULTS

Time series data on consumer prices of reasonable length are available for Massachusetts, Charleston and Philadelphia. Rothenberg (1979) provides annual data on a prices index covering 15 farm products over the period 1750–1855. In Cole (1938) monthly data on commodity price indices for Charleston and Philadelphia over the periods 1739:1–1861:12 and 1731:1–1861:12, respectively. On the basis of this index time series we calculate the inflation rate.

We investigate Hayek's hypothesis relying on a fairly standard time series approach. The inflation rate $\pi_t$ is modelled with an ARMA type process which includes a dummy variable $D_t$:

$$\pi_t = \alpha_0 + \sum_{i=1}^{n} \alpha_i \pi_{t-i} + \sum_{i=1}^{n} \beta_i u_{t-i} + \gamma D_t + \varepsilon_t$$

$$D_t = \begin{cases} 1, & \text{if } t \geq 1791 \\ 0, & \text{if } t < 1791 \end{cases}.$$

With the help of the dummy variable we model the hypothesised permanent shift in the inflation rate after the introduction of a single currency in 1791. The autoregressive parameters are $\alpha_{t-i}$ and $\beta_{t-i}$ denote the moving average coefficient $t_5$.

For Massachusetts, Charleston and Philadelphia we receive the following estimation equations:

$$\pi_t^M = -6.60 + 0.28\pi_{t-3}^M + 0.29u_{t-2} + 5.22D_t + \hat{\varepsilon}_t,$$
$$\quad (1.74)^* \quad (3.27)^{***} \quad (2.90)^{***} \quad (1.13)$$

$$\pi_t^C = -5.45 + 0.75\pi_{t-2}^C + 0.26u_{t-2} + 0.19u_{t-4} + 9.81D_t + \hat{\varepsilon}_t,$$
$$\quad (2.16)^{**} \quad (27.29)^{***} \quad (6.85)^{***} \quad (5.41)^{***} \quad (3.22)^{***}$$

$$\pi_t^P = -5.33 + 0.66\pi_{t-2}^P + 0.12u_{t-1} + 7.63D_t + \hat{\varepsilon}_t,$$
$$\quad (2.11)^{**} \quad (7.41)^{***} \quad (3.44)^{***} \quad (2.73)^{***}$$

respectively, where t-statistics are in parantheses and *, **, *** indicate statistically significant coefficients at the 10, 5 and 1 per cent level. With the exception of the coefficient of the dummy variable in the equation for Massachusetts the parameters are significant and positive. This supports the hypothesis that the introduction of a single currency in 1791 resulted in a higher level of US inflation rate compared to the period before 1791.

## CONCLUSIONS

This study makes a case in favour of Hayek's proposal for the denationalisation of money, as it shows that the regime switch to a single currency led to a higher inflation rate in 1791 in North America. One is tempted to say that the same happened in Germany when the euro was introduced as the single European currency. This historical example however can hardly justify abandoning the euro or even to privatise the money supply process in principle. With regards to the euro one has to admit that there might have been a hidden jump in consumer prices upon the introduction of the single currency, but the European Central Bank is not facing an inflation problem. From a global perspective there seems to be evidence that inflation as a problem of economic policy has faded away anyway. With regards to Hayek's intellectual challenge 'free banking' would cut off hundreds of years of cultural development of capital markets. It has taken the oldest central bank, the Bank of England, which was founded as a private institution and nationalised in 1946, half a century to become operationally independent from the government. A return to 'free banking' appears not only unthinkable, but also contradicts Hayek's spirit against discretionary economic policy. This does not mean that the current institutional arrangement is the best of all possible worlds, but the findings of this study do not call for action in the sense of joining the 'free money movement' within the nearer future.

## NOTE

1.  Coase showed that even the lighthouse used to be a private good.

## REFERENCES

Buiter, W.H. and N. Panigirtzoglou (2003), 'Overcoming the zero bound on nominal interests rates with negative interest on currency: Gesell's solution', *Economic Journal*, **113** (490), 723–46.

Cole, Arthur Harrison (1938), *Wholesale Commodity Prices in the United States: 1700–1861*, Cambridge, MA: Harvard University Press.

Gesell, S. (1916), *The Natural Economic Order*, rev. edn 1958, London: Peter Owen.

Glaser, D. (1997), 'An evolutionary theory of the state monopoly over money', in K. Dowd and R.H. Timberlake (eds), *Money and the Nation State*, New Brunswick, NJ and London: Transaction Publishers.

Gorton, G. (1999), 'Pricing free bank notes', *Journal of Monetary Economics*, 44, 33–64.

Grubb, F. (2002), 'Creating the U. S. Dollar Currency Union, 1748–1811: A Quest for Monetary Stability or a Usurpation of State Sovereignty for Personal Gain?', University of Delaware Economics Department working paper 00–02.

Hayek, Friedrich A. von (1976), *Denationalisation of Money*, London: Institute of Economic Affairs.

Hayek, Friedrich A. von (1990), *Denationalisation of Money – The Argument Refined*, London: Institute of Economic Affairs.

Neldner, M. (2003), 'Competition necessarily tends to produce excess: the case of free banking in Switzerland', *German Economic Review*, **4** (3) 289–408.

Rothenberg, Winifred B. (1979), 'A price index for rural Massachusetts, 1750–1855', *Journal of Economic History*, (December), 975–1001.

# 7. Money and reciprocity in the extended order – an essay on the evolution and cultural function of money

## Walter W. Heering*

*Money is indispensable for extending reciprocal cooperation beyond the limits of human awareness – and therefore also beyond the limits of what was explicable and could readily recognised as expanding opportunities.*

Friedrich August von Hayek (1988, p. 104)

Money, according to *Friedrich A. von Hayek*, is an eminent cultural achievement, which has developed spontaneously along with evolution of what he termed the 'extended order'. Three aspects of this view on money are of special interest here. First, money was and is mostly misunderstood and is still badly understood even by specialists in the field (Hayek 1988, pp. 101–102). Second, money cannot be managed or handled deliberately; attempts to do so in the past have produced devastating effects. Indeed, *Hayek* saw money as one of those regrettable examples, where intervention by the state prevented more efficient arrangements (Hayek 1988, pp. 103–104). Third, money is a necessary prerequisite (in the same sense as is law, morality, etc.) for a modern liberal society (Hayek 1988, p. 104).

In their contribution to this volume, *Martin Bohl* and *Jens Hölscher* have focused on the second of these three points: On *Hayek's* deep distrust in the ability and honesty of state agencies to manage money properly, which culminated during the mid-1970s period of high inflation in his radical proposal, 'almost a bitter joke', as he himself put it (Hayek 1984, p. 29), to 'denationalise' money, i.e. to abandon the state monopoly for issuing money in favour of a system of competing private monies (Hayek 1976; 1978). *Bohl* and *Hölscher* seem to sympathise with this plan. In contrast, I am rather sceptical, and some reasons for this scepsis will become clear – or so I hope – in the course of the chapter. Anyway, I first want to concentrate on the third point, which seems to me the more general and important one. In doing so I am not only hoping to throw some new light on the second aspect but also to narrow down the relevance of the first one, viz. enhancing our understanding of money.

More concretely, after introducing the concept of reciprocity (section 2), I will argue four theses:

1. Money enables economic cooperation in an extended order by establishing a complex network of general reciprocity. In this way money is one driving factor in the transformation of large modern societies into communities by reconciling general reciprocity with the market principle of equivalence (sections 3 and 4).
2. The use of money is generally based on two principles or rules: (1) the 'rule of acceptance', and (2) the 'rule of access'. In the first place, these rules seem to have been established spontaneously, by trial and error. More sophisticated monetary systems, however, seem to require a more conscious management (sections 5 and 6).
3. Monetary systems can be distinguished by the way they deal with the rule of access. Importantly, there is a trade-off between the degree by which the rule is fulfilled and the elasticity/flexibility of the monetary system. Flexibility therefore comes at a price of potential instability and vice versa (section 6).
4. Finally coming back to *Hayek*, I will outline why we should be more optimistic than he was about the future success of designing and implementing a monetary constitution allowing reasonable degrees of both flexibility and stability. Indeed, such a process appears to be already under way and we should not be too impatient about its short-term success (sections 7 and 8). Section 9 concludes.

Overall, my assessment of some of *Hayek's* late monetary ideas leads to an ambivalent result. Any open-minded economist must certainly be impressed by the originality and thoroughness of his thinking, often being in sharp contrast to streamlined modern monetary theory. His famous warning against any kind of 'pretence of knowledge' and thus against any complacency is timeless and of utmost importance for monetary management of our times, where once again technocratic tendencies and illusions of monetary fine-tuning seem to show up. Nevertheless, my own research into monetary questions leads me to believe that his policy recommendations are not only impracticable but also undesirable in the end. To make my point, let me first develop what seems to me an appropriate general perspective on money.

## PRELIMINARIES

Communities are based on the rights and obligations of their members, which eventually turn out to determine a specific distribution of available (and producible) goods, i.e. the contribution and claim of any individual to wealth and welfare. In any given community there will be a set of norms, rules and procedures, commonly accepted by the majority of its members, which specify the valuation of the contribution of the individual members and therefore define what each member has to contribute and is entitled to receive. In its broadest meaning, 'fairness' may be conceived as the idea that the allocation of goods between the community members meets the criteria of this set. Fairness in this sense does not necessarily imply equality of distribution. For instance, some members of the community may have higher social status than others, and are therefore granted a larger fraction of total income and/or wealth. As long as this is socially accepted, it doesn't disturb fairness. I consider *reciprocity* as just a mode of distribution which ensures fairness, meaning that no member can make his living at the expense of others according to the values accepted by the community as a whole. Without such a commonly shared sense of fairness, I strongly believe, no community would be viable for long. Put in technical terms, more familiar to economists: reciprocity implies that members of the community by and large remain in their respective intertemporal budget constraints. Reciprocity is a common feature of all types of community; we may even say that it is what turns societies into communities, to use (without its romantic connotation) a famous distinction introduced by the German sociologist *Ferdinand Tönnies* (1887). What differs, however, is the mode of enforcement. I will argue that money is the medium by which reciprocity is established in large, anonymous and liberal ('modern') societies.

## ON THE MEANING OF RECIPROCITY

An explicit and precise definition of reciprocity is seldom found in the broad literature, which includes writings from sociologists, anthropologists, biologists, philosophers, historians, and, more recently, economists. The reluctance to define clearly what is to be discussed has been criticised early on by *Alvin Gouldner*, apparently without much impact (Gouldner 1960). A notable exception is *Rachel E. Kranton*, who starts her stimulating article with a fairly precise definition: '*Reciprocal exchange* is informally enforced agreements to give goods, services, information, or money in exchange for future compensation in kind' (Kranton 1996, p. 830). I will here adopt a similar definition, trying to improve on hers using ideas found in more implicit and informal notions of the concept: *Reciprocity is the social attitude within a group of people to respond in kind ('pay back in one's own coin') at some later date and with approximately the same value, a behaviour which is not formally enforced.*

Reciprocity in the sense I use the term here is an essential requirement of living within a society given some degree of division of labour. I do not address some rather incidental forms of unilateral transfers. In sociological jargon, I deal with 'gifts' (*'Gaben'*) rather than 'presents' (*'Geschenke'*) (Paul 2002). Also, in contrast to some authors, I refrain from linking the observable phenomenon of reciprocal behaviour directly to its potential but unobservable motives. *Ernst Fehr, Simon Gächter* and *Georg Kirchsteiger*, for example, take 'reciprocity motives' as a primitive concept in their analysis (Fehr et al. 1997). Certainly, it is methodologically preferable to separate facts from their underlying causes.

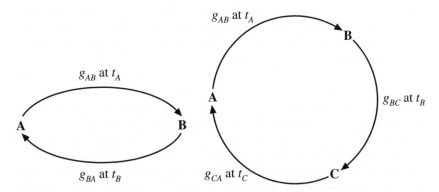

(a)  Bilateral (simple) reciprocity   (b)  Multilateral (general) reciprocity

*Figure 7.1   Bilateral and multilateral reciprocity*

We may speak of *bilateral* reciprocity if only two parties are involved (Figure 7.1a): $A$ gives some $g_{AB}$ at some date $t_A$ to $B$, whilst the latter reciprocates with $g_{BA}$ at $t_B > t_A$. More important, however, are forms of *multilateral* reciprocity (Figure 7.1b), in which the condition of fairness is fulfilled even if the service an individual does to a second member of the community, is reciprocated by a third member, etc.: So $A$ may give $g_{AB}$ at $t_A$ to $B$, then $B$ gives $g_{BC}$ at $t_B$ to $C$, while the latter reciprocates to $A$ with $g_{CA}$ at $t_C$. Obviously, with more than three actors the resulting network of reciprocity quickly becomes quite complex. Another distinction is drawn in the literature between *positive* and *negative* reciprocity. While the first one refers to rewarding of good behaviour, the latter term implies punishing bad behaviour. 'I'll scratch your back if you'll scratch mine!' (Kranton 1996, p. 830, emphasis in original) is the prototype of a positive reciprocity, while the biblical motto 'An eye for an eye, a tooth for a tooth!' describes the typical case of negative reciprocity.

Reciprocal exchange, by our definition, is not formally enforced. This very aspect is an important feature of the arrangement, which enables its efficiency.[1] Nevertheless, a vital problem of such an arrangement is how to ensure that partners actually reciprocate and, by and large, in equivalent amount. Normally, the enforcement mechanism is based on repetition: the fact that actors know that they will depend on each other in the future makes them inclined to cooperate. It has been shown that if a group is small, so that social monitoring is easy, and if each actor cares for the future, which is tied to the solidarity of the group, then the problem of non-cooperative behaviour can be overcome by repeating the game, even if the stage game is of the type of a Prisoners' Dilemma (Axelrod 1984; Kreps 1990, etc.). In this perspective the romantic characterisation of reciprocity, often found in sociological and anthropological writings on traditional and archaic communities, loses much of its glory. In fact, reciprocal behaviour has even been observed in non-human evolution (Trivers 1971; Esser 1993; Matsui 1996). As *Oliver Williamson* (1993) has remarked, reciprocity is entirely profane; it is simple calculative behaviour and must therefore not be confused with 'trust' or 'altruism' in the proper sense (and as the terms are used in common language), the most important feature of which is non-calculativeness.

Whatever the virtues of small-group solidarity, as the group size grows and the group becomes more differentiated and sophisticated, any straightforward cooperative solution becomes increasingly infeasible (Araujo 2004). This may be the reason why often even the term 'reciprocity' is reserved for traditional and archaic communities. However, more recently, researchers from different academic disciplines have acknowledged, as *Georg Simmel* had already done a century ago, that even modern societies must rely on reciprocity. What has rarely been realised, however, is that modern payment systems are nothing else than large and complex networks of multilateral reciprocity. Here, however, reciprocity is an unintended rather than an intended result. This was one of the main themes of *Simmel*, whose brilliant 'Philosophie des Geldes' ('Philosophy of Money') was first published in 1900 (also see Simmel 1896).

## DIGRESSION: ANOTHER APPROACH ON 'MONEY AND RECIPROCITY'

Before presenting my own approach, I should perhaps comment a bit on another research programme, which (quite accidentally) runs under the same title as mine, viz. 'Money and Reciprocity'. At the 2002 annual conference of the 'Verein für Socialpolitik' in Innsbruck two colleagues from the University of Zurich, *Thorsten*

*Hens* and *Bodo Vogt*, presented a paper with this very title (Hens and Vogt 2003). However, the authors there deal with an issue completely different from mine. Roughly speaking, my intention is to derive '*reciprocity by money*', while they in fact look for '*money by reciprocity*'. Both approaches deal with acceptance of money, but while I argue that the latter establishes a network of generalised reciprocity, they argue that reciprocal behaviour may support money's acceptance.

Although there may be some element of truth in their hypothesis, their conceptualisation is open to debate. Straightforwardly, the authors define reciprocity with regard to money as the tendency to accept money as a consequence of having had the experience of others accepting it. Analytically, the crucial aspect is that, while purely selfish market participants would only care for expected future net benefits from accepting money, reciprocity implies that participants also take their past experiences with other participants into account. Based on laboratory experiments at the University of Zurich, the authors conclude that this type of reciprocal attitude has a role to play. Unsurprisingly, positive reciprocity seems to render the monetary system more stable than could be expected from a standard game with selfish individuals, whilst negative reciprocity tends to make the monetary system more unstable and prone to break down. The second feature is somewhat unexpected and rather implausible; it certainly can be explained by the extremely rigid set-up of the market game which is adopted. In particular, in a more realistic scenario a money holder meeting a potential trade partner not willing to accept money would probably have no difficulty to find another partner who will. Furthermore, the way *Hens* and *Vogt* define (negative) reciprocity in a monetary system implies a potential degree of instability which is anyway doubtful. Nevertheless, I may admit that there is possibly an interaction between my 'reciprocity by money' and their 'money by reciprocity', which works in both directions. This interaction is, however, not studied in what follows.

## MONETARY TRADE AS NETWORK OF GENERAL RECIPROCITY

*Karl Polanyi* (1957) distinguished between three modes of 'social integration':

1.  *Reciprocity*, which relies on personal relationship;
2.  *Redistribution*, which relies on the existence of a central power;
3.  *Exchange*, which relies on price-determining markets. Because the latter means that there is room for negotiation about terms of trade, it implies, which *Polanyi* himself does not mention explicitly, that market partners mutually respect themselves as 'equal' with regard to their roles in the market game.

This classification, although probably not exhaustive, is useful because it makes clear that social interaction and integration can be based on quite different relationships between members of a society. Nevertheless, the labels chosen miss the crucial point that all forms of social integration imply some form of reciprocity. And indeed, it can be argued that market exchange mediated by money (some kind of fiat money, to be more specific) establishes the most complex and sophisticated system of reciprocity ever observed so far. As '[a] behavior (a perception/action pair) is called a *culture* of the society if the majority of its members subscribe to that behavior' (Matsui 1996, p. 290 emphasis in original), we here have a cultural achievement of first order.

That a monetary economy is complex and sophisticated rarely needs any explanation, but that monetary trading implies a network of reciprocity may not be so obvious. Here is a simple way to see it (Kocherlakota 1998a): imagine an alien from another solar system visiting a monetary economy here on earth. Suppose further that the alien has a blind spot for the monetary flows paralleling the material flows of goods and services, because he is only capable of perceiving intrinsically useful items (he looks behind the 'veil of money'). What he would see is person *A* giving something of value to person *B*, who in turn gives something to another person *C*, and so on. However, no visible quid pro quo is provided, which is just what has been described as multilateral reciprocity. According to the perception of this creature, a society based on monetary trade appears as a large network of 'gift-exchange'.

From this perspective, money is no more nor less than a receipt for gifts given to other community members and thus an entitlement (in a sense) to receive gifts of the same values from others. Money figures as a medium of *collective memory*. Remarkably, the word 'Money' etymologically seems to stem from 'Mnemosyne', the Greek goddess of memory and the muses ('Mneme' = memory). If any receipt eventually is redeemed by the original issuer against his goods or services, then multilateral reciprocity is realised, no matter how long the chain of transactions falling in between and how they vary in terms of substances, dates, spaces and persons. Regarding its *content*, money thus represents an entitlement (or claim) to goods and services from other members, which a person acquires by her own delivery of same value.

However, with regards to its *form*, money is no claim at all, because nobody exists who is legally in charge to honour it. This odd dialectic is responsible not only for much confusion in the thinking on money, but also explains the efficiency of the monetary arrangement as well as its fragility.

## MONEY'S ROLE IN MAKING COMMUNITY

What makes this simple idea of 'reciprocity by money' to appear so counterintuitive? Obviously, we seldom look at modern market economies as networks of reciprocal exchange. Sure, we recognise that there are lots of reciprocal elements even in our society. But we normally tend to associate those elements not with the core of the society but rather with its periphery. The core, instead, is based primarily on what more appropriately may be termed *equivalence*, which is established by way of legally binding contracts, which free and formally equal private owners enter in order to gain mutual benefits. Since this, under given conditions, is the only way to realise an exchange of goods and services, contributions of both parties are equivalent in the sense that nobody would be willing (and cannot be forced) to enter into a commitment against his own interest. Equivalence requires bilateral balancing of value between any pair of trade partners. Nobody can legally enforce a claim, which she holds against one person, towards a third person, if this is not contractually agreed upon (or imposed by law). By this, equivalence obviously constitutes a restriction on trade, but it still allows intertemporal exchange between any two partners. Yet, this would imply one of them accepting another's promise to deliver goods tomorrow for receiving goods today. Let us see whether this can work.

Modern societies are made up of large numbers of fairly differentiated, sophisticated, anonymous and more or less egoistic individuals. Personal relationships and commitments, which have been and still are predominant in other societies, are undermined and obsolete to a large degree and reserved for private, intimate spheres of life. The downsides of this development are obvious and often condemned: generally, social cooperation is much more difficult to establish (Hollis 1998). Importantly, however, we should not overlook the remarkable positive impact. No other society hitherto has been able to simultaneously generate a comparable degree of individual freedom and a comparable level of general welfare. Fundamental prerequisites are *individuality* and *anonymity* of members of the society, bound to their *private property*. Jointly these elements not only guarantee citizens their private sphere, but are also necessary for the functioning of *competitive markets*. Note in particular that anonymity implies the absence of personal preferences between market participants, commonly regarded as a necessary condition of perfect competition (Heering 1999b; Heering and Pfirrmann 2002). The importance of all this can easily be seen when looking at societies dominated by patronage, which nowadays applies to Russia and other states of the former Soviet Union as well as to many developing countries.

Be that as it may, under the conditions set out, intertemporal exchanges of goods and services even between two actors are extremely risky activities for those who have to give valuables for personal promises. Such deals cannot therefore happen very often. What is required then is not only equivalence, but equivalence that must be settled instantaneously: actors will only be ready to part with their own goods if simultaneously they receive something of equal value. This is *W. Stanley Jevons'* famous condition of 'double coincidence of wants' (Jevons 1875, p. 57). In a way explained in the next section, money provides a means for overcoming this problem. It acts as a *device to reconcile the principle of multilateral reciprocity with the principle of equivalence* within the limits of a given payment community ('*Zahlungsgemeinschaft*', to use a term of *Max Weber* (1922)). By accepting money and only money as means of payment in exchange for their goods and services, members of the community jointly establish a social accounting system (Schumpeter 1970). Equally important, at the same time a very effective and efficient enforcement mechanism is created.

We are now able to see, how money can establish *multilateral reciprocity*:

1. Money simulates equivalence. Since money is generally valued on all markets it fulfils the role of a placeholder as an option for goods in general. As *Karl Marx* rightly observed, it functions as 'general equivalent' (Marx 1867 [1970]). Since payment with money is final, the receiver of money must not care about the honesty or credibility of the person she gets it from. Money allows any bilateral imbalance to be settled immediately, so that equivalence is quid pro quo.
2. Moreover, by its universality with regards to the persons to whom it may be transferred in exchange for goods, money creates multilateralism in payment, i.e. multilateral exchange. Also, in general, dates of giving and receiving goods and service for any individual actor differ.
3. Finally, as nobody is obliged to accept money in exchange for his goods, reciprocation induced by money is not formally enforced, but constitutes an informal social arrangement.

Notice that these are exactly the criteria listed in the definition at the outset!

Money, to summarise our discussion so far, is a social institution, enabling large societies of anonymous private owners to realise multilateral reciprocity without the pertinent restrictions on personal freedom and on competition, which characterise small, tight-knit communities. Put shortly and pointedly, like the rule of law, money is one of the essential devices to transform modern societies into communities. However, this mode of cooperation does not come without a cost, in material as well as in immaterial terms. Immaterial costs are, to some extent at least, the losses of personal relationships in modern societies. This, in turn, disables some forms of transactions, which could indeed be more efficient than monetary trade, a perspective hitherto rarely acknowledged in mainstream economic theory (Prendergast and Stole 2001).

## RULES OF THE MONEY GAME

What are the principles allowing this transformation? Money, starting with the trivial, fulfils several functions in a modern market economy: it is a means of payment, a medium of exchange, a store of value and a unit of account, as we have been taught by generations of economists. There have been endless discussions on the meaning and importance of these features, and most economists have long been used to consider the medium-of-exchange function as the most important one (Kiyotaki and Wright 1992). This follows straightforwardly from the widely accepted interpretation of money as a device for overcoming physical restrictions on trade due to an 'absence of double coincidence of wants'; for two individuals to become engaged in bilateral exchange both must offer something that is wanted by the other. However, more recent research has recognised that the 'problem of coincidence' is not the only and not even the most pressing one to plague modern liberal societies. More important is what may be called a 'problem of commitment', which prevents exchange of goods and services against personal promises to reciprocate in kind (Gale 1982; Wallace 2000a).

There appears to be a vivid convergence in the micro-foundation of money. Essentially, money in modern theory is conceptualised as a device enabling a complex multilateral network of reciprocal transactions among relatively selfish and anonymous members of a large, sophisticated modern society.[2] More analytically, society's complexity can explain the ubiquitous existence of lack of double coincidence of wants. In itself, however, this does not create a serious obstacle to cooperation; it could, in principle, be overcome by personal promises, as the case of traditional communities demonstrates. It is the anonymity and selfishness of its members which are responsible for general absence of personal trust (technically, individual actors are unable to enter binding commitments) preventing personal loans. Note that legal enforcement will not be of much help either, since for the bulk of small transactions the fixed costs of legal enforcement can be expected to exceed their value. Jointly these elements explain why money as a final, anonymous means of discharging obligations can be welfare improving. If all members of the society always honour their promises, no money would ever be necessary (Gale 1982). Rephrasing and inverting the famous biblical verdict, *Nobuhiro Kiyotaki* and *John H. Moore* recently have set the provoking thesis that 'evil is the root of all money' (Kiyotaki and Moore 2002).[3] The focus of research has thus shifted from a technical to a social restriction and (not always in words but anyway in tenor) from the medium-of-exchange to the means-of-payment function of money (Moini 2001). However, money can play its role only if generally accepted (Heering 2003a). Hence the primary necessary condition for any viable monetary system is to establish and maintain the acceptance of money. At present, we do not know very much about how this can be achieved.

Let me illustrate the foregoing informal argument by way of a simple model. Consider the following asymmetric, sequential, one-shot Prisoners' Dilemma game, which is sometimes called *game of trust* (Kreps 1986; Berg et al. 1995), but may more appropriately be labelled *game of promise*.[4] We assume an economy with one consumption good and two periods. There are two individuals $A$ and $B$ with endowments *(1, 0)* and *(0, 1)* respectively; the first (second) number stands for endowment in period 1 (2). Both individuals would benefit from an intertemporal agreement to exchange $\frac{1}{2}$ of $A$'s endowment today for $\frac{1}{2}$ of $B$'s endowment tomorrow, implying that $A$ strictly prefers *($\frac{1}{2}$, $\frac{1}{2}$)* to *(1, 0)*, while $B$ strictly prefers *($\frac{1}{2}$, $\frac{1}{2}$)* to *(0, 1)*. However, as usual, both individuals always prefer more to less. Thus their complete preference orderings over possible outcomes may be written as

$$(\tfrac{1}{2}, \tfrac{1}{2}) \succ_A (1, 0) \succ_A (\tfrac{1}{2}, 0) \text{ and } (\tfrac{1}{2}, 1) \succ_B (\tfrac{1}{2}, \tfrac{1}{2}) \succ_B (0, 1)$$

respectively, where $a \succ b$ indicates that $a$ is strictly preferred to $b$.

Each of the two actors has two options, as indicated in Figure 7.2 below.

The problem for $A$ in this environment is that in exchange for her today's goods she can only get a promise for tomorrow's goods (Gale 1982). Thus she faces a choice between accepting or not accepting such a promise. In the second round then $B$ has to decide whether he will keep or break the promise. $B$ will, of course, be eager to convince $A$ to trust his promise. However, $A$ will realise that this is only 'cheap talk'. For if $B$ is given the choice, he certainly will decide to abuse $A$'s trust because that is what his preference ordering tells him; obviously, this is an example of *time inconsistency*. As a consequence, no contract will be signed. The only incentive-compatible equilibrium is *autarky*. Note also that under strict anonymity of the players even repeating the game as such could not make any difference to this result.

The *problem of commitment* (which is a problem of incentive and possibly of memory) can be solved by one single and simple device. If $B$ backs his promise by handing over to $A$ some object $x$, which $A$ knows that $B$ would

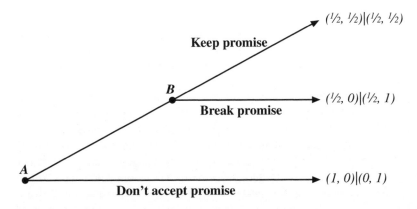

*Figure 7.2   The promise game*

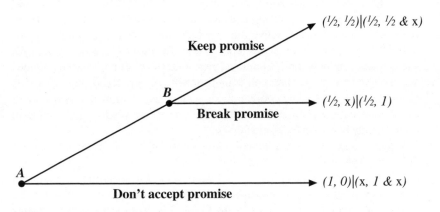

*Figure 7.3   The promise game with collateral*

like to or must have returned, this object functions as a reminder as well as an enforcement device (Ostroy and Starr 1990). The threat of not returning $x$ will make **B** inclined to honour his commitment. The payoffs of the game now are as in Figure 7.3.

Preferences of **A** and **B** are now assumed to be:

$$(\tfrac{1}{2}, \tfrac{1}{2}) \succ_A (1, 0) \succ_A (\tfrac{1}{2}, x) \text{ and } (\tfrac{1}{2}, \tfrac{1}{2} \& x) \succ_B (\tfrac{1}{2}, 1) \succ_B (x, 1 \& x)$$

respectively. Since $x$ is such that **B** prefers *($\tfrac{1}{2}$, $\tfrac{1}{2}$ & **x**)* to *($\tfrac{1}{2}$, 1)*, the trick is done. **B**'s promise is now credible. Note, that a simple promissory note won't do, because, whilst a reminder, it hardly can be used as an effective medium of enforcement. Object $x$ acts as a medium of collective memory or record-keeping and simultaneously as a medium of punishing. Although this model illustrates important functions of money, *x* in our example is still *not* money; it is just a *collateral*, which does not alter the fact that *B* has a personal commitment towards *A*. In a more complex environment this device would not be of much help.

For an object to become money in the proper sense, some additional features must come in: First, the object must not function as a reminder of a personal, bilateral commitment. It acts as an anonymous medium of memory, the handing over of which immediately clears the debt somebody has entered into by receiving goods. Second, acceptance of the object in exchange is warranted solely by expectation that all other members of the trading community will do the same; and third, non-acceptance will be punished by ostracism from the trading and payment community. A generalised model can capture these three moments: (1) There are many actors, who meet at random. The probability, with which two peculiar actors meet more than once, can be interpreted as an index of anonymity. (2) Money is introduced as a token, which is of no use as such, i.e. enters neither preferences nor technology. It is therefore accepted only if it can be used to buy others' goods. Obviously this requires that the game is (at least potentially) infinitely repeated. (3) If all actors accept money and only money in exchange, then punishment for non-acceptance occurs by exclusion from the trading community. It is then easy to show that such a game can have a cooperative equilibrium, although the repeated original game of promise may have none (Araujo 2004).

Whilst, so far, we have assumed that money *is* generally accepted, next we ought to explore the logic of this social behaviour. To establish multilateral reciprocity, a monetary system must follow some rules. Assume the equilibrium price vector of an intertemporal general equilibrium model (in the version of *Kenneth Arrow* and *Gerard Debreu*) is given. This analytical trick allows us to concentrate fully on the *logistic* problem of realising the equilibrium allocation by bilateral trade, which is the basic task for money to fulfil (Ostroy 1973; Anderlini and Sabourian 1992). A set of bilateral transactions can then be shown to exist, each of them involving money on one side, by which the equilibrium allocation of goods is achieved in an efficient way. For money to enable this process, however, it must be generally accepted in transaction. For this to happen two basic rules have to be satisfied. The first rule is straightforward.

**Rule 1 (acceptance)** *Each market participant shall accept money and only money in exchange for own goods and services or claims thereon.*

It may seem that this rule begs the question, because it already entails the solution. But the problem is exactly *how* the rule of acceptance can be guaranteed if not formally enforced. With this respect, note that rule 1 is actually *self-enforcing* (a *Nash equilibrium*), where enforcement takes place via threat of exclusion from future trade. However, there always exists an alternative Nash equilibrium, in which nobody accepts money. Indeed, there is a particular risk in accepting money, because its future value in term of goods cannot be negotiated in advance (Giannini 1995). To minimise this risk we must have:

**Rule 2 (access)** *No market participant shall get access to money otherwise than by exchanging goods and services or claims thereon for it.*

If rule 2 is not met, rule 1 will probably not be adopted in the first place, since it loses its punishing potency. Market participants must then be afraid of receiving less than they give and will therefore not accept money in exchange for their goods and services. Therefore, rule 2 becomes pivotal in any monetary system. Unfortunately, rule 2 as such is generally not self-enforcing; it has to be backed by some more explicit measures.

## EVOLUTION OF MONETARY SYSTEMS

Having explained the logical structure of monetary trade, we next ask *how* the underlying rules have been established and how their application has developed over time.

Originally, the rules of the 'money game' (the term is *Thomas Crump's* (1981, 32)) and compliance with them evolved, as far as we know, spontaneously, without any explicit agreement and even without understanding their logic. The fact that today their understanding is still incomplete is ample evidence for this. Nevertheless, although the exact historical origin of money is still in the dark, what can be said with some confidence is that there seems to have been several routes (Wray 2000). Quite often trading actors seem to have adopted objects which already have been used in paying off non-trade (ritual or administrative) obligations (Goodhart 2002). In many primitive communities, exchange took the form of goods for some naturally scarce tokens (cowries on many Pacific islands, big stones on the Yap Island, etc. (Crump 1981; Davies 1994)). In medieval Europe, networks of merchants from different areas invented a quite sophisticated system of clearing based on personal IOUs, pretty tough sanctions and under the protection of the official law (Boyer-Xambeu et al. 1994). In more open and less close-knit environments, particularly in trade between communities, valued commodities have been widely used. For centuries precious metals became the dominantly used means of payment and media of exchange in long-distance and large-volume trade between different populations and cultures. However, internally these modes of payment were often substituted by token coins, later by private banknotes qua claims on deposited metal and still later also by official central bank notes (Crump 1981). With the emergence of nation states during the nineteenth and at the beginning of the twentieth century inconvertible fiat money became more and more usual (Helleiner 2003). Obviously, the concrete mode of transaction and payment varied widely depending on facilities and costs of monitoring and available sanction technologies. Moreover, throughout history, monetary systems have been regulated and managed by the state or by private clubs in different degrees.

In theory this diversity of developments was reflected by two opposing hypothesis about the origin of money (Hart 1986; Goodhart 1998). One approach, mostly associated with *Georg Friedrich Knapp's* 'State theory of money', but more appropriately traced to *Adam Müller*, maintains that money is a creature of the state or legal system (Müller 1816; Knapp 1905). The other idea goes back at least to *David Hume* (1740), but is attributed to *Carl Menger* (1871; 1909) and was elaborated by *Ludwig von Mises* (1912); it is also the one favoured by *Hayek*. *Robert Nozick* called it 'invisible-hand explanation' (Nozick 1974 [1995], 18; also see Langlois 1986 and Vaughn 1987). Money, according to this approach, evolved endogenously from market interaction of private actors without any intention. It is, to quote *Adam Ferguson's* famous statement from 1767, 'the result of human action, but not the execution of any human design' (quoted from Vaughn 1987, 169).[5] Against the rapidly growing popularity of *Knapp's* 'State theory of money' shortly after its first publication, *Menger* insisted that '[m]oney was not created by legislation; it is not originally a governmental but a social phenomenon' (quoted from Issing 1997, 186).

There are some confusing elements in this still ongoing debate. There is concern about history compared to theory, which *Joseph A. Schumpeter* had already mentioned (1970). A theory should of course not contradict the broad historical facts, but there is no need why it should confirm any singular and accidental aspect of the different courses of history. *Nozick*, for instance, is quite explicit that his preference for invisible-hand theories is mainly a methodological choice; he is looking for minimal explanations. No doubt, *Menger's* theory of money fits in as has subsequently been shown by *Robert Jones* (1976) and *Seonghwan Oh* (1989). Furthermore, a distinction should be drawn between means of payment in general and trade-related money. Whatever the origin of the former, *Menger's* theory again fits into an explanation of the latter. Does this mean that *Menger* was right after all? Not entirely, I would argue.

Analytically the issue boils down to the question, whether monetary trade can best be conceptualised by a pure co-ordination game or rather by a game of the Prisoners' Dilemma type (Steiner 1978; Lagerspetz 1984). The foundation of the money game by the two rules introduced above throws some new light upon this question. First note that the rule of acceptance (rule 1) as such is entirely conventional. It does not entail any conflict of interest, and compliance with it can therefore be rationalised by a pure *coordination game*. In this respect *Hume* (1740) rightly compares money to language. On principle, *Menger's* idea can be used to explain the dynamic properties of this game, which, under reasonable conditions leads to a monetary Nash equilibrium. Those historical facts which have been sketched above may, however, have served as 'focal points' (Schelling 1960), by which the search process was significantly shortened.

The same reasoning, however, does not apply to the rule of access (rule 2). Obviously, in the corresponding game each actor has a clear incentive to violate the rule. For if all other actors stick to the rule, he can gain most if he extends his own access to money. And if all others violate the rule, then he will have to join them for otherwise he will turn out as the only fool. Thus the underlying game is of the type of a *Prisoners' Dilemma* with each actor's dominant strategy being to violate the rule of access. But if all actors do acknowledge this ubiquitous temptation, they will not accept money in the first place. Violation of rule 2 eventually provokes abandonment of rule 1. Only a non-monetary equilibrium is then feasible.

The money game, therefore, is generally not a pure coordination game. It is, to be sure, in principle possible to design a monetary system in which the rule of access cannot be violated. If an object is chosen as money, which is absolutely fixed in quantity (it cannot be reproduced, either publicly or privately, implying that counterfeiting is not possible) and all existing items are registered, then, provided that rule 1 is strictly followed, the only way an actor could violate rule 2 is by individual theft. Whilst this may pose a problem for the legal system, it is no problem of the monetary system, because it leaves the aggregate money volume unchanged. Moreover, as long as the nominal value of money is not higher than its production costs, the rule of access will also be automatically honoured. Money of this type clearly could have and apparently has developed spontaneously, without any deliberate agreement. The only problem was that real monetary objects have always been exposed to much cheaper forgeries. Those troubles increased when money became fiduciary.

Monetary systems can be characterised by the way they deal with the rule of access, as the table at the end of the chapter indicates. Remarkably, the most primitive money is, in a sense, an ideal one. Actually, it is the type incorporated in most microeconomic models of money. However, this type of money can only fit a fairly stationary environment. Generally, there exists a potential trade-off between the elasticity of a monetary system and its long-run stability requiring rule 2 to be met. Experience shows that arrangements in which the rule is automatically fulfilled are those with long-run price stability but serious short-run instability, while more flexible systems are prone to long-run instability. The synopsis indicates that there is no easy way out of this dilemma.

## PUBLIC OR PRIVATE MONEY?

What, if anything, follows from our reasoning for the question of a public monopoly over money? As I said at the beginning, I am more optimistic than *Hayek* was about the future prospect of designing and implementing a monetary system which allows a reasonable degree of both flexibility and stability. At the same time I am much more pessimistic than he was regarding the potency of private competitive monies to solve the commitment problem which actors in large, complex economies face.

To begin with the pessimistic part of my argument: As far as I am aware, neither *Hayek* nor any other proponent of the 'Free Money Movement' has ever made any serious attempt to explain why money is essential in the first place. Most of them seem to accept (as do at least 95 per cent of all economists) *Menger's* (and others') thesis that it was the inconvenience of barter which led to the evolution of money (Dowd 1988; 2000). Although *Hayek* emphasised the eminent cultural role of money in enabling cooperation in a liberal market economy, he never explored this role in a systematic way. As a consequence there has been a tendency to trivialise the phenomenon of money. Indeed, if the main obstacle for money to overcome is the lack of double coincidence in bilateral trade, then the money game can be reduced to the pure co-ordination game underlying the rule of acceptance. In this perspective there is no need for any *force majeure*. The monopoly over money must appear as an usurpation in the state's self-interest only (Hayek 1978; Glasner 1998).[6] But if lack of double coincidence was the only problem money has to solve, then it should be possible for private actors to arrange other modes of payment. Accordingly the state's prerogative of issuing money would lose its power, which depends on private actors voluntarily accepting money. Ironically, therefore, the whole argument implicitly assumes that the state *is* capable to enforce acceptance of its money, contradicting the conviction held by other Austrian scholars (especially Mises 1912, pp. 43–54).[7] Realising that there is more to the rationale of money than bypassing the banal technical restriction of lacking double coincidence, which anyway hardly could count as one of the greatest cultural achievements of mankind, the matter becomes more complicated as outlined. I am not at all convinced that the 'commitment problem', which in a modified version (or on another level) reoccurs in the rule of access, can, on balance, be better solved by private money issuers than by state authority.

Now for the optimistic part of my argument: The main idea can be taken from *Hayek's* own discussion of the rule of law:

> Life of man in society ... is made possible by the individuals acting according to certain rules. With the growth of intelligence, these rules tend to develop from unconscious habits into explicit and articulated statements and at the same time to become more abstract and general. Our familiarity with the institutions of law prevents us from seeing how subtle and complex a device the delimitation of individual spheres by abstract rules is. If it had been deliberately designed, it would deserve to rank among the greatest of human inventions. But it has, of course, been as little invented by any one mind as language or money or most of the practices and conventions on which social life rests. (Hayek 1960, p. 148)

Essentially, *Hayek* here says that although the rule of law has developed spontaneously and unintentionally, it has been domesticated and cultivated at some stage by human will. Most interesting in our context is the parallel between money and law, or (perhaps more accurately) between the monetary and the legal systems, he draws. The analogy has often been suggested (Illing 2000; Heering 2003a; Spahn 2002). That money should have a status similar to the law was anticipated by the French bishop and philosopher *Nicolas Oresme*, writing around 1360 that 'moneta debet esse quasi quaedam lex et quaedam ordinatio firma' (quoted from Duisenberg 2002, p. 3). Yet so far no systematic treatment exists, notwithstanding some first thoughts (Voigt 2002; Goodhart 2002; Goodhart and Meade 2003; Heering 2003a). In my opinion quite a few lessons can be learned from comparing the monetary system with its legal counterpart. Here are some.

First, legal system and monetary system are both 'collective goods' in a straightforward and intuitive sense.[8] Both establish rules of conduct, which regulate the relationships among private actors and between them and state representatives. Both lines are of equal importance and to emphasise one to the neglect of the other is dangerous. Moreover, both sets of rules are generally acceptable only because of their neutrality regarding the great variety of individuals (their status, wealth, background, education, opinions, etc.) within a modern society. We know that this neutrality is often violated in both systems, that officials from time to time have even bent the law and that governments have often abused the monetary system in their own interest. However, would the same authors who request replacement of public money by private money also suggest the same consequence for the law? Of course, this is a rhetorical question. As *Otmar Issing* put it: 'If it does not seem advisable – and here everybody will agree – to restore law – that is, legislation and jurisdiction – to this "pre-governmental" state, to leave its development to private competition, how can one recommend private currency competition?' (Issing 1997, p. 187) Examples of abuse of governments' monopoly as such are not at all sufficient reason for abandoning public provision of money altogether.[9] Interestingly, even strictly liberal economists and philosophers such as *Irving Fisher, Henry Simon, Walter Eucken, James Buchanan, Geoffrey Brennan, Milton Friedman* and others did not intend to go so far.[10]

Second, central banks have recently been granted a significant degree of autonomy from their government. Debates about the suitable degrees of independence, accountability and transparency still continue, though (Amtenbrink 1999; Eijffinger and Hoeberichts 2000; Winkler 2000; Cukierman 2001; Geraats 2002). There seems to be no clear-cut answer. A look at the legal system may here be helpful in providing some guidelines for further discussion. Under the rule of law, jurisdiction has an independent status with respect to legislation and executive power; only constitution and law restrict it. Independence is required because interpretation and application of the law to concrete cases must be neutral towards any natural person or legal entity, in order for the legal system to be generally accepted and thus being able to achieve its goal of allowing individuals with conflicting interests and opinions to live peacefully together. Since legislative as well as executive bodies are legal entities, their possible interference with jurisdiction must be prevented in the same way as the interference of any other natural person or legal entity. Looking back on centuries of successful operation of an independent jurisdiction, monetary economists should have much to learn from this experience. To suppose the learning should rather be the other way round, as is sometimes suggested (Voigt 2002), seems to me very odd indeed. There is, however, a general rational behind independence of public agencies: rules of conduct aim at efficiency by increasing the scope for cooperation. Since efficiency-improving measures, by definition, entail no distributional conflict, it can, indeed should, be left to public but non-governmental authorities. Whenever distributional conflicts are involved, on the other hand, the legitimate democratic bodies should deal with these (Blinder 1997; Majone 1997).

Third, as *Hayek* emphasises, the rules of law have become more conscious over time, and were deliberately adjusted to a permanently changing environment. This has also been an important part of cultural evolution. I cannot see any reason why the same process should not apply to money. Already in 1909 *Carl Menger* wrote that 'just as common law was endorsed by legislation, the institution of money ... was refined and adjusted by government recognition and regulation to meet the manifold and changing requirements of transactions' (quoted from Issing 1997, p. 186 f). Of course, state and society had to go through lengthy and often painful experience to learn the principles of law and how these principles are best formulated and applied. Failures and drawbacks have been almost inevitable. We should certainly not be too impatient with the same process with regards to money, which has just taken off.

## CHALLENGES FOR MODERN MONETARY POLICY

It is completely true that emperors of all times have abused their prerogative power over money to exploit their subjects and sometimes even provoked breakdowns of the monetary system. But the most serious challenges did not occur before the twentieth century. To understand why, we have to recognise three main factors explaining the dilemma of modern monetary policy. Understanding the underlying tensions should put us in a better position to cope with them.

First, there is the emergence of purely fiat money, which followed the abandonment of the gold standard. The first blow came with World War I, when all engaged countries at least temporarily suspended convertibility of their currencies into gold. In 1933 the convertibility of the US dollar into gold coins for private actors finally ended, and in 1971 even foreign governments were denied conversion of their dollar reserves into gold (Friedman and Schwartz 1986; Kohn 2004). Existence of manipulative domestic currencies created an obvious temptation for governments, which they first had to learn to deal with.

Second, we have to consider why this facility led to inflationary outbursts, the last of which occurred in the 1970s. The essential moment seems to be the emergence of mass democracies, taking place at about the same time as when countries went off the gold standard (Giannini 1994; Helleiner 2003). This factor amplified the new temptation on governments, which they often failed to resist. This explains why governments of any colour were prone to opportunism. All in all it didn't matter which party was in charge.

Third, we have to acknowledge that the Great Depression of the early 1930s had a traumatic impact on public and on governments (Giannini 1994). The latter saw themselves under great political pressure to act somehow against the dramatic consequences. As is well known, the theories of *John Maynard Keynes*, among others, purported to provide the means and the rationalisation of that kind of political activism. Clearly, a domestic monetary arrangement based purely on fiat was a necessary requisite.

While Keynesian illusions during the following experience of 'stagflation' soon faded away, liberal societies will have to live with the other two factors, for good or bad. However, several comments are in order:

## The role of central banks

To be sure, there are quite a few economists who still are in favour of central banks taking responsibility for short-run stabilisation policy. Yet this reflects a widespread misconception of money, its role in society and the requirements needed to safeguard this role. Money, like the law, should not be made (and can only be made so at high social costs) an object of political manipulations or experiments (Hayek 1984, p. 41). Indeed, monetary policy as we are familiar with it, a notion that came up during the twentieth century, should be abandoned altogether. Money has one and only one role in society, to facilitate and smooth out mutually beneficially market transactions, and central banks should be committed to serve this task as efficiently as possible without jeopardising money's general acceptance, on which its efficiency-enhancing function rests. Sure, in a world of uncertainty and continuous change, some experimentation is always required. Monetary management, as well as the law, has to be improved constantly to fit existing conditions better as well as adapted to new conditions, but significant erratic changes within short time intervals should be avoided as far as possible. In particular, this requires a strict separation between monetary management and fiscal policy, the most urgent task in *Hayek's* proposal (1978, p. 117).[11]

## Price stability and rule of access

At the very moment, inflation seems to be no issue; many observers instead are raising concerns about risks of deflation. It must be emphasised, though, that (open) inflation is only one possible symptom for violation of the rule of access; incidences of quantity rationing of actors on markets are another (Mises 1912, p. 230). This is one reason why 'inflation targeting', fashionable as it is in these days, might prove not appropriate as a general monetary policy strategy. As a matter of fact, governments (central banks) can easily stabilise any price level they choose, simply by pegging the money price of a corresponding basket of commodities. Variants of this idea have been suggested since termination of the gold standard, and *Hayek* once (1943) promoted a 'commodity reserve currency'. Yet, I doubt that this would be a wise policy. Practitioners of central banking never showed much inclination to adopt it and *Hayek* has dissociated himself from it in his later work (Hayek 1978, p. 48). That price level stability as such may be a misleading policy guide is also suggested by the following episode: In 1925 *Hayek* criticised US monetary policy during the prosperous period of the 1920s as too easy, although inflation was quite low. He argued 'that the injection of money through credit markets must result in a misallocation of resources despite the price-level stability', and this diagnosis 'was the basis for his prediction that the money-induced boom would eventually lead to a bust' (Garrison and Kirzner 1987, p. 126). As we know, his prophecy turned out to be right.

**Central banks in a modern, democratic state**

Even if one must concede that a lot of risks still exist, we must not underrate the remarkable learning process which governments and public have gone through during recent decades. The fact that most central banks now are granted a high degree of autonomy from their government is a promising sign. The intensive debate about status and organisation of central banks, we are witnessing, is another. Moreover, whilst the downsides of modern mass democracy are pretty obvious, it has important positive and promising aspects too: The state corresponding to this political arrangement is clearly no longer the *Leviathan*, challenged by early liberals. Modern states have a highly complex structure, which renders it very difficult to believe in any theory of conspiracy, whereby a monolithic power pursues a well-defined and unique interest in plundering and cheating people. This caricatured vision, nevertheless, still seems to stimulate many liberal political philosophers and economists. Of course, we should always be aware of the risks a modern monetary system is prone to. In the end, it is probably the consciousness of private actors that a stable, well-accepted currency fits market activities best, at least in the longer run ('stability culture' as it has been labelled), which jointly with appropriate institutions and their suitable staffing provide the proper safeguard for an efficient monetary arrangement.

## CONCLUSION

Undoubtedly, our sense of money, monetary systems and the requirements of their proper functioning has been enlarged and deepened substantially during the last fifty years or so. It can, however, be argued that this progress owes much more to practical experience than to economic theories and academic research. Although money is presumably one of the central social institutions which have evolved without having been intentionally invented by mankind, it has now reached a degree of sophistication, which seems to make necessary a more conscious and deliberate management. In this respect money doesn't stand alone, though. It follows the track of the legal system.

*Hayek's* ideas remind us that our knowledge of money and the economy is (still?) far too incomplete to allow perfect designing of the monetary system by reason only. Whether or not we follow him in his proposal to leave it to the market to decide on a suitable arrangement, his fundamental point remains true. It means, in particular, that any ambition for using money as an instrument in short-term stabilisation of the economy is hopeless. In academia as well as among practitioners there still are serious conceptual failures concerning money's role in society and the economy, which block further insights into the requirements of an appropriate system, not to mention the pertinent political obstacles for implementation. At present, monetary policy research seems to be more concerned with technicalities (How can price stability best be achieved? What are the appropriate price index and definition of its stability? Is monetary targeting more effective than direct inflation targeting, etc.?) rather than taking seriously the fundamental challenge of providing a framework in which the proper role of money can best be fulfilled. Of course, handling technical details is important. But without having a clear understanding of the fundamental issues it is at risk of becoming purely technocratic in pretending technical solutions to non-technical problems.

I wholeheartedly agree with *Hayek* and others that money is too important (and too special) to let government have its way. Money must be removed from government's playing field. From my understanding of money, however, I doubt very much that *Hayek's* positive proposal is realistic and, even if it would be, that it is desirable. I prefer the only available alternative, which takes the evolution of the legal system as a model. This leads to the monetary constitution approach. A monetary constitution describes the institutional set-up of a monetary system; it determines the legal status of monetary authorities vis-à-vis legislative and executive on one hand and vis-à-vis other monetary and financial institutions on the other, and it defines aims, rules and procedures of the internal decision-making in pursuing monetary policy. Serious discussion of the idea goes back to the aftermath of the world-wide banking crises in the early 1930s (Lutz 1936; Bernholz 1989, 2003) and was revitalised in the early 1960s at the dawn of the inflationary outburst in particular by scholars of the Chicago School (Friedman 1959; Yeager 1962; Brennan and Buchanan 1981). It was a direct reflex of and a logical reaction to the challenge posed by the advent of fiat money. In recent years the issue has gained further momentum not only by the intensive debate on the legal and political status of central banks but also by the process of European monetary integration speeding up in the 1990s (Claassen 1984; Blackburn and Christensen 1989; Blinder 1996; Bofinger and Ketterer 1996; Issing 1998). Nevertheless, still missing is a solid formulation and foundation of the concept. Only with such a legal framework, however, will it be possible to equip monetary authorities with the necessary power and scope to manage the monetary system in the most efficient way to provide sufficient liquidity to the economy subject to the hard constraint of not violating the rule of access. On balance, I don't share *Hayek's* pessimism that this is a 'mission impossible'.

*Table 7.1   Synopsis of monetary systems*

| | | | | Stability? | |
|---|---|---|---|---|---|
| Money type | Money media | Money stock | Rule 2 met? | short-run | long-run |
| **Primitive money** | Scarce objects (cowrie, Yap stones, etc.) | Inelastic (given stock) | Yes | Yes | Yes |
| **Commodity money** | Producible valuables (precious metals) | Weakly elastic according to technology | Yes | No | Yes |
| **Fiduciary money** | Claims on issuer's valuables | Weakly elastic subject to reserve requirements | Yes | No | Yes (?) |
| **Government money** | Fiat money (notes, coins) | Perfectly elastic | No | Yes | No |
| **Central bank money** | Fiat money (notes, coins) | Perfectly elastic | Yes (?) | Yes | Yes (?) |

## ACKNOWLEDGEMENT

* I would like to thank Ursula Backhaus and Leland Yeager for helpful comments on a former draft. Obviously the usual absolution does apply

## NOTES

1.  One way to interpret the misery of socialism is that it tries to enforce reciprocity by formal law, which has, at the end of the day, proved to be an impossible task.
2.  The list of contributions along these lines is long and includes *Ferdinando Galiani* (1751), *Henry D. Macleod* (1889), *Joseph A. Schumpeter* (1954, 1970), *Joseph M. Ostroy* (1973), *Martin Shubik* (1973), *Charles A. E. Goodhart* (1975, 1989, 1998), *S. Herbert Frankel* (1977), *Douglas Gale* (1982), *Dan Bernhardt* (1989), *Robert M. Townsend* (1989), *Walter W. Heering* (1991, 1999a, 1999b, 2002a, 2002b, 2003a, 2005), *Narayana R. Kocherlakota* (1998a and 1998b), *Narayana R. Kocherlakota and Neil Wallace* (1998), *Neil Wallace* (1997, 2000a and 2000b), *Peter Bernholz* (2000); *Mostafa Moini* (2001), *Heinz-Peter Spahn* (2001, 2002, 2003), *Leland B. Yeager* (2001), *Nibohuri Kiyotaki* and *John H. Moore* (2002), *Luis Araujo* (2004). Reference here is only to economists.
3.  Note, however, that the bible says '[t]he *love* of money is the root of all evil' (I Timothy 6:10, italics added).
4.  The model intends to formalise *David Hume's* (1740) classic statement: 'Your corn is ripe today; mine will be so tomorrow. 'Tis profitable for us both that I shou'd labour with you

today, and that you shou'd aid me tomorrow. I have no kindness for you, and know that you have little for me. I will not, therefore, take any pains on your account; and should I labour with you on my account, I know I shou'd be disappointed, and that I shou'd in vain depend upon your gratitude. Here then I leave you to labour alone: You treat me in the same manner. The seasons change; and both of us lose our harvests for want of mutual confidence and security' (quoted from Hollis 1998, p. 41).

5.  'The most obvious examples of spontaneous order are the use of language and, among economic phenomena, the use of money. Money, the most commonly accepted medium of exchange, came to be accepted, commonly accepted, and then most commonly accepted as a result of a long sequence of actions on the part of a multitude of individual traders none of whom *intended* to create the institution of money' (Garrison and Kirzner 1987, p. 121 emphasis in original).

6.  In 1960 *Hayek* wrote: 'Why, it is sometimes asked, should we not rely on the spontaneous forces of the market to supply whatever is needed for a satisfactory medium of exchange as we do in most other respects? It is important to be clear at the outset that this is not only politically impracticable today but would probably be undesirable if it were possible. ... [I]f men had not come extensively to use credit instruments as money or close substitutes for money, we might have been able to rely on some self-regulating mechanism. This choice, however, is now closed to us' (Hayek 1960, p. 324). And in a note (p. 520) he added: 'Though I am convinced that modern credit banking as it has developed requires some public institutions such as the central bank, I am doubtful whether it is necessary or desirable that they (or the government) should have the monopoly of the issue of all kinds of money.'

7.  It may be argued, following *Knapp* (1905, p. 85), that the state can always enforce acceptance of its money by demanding payments to itself (e.g. taxes) to be made in this money (Lerner 1947; Wray 2000). As *Ross M. Starr* (1974) has shown, there is no doubt that acceptance by the state may, on principle, induce general acceptance of any money. The critical issue, however, is whether this inducement is strong enough to act as effective enforcement device. Such enforcement must work through discrepancies between the value of purchases by the state from individual private actors with its money and their individual tax duties payable in the same money. To meet tax requirements the public has to reallocate the stock of state money, and the most straightforward way to achieve this is by selling to and buying from each other. That the state normally also claims a percentage of every sale's value as indirect tax obviously supports the mechanism. It is easy to see how this may lead to a general acceptance of state money, because anybody selling something for this money can expect that others will have to do so too to meet their tax requirements. But this mechanism is far from compelling. The case of Russia in recent years suggests that it may work very badly if at all (Woodruff 1999). It requires, of course, the state to be able to enforce tax payment in its money. Moreover, enforcement itself seems to presuppose what it intends to establish, namely the general acceptance of money. For only if state money is generally accepted by market participants will it be possible to enforce tax payment in it. Although the legal tender status of money may serve as a focal point in the sense of *Thomas Schelling*, it is questionable that it is generally sufficient to enforce acceptance of state money.

8.  There have been lots of discussions about the 'public' nature of money (e.g. Salin 1984; Vaubel 1984; White 1999). Unsurprisingly, thorough investigation reveals that money is not a 'public good' in the narrow technical sense the term was introduced by *Paul A. Samuelson* (1954) and elaborated by *Richard A. Musgrave* (1959). Conceding that, I should perhaps make more explicit in which sense I here use the term 'collective good': With regards to money we have to distinguish between the monetary system, essentially a network for settling payments, and the medium by which payment is made, the key, so to say, enabling individuals to use the network (Clower 1969; Moini 2001). Access to the latter has to be strictly limited to legitimate claims (and may be subject to the charging of a fee, normally in the form of interest), implying that means of payment (as distinguishable items) are certainly pure 'private goods'. But apart from those safeguards, which make sure that only 'authorised' individuals get access to the network, the monetary

system doesn't suffer from rivalry in consumption of its services. Provided that 'society' can produce monetary services at zero marginal cost (which is, although obviously not entirely accurate for real monetary systems, the usual assumption in monetary theory), standard welfare theory suggests that monetary services should be delivered to individual actors free of any charge (Friedman 1969).

Moreover, as with other networks, rather than consumptive rivalry we would expect social benefits from using money to increase with the number of participants (Issing 2000, p. 18). Technically, therefore, services of the monetary network may best be conceived as 'club goods' (a concept invented by *James M. Buchanan* (1965)), where the number of club members may potentially be infinite. Let $m$ stand for individual 'real' money holding at some point in time (assuming that all actors are alike in this respect) and $N$ for the number of actors participating in the money game ('club members'), then $M = Nm$ denotes aggregate 'real' money balances. Increasing $M$ by enlarging the size of the club may then be beneficial for any number $N$, but there will probably be some value of individual money balances $m^*$, beyond which individual money holdings can only be increased by generating negative externalities which reduce money's benefits to all (Heering 2003b). Nevertheless, nobody meeting the safeguarding requirements, and to the extent she or he does, should be excluded and everybody should be treated alike. Provision of law services is obviously similar: only authorised persons can consume them (apart from a few very basic and fundamental rights, which have been stipulated to apply to any human being), but apart from that proviso the law should be neutral to all (natural and legal) persons under its jurisdiction. This neutrality (or fairness) in the sense of impartiality is required for efficient functioning of the monetary as well as the legal system simply because their general voluntary acceptance depends on it. It is this feature that I am prepared to take as responsible for their inherently collective nature. In the case of money, impartiality is captured by strict compliance with the rule of access. More formally, it has been argued that compliance with the rule involves a conflict of interest of a Prisoners' Dilemma type, which can hardly be resolved spontaneously. Indeed, the PD-paradigm is used to conceptualise collective goods in a broad sense (Mueller 1989, p. 10f).

Yet, their 'collective' nature is still not in itself sufficient reason for having services provided by the state. Although used synonymously with 'public good' in most of the literature, the term 'collective good' is adopted here exactly to avoid the plainly wrong association of a necessary intervention by the government or 'the state'. The only association I would draw is that provision of collective goods is based on some sort of *collective agreement*, whatever its extent, nature and source. In history there were monetary systems for which the rule of access was (nearly) automatically fulfilled. In those cases enforcement of the rule must not have been grounded on explicit agreement, and its nature may even have not been understood. On the other hand, there were also systems in which fulfilment of the rule was based on collective agreement between members of a rather narrow group of merchants with a strict business codex and tough sanctions. Although backed by legal protection of local authorities and denominated in the official money of account, these payment systems were run privately. But considering more sophisticated monetary systems with fiat money for all members of a nation state or even beyond, I cannot see how any person or any body below the highest level of political authority may possibly be able to organise and operate them. As with law this is not so much a matter of pure logic but of practicability, given structures and costs of governance and enforcement in the world we live in.

9.  In his contribution to this volume *Christian Schubert*, rightly in my opinion, points to a certain ambiguity (or even inconsistency) in *Hayek's* treatment of judge-made law, in particular in the context of Anglo-Saxon common law tradition: *Hayek's* view of judges as 'cognitive heroes' without any tension to egoism due to a superior process of socialisation is not easily made compatible with his overall assumption regarding the cognitive limitation and fundamental subjectivism of human beings. Whilst this ambiguity poses a problem for *Hayek's* theory, I think that he is, at least partly, right as a matter of facts. Contrary to what some extreme institutionalists think, an appropriate set-up of formal institutions is necessary but not sufficient for proper conduct. At the end of the day, we always have to

rely on the professional expertise and personal integrity of agents who design and/or operate an institution (Popper 1945, p. 151). That this also applies to the 'art of central banking' is increasingly recognised (Heering 2002a, 2002b). The fact that *Hayek* was aware of it makes his monetary suspicion even more odd.

10. In 1959 *Milton Friedman* argued: 'Something like a moderately stable monetary framework seems an essential prerequisite for the effective operation of a private market economy. It is dubious that the market can by itself provide such a framework. Hence, the function of providing one is an essential governmental function on a par with the provision of a stable legal framework' (Friedman 1959, p. 8). In an excellent review almost thirty years later, he found no convincing argument to change his mind (Friedman and Schwartz 1986). Moreover, in this context as well as in other writings (Friedman 1984), *Friedman* explicitly expressed his sceptical view on *Hayek's* proposal.

11. One of the buzzwords in contemporary economic policy debates is 'policy mix', which is exactly the opposite of what is necessary according to *Hayek*, and I think he's quite right in this. Already in his *Constitution of Liberty*, he was very concerned about the dominance of fiscal over monetary policy: 'A monetary policy independent of financial policy is possible so long as government expenditure constitutes a comparatively small part of all payments and so long as the government debt ... constitutes only a small part of all credit instruments. Today this condition no longer exists. In consequence, an effective monetary policy can be conducted only in co-ordination with the financial policy of government. Coordination in this respect, however, inevitably means that whatever nominally independent monetary authorities still exist have in fact to adjust their policy to that of the government. The latter, whether we like it or not, thus necessarily becomes the determining factor' (Hayek 1960, p. 327).

# REFERENCES

Amtenbrink, Fabian (1999), *The Democratic Accountability of Central Banks. A Comparative Study of the European Central Bank*, Oxford and Portland: Hart Publishing.

Anderlini, Luca and Hamid Sabourian (1992), 'Some notes on the economics of barter, money and credit', in Caroline Humphrey and Stephen Hugh-Jones (eds), *Barter, Exchange and Value. An Anthropological Approach*, Cambridge: Cambridge University Press, pp. 75–106.

Araujo, Luis (2004), 'Social norms and money', *Journal of Monetary Economics*, **51**, 241–56.

Axelrod, Robert (1984), *The Evolution of Cooperation*, New York: Basic Books.

Berg, J., J. Dickhaut and K. McCabe (1995), 'Trust, reciprocity, and social history', *Games and Economic Behavior*, **10**, 122–42.

Bernhardt, Dan (1989), 'Money and loans', *Review of Economic Studies*, **56**, 89–100.

Bernholz, Peter (1989), *Geldwertstabilität und Währungsordnung*, Tübingen: Mohr Siebeck.

Bernholz, Peter (2000), 'Zahlungsmittel und Dezentralisierung ökonomischer Aktivitäten', in Jürgen von Hagen und Johann Heinrich von Stein (eds), *Obst/ Hintner: Geld-, Bank- und Börsenwesen. Handbuch des Finanzsystems*, 40th edn, Stuttgart: Schäffer-Poeschel, pp. 38–58.

Bernholz, Peter (2003), *Monetary Regimes and Inflation: History, Economic and Political Relationships*, Cheltenham, UK and Northampton, US: Edward Elgar.

Blackburn, Keith and Michael Christensen (1989), 'Monetary policy and policy credibility: theories and evidence', *Journal of Economic Literature*, **27**, 1–45.

Blinder, Alan S. (1996), 'Central banking in a democracy', *Federal Reserve Bank of Richmond Economic Quarterly*, **82** (4), 1–14.

Blinder, Alan (1997), 'Is government too political?', *Foreign Affairs*, **76**, 115–26.

Bofinger, P. and K.-H. Ketterer (eds) (1996), *Neuere Entwicklungen in der Geldtheorie und Geldpolitik. Implikationen für die Europäische Währungsunion. Festschrift für Norbert Kloten*, Tübingen: Mohr Siebeck.

Boyer-Xambeu, Marie-Thérèse, Ghislain Deleoplace and Lucien Gillard (1994), *Private Money & Public Currencies. The 16th Century Challenge*, translated from French, Armonk and London: M.E. Sharpe.

Brennan, Geoffrey H. and James M. Buchanan (1981), 'Monopoly in money and inflation: the case for a constitution to discipline government', Institute of Economic Affairs Hobart Paper 88, London.

Brennan, Geoffrey H. and James M. Buchanan (1985), *The Reason of Rules. Constitutional Political Economy*, reprinted 2000, Indianapolis: Liberty Fund.

Buchanan, James M. (1965), 'An economic theory of clubs', *Economica*, **32**, 1–14.

Claassen, Emil Maria (1984), 'Monetary integration and monetary stability: the economic criteria of the monetary constitution', in Pascal Salin (ed.), *Currency Competition and Monetary Union*, The Hague: Martinus Nijhoff Publishers, pp. 47–58.

Clower, Robert W. (1969), 'Introduction' in Robert W. Clower (ed.), *Monetary Theory. Selected Readings*, Harmondsworth: Penguin Books, pp. 7–21.

Crump, Thomas (1981), *The Phenomenon of Money*, London: Routledge & Kegan Paul.

Cukierman, Alex (2001), 'Are contemporary central banks transparent about economic models and objectives and what difference does it make?', Economic Research Centre of the Deutsche Bundesbank discussion paper 05/01.

Davies, Glyn (1994), *A History of Money. From Ancient Times to the Present Day*, Cardiff: University of Wales Press.

Dowd, Kevin (1988), 'Automatic stabilizing mechanisms under free banking', reprinted 1993 in Kevin Dowd, *Laissez-faire Banking*, London and New York: Routledge, pp. 25–40.

Dowd, Kevin (2000), 'The invisible hand and the evolution of the monetary system', in John Smithin (ed.), *What is Money?*, London and New York: Routledge, pp. 139–56.

Duisenberg, Willem F. (2002), 'Der Internationale Karlspreis zu Aachen 2002. Dankesrede von Willem F. Duisenberg, Präsident der Europäischen Zentralbank, Aachen, am 9. Mai 2002', printed in *Deutsche Bundesbank, Auszüge aus Presseartikeln*, 22, 17 May, 3–5.

Eijffinger, S.C.W. and M.M. Hoeberichts (2000), 'Central bank accountability and transparency: theory and some evidence', Deutsche Bundesbank Economic Research Centre discussion paper 06/00.

Esser, Hartmut (1993), *Soziologie. Allgemeine Grundlagen*, Frankfurt/Main and New York: Campus Verlag.

Fehr, E., S. Gächter and G. Kirchsteiger (1997), 'Reciprocity as a contract enforcement device: experimental evidence', *Econometrica*, **65**, 833–60.

Frankel, Herbert S. (1977), *Money – Two Philosophies. The Conflict of Trust and Authority*, Oxford: Basil Blackwell.

Friedman, Milton (1959), *A Program for Monetary Stability*, New York: Fordham University Press.

Friedman, Milton (1969), *The Optimum Quantity of Money and Other Essays*, Chicago: Aldine.

Friedman, Milton (1984), 'Currency competition: a sceptical view', in Pascal Salin (ed.), *Currency Competition and Monetary Union*, The Hague: Martinus Nijhoff Publishers, pp. 42–46.

Friedman, M. and A.J. Schwartz (1986), 'Has government any role in money?', *Journal of Monetary Economics*, **17**, 37–62.

Gale, Douglas (1982), *Money: In Equilibrium*, Cambridge and New York: Cambridge University Press.

Galiani, Ferdinando (1751), *Della Moneta* [German title *Über das Geld*], translated with commentary by Werner Tabarelli 1999, Düsseldorf: Verlag Wirtshaft und Finanzen.

Garrison, R.W. and I.M. Kirzner (1987), 'Friedrich August von Hayek', reprinted in John Eatwell, Murray Milgate and Peter Newman (eds), *The New Palgrave: The Invisible Hand*, London and Basingstoke: Macmillan, pp. 119–30.

Geraats, Petra M. (2002), 'Central bank transparency', *Economic Journal*, **112**, F532–F565.

Giannini, Curzio (1994), 'Confidence costs and the institutional genesis of central banks', Banca d'Italia, Temi di Discussione del Servizio Studi, No. 226.

Giannini, Curzio (1995), 'Money, trust, and central banking', *Journal of Economics and Business*, **47**, 217–37.

Glasner, David (1998), 'An evolutionary theory of the state monopoly over money', in Kevin Dowd and Richard H. Timberlake, Jr. (eds), *Money and the Nation State. The Financial Revolution, Government and the World Monetary System*, New Brunswick and London: Transaction Publishers, pp. 21–45.

Goodhart, Charles A.E. (1975), *Money, Information and Uncertainty*, reprinted 1984, London and Basingstoke: Macmillan.

Goodhart, Charles A.E. (1989), 'The development of monetary theory', in David T. Llewellyn (ed.), *Reflections on Money*, London and Basingstoke: Macmillan, pp. 25–36.

Goodhart, Charles A.E. (1998), 'The two concepts of money: implications for the analysis of optimal currency areas', *European Journal of Political Economy*, **14** (1998), 407–32.

Goodhart, Charles A.E. (2002), 'The constitutional position of an independent central bank', *Government and Opposition*, **37**, 190–210.

Goodhart, C.A.E. and E. Meade (2003), 'Central banks and supreme courts', London School of Economics, mimeo revised draft, September.

Gouldner, Alvin W. (1960), 'The norm of reciprocity: a preliminary statement', *American Sociological Review*, **25**, 161–78.

Hart, Keith (1986), 'Heads or tails? Two sides of the coin', *Man*, N.S., **21**, 637–56.

Hayek, Friedrich A. von (1943), 'A commodity reserve currency', reprinted 1949 in Friedrich A. von Hayek, *Individualism and Economic Order*, London: Routledge & Keegan Paul, 209–19.

Hayek, Friedrich A. von (1960), *The Constitution of Liberty*, London and Henley: Routledge & Keegan Paul.

Hayek, Friedrich A. von (1976), '*Denationalisation of money. An analysis of the theory and practice of concurrent currencies*', Institute of Economic Affairs Hobart Paper 70, London.

Hayek, Friedrich A. von (1978), '*Denationalisation of Money – The Argument Refined*.

*An Analysis of the Theory and Practice of Concurrent Currencies'*, Institute of Economic Affairs, Hobart Paper 70, London.

Hayek, Friedrich A. von (1984), 'The future unit of value', in Pascal Salin (ed.), *Currency Competition and Monetary Union*, The Hague: Martinus Nijhoff Publishers, pp. 29–42.

Hayek, Friedrich A. von (1988), *The Fatal Conceit. The Errors of Socialism*, in *The Collected Works of Friedrich August Hayek*, vol. 1, edited by W.W. Bartley III, 1998 paperback edn, London: Routledge.

Heering, Walter (1991), *Geld, Liquiditätsprämie und Kapitalgüternachfrage. Studien zur entscheidungstheoretischen Fundierung einer Monetären Theorie der Produktion*, Regensburg: Transfer Verlag.

Heering, Walter (1999a), 'Privateigentum, Vertrauen und Geld. Überlegungen zur Genese von Zahlungsmitteln in Marktökonomien, oder: Wie man in Berlin, Bremen und anderswo über Geld denkt!' in Karl Betz und Tobias Roy (eds), *Privateigentum und Geld. Kontroversen um den Ansatz von Heinsohn und Steiger*, Marburg: Metropolis, pp. 99–143.

Heering, Walter (1999b), *'Erneut gelesen: Frank Hahns Kritik an einer Walrasianischen Fundierung der Geldtheorie. Zugleich eine Retrospektive auf einige Aspekte des Projektes 'Mikrofundierung der Makroökonomik'*, Freie Universität Berlin and Arbeitsstelle Politik und Technik, papers 2/99.

Heering, Walter (2002a), 'Politik und Ökonomie der Europäischen Währungsunion. Perspektiven des Abschieds von nationaler Wirtschaft und nationalem Geld', in Peter März (ed.), *Die zweite gesamtdeutsche Demokratie. Ereignisse und Entwicklungslinien – Bilanzierungen und Perspektiven*, München: Olzog Verlag, pp. 347–77.

Heering, Walter (2002b), *Europäische Geldpolitik*, Frankfurt am Main: Fischer Taschenbugh Verlag.

Heering, Walter (2003a), 'Acceptance of money and price level stability. Reflections on monetary constitution', mimeo, Brighton Business School.

Heering, Walter (2003b), 'On the notion of monetary optimum. A suggested interpretation', Brighton Business School/University of Brighton discussion paper series on economic and social transition, PEST No. 1, Brighton.

Heering, Walter (2005), *Geld*, Frankfurt am Main: Fischer Taschenbuch Verlag (forthcoming).

Heering, Walter and Oliver Pfirrmann (2002), 'Private ownership and markets: limits to privatization in the transition process', in Oliver Pfirrmann and Günter H. Walter (eds), *Small Firms and Entrepreneurship in Central and Eastern Europe – A Socio-Economic Perspective*, Heidelberg and New York: Physica, pp. 47–72.

Helleiner, Eric (2003), *The Making of National Money: Territorial Currencies in Historical Perspective*, Ithaca, NY: Cornell University Press.

Hens, T. and B. Vogt (2002), 'Money and Reciprocity', IEW/University of Zurich working paper 138.

Hollis, Martin (1998), *Trust within Reason*, Cambridge: Cambridge University Press.

Illing, Gerhard (2000), 'Zentralbankverfassungen', in Jürgen von Hagen and Johann H. von Stein (eds), *Obst/Hintner: Geld-, Bank- und Börsenwesen. Handbuch des Finanzsystems*, 40th edn, Stuttgart: Schäffer-Poeschel, 1620–39.

Issing, Otmar (1997), 'Hayek's suggestion for currency competition: a central banker's view', in Stephen F. Frowen (ed.), *Hayek: Economist and Social Philosopher. A Critical Retrospect*, Basingstoke and London: Macmillan, pp. 185–93.

Issing, Otmar (1998), 'Die Europäische Zentralbank. Das Problem der Glaubwürdigkeit', in Dieter Duwendag (ed.), *Finanzmärkte im Spannungsfeld von Globalisierung, Regulierung und Geldpolitik*, Berlin, pp. 179–92.

Issing, Otmar (2000), 'Hayek, Currency Competition and European Monetary Union', Institute of Economic Affairs occasional paper 111, London.

Jevons, W. Stanley (1875), 'Money and the mechanism of exchange', reprinted 1989 in Ross M. Starr (ed.), *General Equilibrium Models of Monetary Economies. Studies in the Static Foundations of Monetary Theory*, Boston: Academic Press, 1989, pp. 55–65.

Jones, Robert (1976), 'The origin and development of media of exchange', *Journal of Political Economics*, **84**, 757–75.

Kiyotaki, Nibohuri and John Moore (2002), 'Evil is the root of all money', *American Economic Review, Papers and Proceedings*, **92**, 62–6.

Kiyotaki, Nibohuri and Randall Wright (1992), 'Acceptability, means of payment, and media of exchange', reprinted in *Federal Reserve Bank of Minneapolis Quarterly Review*, **16**, 18–21.

Knapp, Georg F. (1905), *Staatliche Theorie des Geldes*, 4th edn, reprinted 1925, Munich and Leipzig: Duncker and Humblot.

Kocherlakota, Narayana R. (1998a), 'The technological role of fiat money', *Federal Reserve Bank of Minneapolis Quarterly Review*, **22**, 2–10.

Kocherlakota, Narayana R. (1998b), 'Money is memory', *Journal of Economic Theory*, **81**, 232–51.

Kocherlakota, N.R. and N. Wallace (1998), 'Incomplete record-keeping and optimal payment arrangements', *Journal of Economic Theory*, **81**, 272–89.

Kohn, Meir (2004), *Financial Institutions and Markets*, 2nd edn, Oxford: Oxford University Press.

Kranton, Rachel, E. (1996), 'Reciprocal exchange: a self-sustaining system', *American Economic Review*, **86**, 830–51.

Kreps, David M. (1986), 'Corporate culture and economic theory', reprinted 1996 in Peter J. Buckley and Jonathan Michie (eds), *Firms, Organizations and Contracts. A Reader in Industrial Organization*, Oxford: Oxford University Press, pp. 221–75.

Kreps, David M. (1990), *Game Theory and Economic Modelling*, 1996 paperback edn, Oxford: Clarendon Press.

Lagerspetz, Eerik (1984), 'Money as a social contract', *Theory and Decision*, **17**, 1–9.

Langlois, Richard N. (1986), 'Rationality, institutions, and explanation', in Richard N. Langlois (ed.), *Economics as a Process. Essays in the New Institutional Economics*, 1989 paperback edn, Cambridge: Cambridge University Press, 225–55.

Lerner, Abba P. (1947), 'Money as a creature of the state', *American Economic Review, Papers and Proceedings*, **37**, 312–17.

Lutz, Friedrich A. (1936), *Das Grundproblem der Geldverfassung*, Stuttgart and Berlin: W. Kohlhammer.

Macleod, Henry Dunning (1889), *The Theory of Credit, vol 1*, Reprinted 1969: Rome: Edizioni Bizzarri.

Majone, Giandomenico (1997), 'From the positive to the regulatory state: causes and consequences of changes in the mode of governance', *Journal of Public Policy*, **17**, 139–67.

Marx, Karl (1867), *Das Kapital. Kritik der politischen Ökonomie, Erster Band, Buch I: Der Produktionsprozeß des Kapitals*, reprint of the 4th edn, 1970, East Berlin: Dietz Verlag.

Matsui, Akihiko (1996), 'On cultural evolution: social norms, rational behavior, and evolutionary game theory', *Journal of the Japanese and International Economies*, **10**, 262–94.

Menger, Carl (1871), 'Grundsätze der Volkswirtschaftslehre', reprinted 1968 in Friedrich A. Hayek (ed.), *Carl Menger: Gesammelte Werke, Band I*, 2nd edn, Tübingen: Mohr Siebeck.

Menger, Carl (1909), 'Geld', reprinted 1970 in Friedrich A. Hayek (ed.), *Carl Menger: Gesammelte Werke, Band IV: Schriften über Geld und Währungspolitik*, 2nd edn, Tübingen: Mohr Siebeck, pp. 1–116.

Mises, Ludwig von (1912), *Theorie des Geldes und der Umlaufsmittel*, 2nd edn, 1924, Munich and Leipzig: Duncker and Humblot.

Moini, Mostafa (2001), 'Toward a general theory of credit and money', *Review of Austrian Economics*, **14**, 267–317.

Mueller, Dennis C. (1989), *Public Choice II. A Revised Edition of Public Choice*, reprinted 1996, Cambridge: Cambridge University Press.

Müller, Adam (1816), *Versuche einer neuen Theorie des Geldes mit besonderer Rücksicht auf Großbritannien*, reprinted 1922, Jena: Gustav Fischer.

Musgrave, Richard A. (1959), *The Theory of Public Finance*, New York: McGraw-Hill.

Nozick, Robert (1974), *Anarchy, State, and Utopia*, reprinted 1995, Oxford and Cambridge, MA: Blackwell.

Oh, Seonghwan (1989), 'A theory of a generally acceptable medium of exchange and barter', *Journal of Monetary Economics*, **23**, 101–19.

Ostroy, Joseph M. (1973), 'The informational efficiency of monetary exchange', *American Economic Review*, **63**, 597–610.

Ostroy, Joseph M. and Ross M. Starr (1990), 'The transactions role of money', in Benjamin M. Friedman and Frank H. Hahn (eds), *Handbook of Monetary Economics, Volume 1*, Amsterdam: North-Holland, pp. 3–62.

Paul, Axel T. (2002), 'Die Legitimität des Geldes', in Christoph Deutschmann (ed.), *Die gesellschaftliche Macht des Geldes*, Wiesbaden: Westdeutscher Verlag, pp. 109–29.

Polanyi, Karl (1957), 'The economy as instituted process', reprinted 1979 in Karl Polanyi, *Ökonomie und Gesellschaft*, Frankfurt am Main: Suhrkamp, pp. 219–44.

Popper, Karl R. (1945), *The Open Society and Its Enemies. Volume I: The Spell of Plato [Die offene Gesellschaft und ihre Feinde. Band I: Der Zauber Platos]*, 7th edn, 1992, Tübingen: Mohr Siebeck.

Prendergast, Canice and Lars Stole (2001), 'Monetizing social exchange', mimeo, University of Chicago.

Salin, Pascal (1984), 'General introduction', in: Pascal Salin (ed.), *Currency Competition and Monetary Union*, The Hague: Martinus Nijhoff Publishers, pp. 1–26.

Samuelson, Paul A. (1954), 'The pure theory of public expenditure', *Review of Economics and Statistics*, **36**, 387–89.

Schelling, Thomas C. (1960), *The Strategy of Conflict*, 16th printing 1997, from the 2nd edn 1980, Cambridge, MA and London: Harvard University Press.

Schumpeter, Joseph A. (1954), *History of Economic Analysis [Geschichte der ökonomischen Analyse]*, 1965, Göttingen: Vaudenhoeck and Ruprecht.

Schumpeter, Joseph A. (1970), *Das Wesen des Geldes, Aus dem Nachlaß von Joseph Alois Schumpeter*, Göttingen: Vaudenhoeck and Ruprecht.

Shubik, Martin (1973), 'Commodity money, oligopoly, credit and bankruptcy in a general equilibrium model', *Western Economic Journal*, **11**, 24–38.

Simmel, Georg (1896), 'Das Geld in der modernen Kultur, Wiederabdruck', reprinted 1995 in Heinz-Jürgen Dahme und Otthein Rammstedt (eds), *Georg Simmel: Schriften zur Soziologie. Eine Auswahl*, 5th edn, Frankfurt am Main: Suhrkamp, pp. 78–94.

Simmel, Georg (1900), *Philosophie des Geldes*, reprinted 1996 in Otthein Rammstedt (ed.), *Georg Simmel: Gesamtausgabe*, vol. 6, 4th edn: Frankfurt am Main: Suhrkamp.

Spahn, Heinz-Peter (2001), *From Gold to Euro. On Monetary Theory and the History of Currency Systems*, Berlin: Springer.

Spahn, Heinz-Peter (2002), 'Die Ordnung der Gesellschaft als Zahlungswirtschaft', in Christoph Deutschmann (ed.), *Die gesellschaftliche Macht des Geldes*, Wiesbaden: Westdeutscher Verlag, pp. 47–72.

Spahn, Heinz-Peter (2003), 'Geld als Institution einer Marktökonomie. Genese und Funktionsbedingungen', in Michael Schmid und Andrea Maurer (eds), *Ökonomischer und soziologischer Institutionalismus*, Marburg: Metropolis, pp. 307–29.

Starr, Ross M. (1974), 'The price of money in a pure exchange monetary economy with taxation', *Econometrica*, **42**, 45–54.

Steiner, Hillel (1978), 'Can a social contract be signed by an invisible hand?', in Pierre Birnbaum, Jack Lively and Geraint Parry (eds), *Democracy, Consensus and Social Contract*, London and Beverly Hills: Sage Publications, pp. 295–316.

Tönnies, Ferdinand (1887), *Gemeinschaft und Gesellschaft*, reprinted 1935, Darmstadt: Wissen schaftliche Buchgesellschaft.

Townsend, Robert M. (1989), 'Currency and credit in a private information economy', *Journal of Political Economy*, **97**, 1323–44.

Trivers, Robert L. (1971), 'The evolution of reciprocal altruism', *Quarterly Review of Biology*, **46**, 35–57.

Vaubel, Roland (1984), 'The government's money monopoly: externalities or natural monopoly', *Kyklos*, **37**, 27–58.

Vaughn, Karen I. (1987), 'Invisible hand', reprinted 1989 in John Eatwell, Murray Milgate and Peter Newman (eds), *The New Palgrave: The Invisible Hand*, London and Basingstoke: Macmillan, pp. 168–72.

Voigt, Stefan (2002), 'Die unabhängige Justiz – eine vernachlässigte Determinante zur Erklärung der Zentralbankunabhängigkeit?', *Schmollers Jahrbuch*, **122**, 207–26.

Wallace, Neil (1997), 'Absence-of-double-coincidence models of money: a progress report', *Federal Reserve Bank of Minneapolis Quarterly Review*, **21** (1), 2–20.

Wallace, Neil (2000a), 'Knowledge of individual histories and optimal payment arrangements', *Federal Reserve Bank of Minneapolis Quarterly Review*, **24** (3), 11–21.

Wallace, Neil (2000b), 'Comment on theoretical analysis regarding a zero lower bound on nominal interest rates', *Journal of Money, Credit, and Banking*, **32**, 931–5.

Weber, Max (1922), *Wirtschaft und Gesellschaft. Grundriss der verstehenden Soziologie*, reprinted 1980, 5th edn, Tübingen: Mohr Siebeck.

White, Lawrence H. (1999), *The Theory of Monetary Institutions*, Oxford: Blackwell.

Williamson, Oliver E. (1993), 'Calculativeness, trust, and economic organization', *Journal of Law and Economics*, **36**, 453–86.

Winkler, Bernhard (2000), 'Which kind of transparency? On the need for clarity in monetary policy-making', European Central Bank working paper no 26.

Woodruff, David (1999), *Money Unmade. Barter and the Fate of Russian Capitalism*, Ithaca, NY and London: Cornell University Press.

Wray, Randall L. (2000), 'Modern Money', in John Smithin (ed.), *What is Money?*, London and New York: Routledge, pp. 42–66.

Yeager, Leland B. (ed.) (1962), *In Search of a Monetary Constitution*, Cambridge, MA: Harvard University Press.

Yeager, Leland B. (2001), 'The perils of base money', *Review of Austrian Economics*, **14**, 251–66.

# Index